DAVE BASSETT

SETTLING THE SCORE

JB
JOHN BLAKE

Published by John Blake Publishing Ltd,
3 Bramber Court, 2 Bramber Road,
London W14 9PB, England

This edition published in Great Britain in 2002

ISBN 1 903402 43 3

All rights reserved. No part of this publication may be reproduced, stored in a retrieval system, or in any form or by any means, without the prior permission in writing of the publisher, nor be otherwise circulated in any form of binding or cover other than that in which it is published and without a similar condition including this condition being imposed on the subsequent purchaser.

British Library Cataloguing-in-Publication Data:
A catalogue record for this book is available from the British Library.

Typeset by Jon Davies

Printed in Great Britain by
Creative Print and Design (Wales), Ebbw Vale, Gwent

1 3 5 7 9 10 8 6 4 2

© Text copyright Dave Bassett/Bernard Bale

Pictures reproduced by kind permission of Empics, JMS Photography, *The Leicester Mercury*, Mike Ford Photography, The Picture Partnership, Popperfoto, NI Syndication and Scott Bairstow/*The Barnsley Chronicle*

Every attempt has been made to contact the relevant copyright holders, but some were unobtainable. We would be grateful if the appropriate people could contact us.

Papers used by John Blake Ltd are natural, recyclable products made from wood grown in sustainable forests. The manufacturing processes conform to the environmental regulations of the country of origin.

Contents

Foreword

I BEGAN MY CAREER WITH HARRY and if it had not been for him I might never have been heard of, let alone have gained an FA Cup winners' medal and played for Wales, or gone to Hollywood! He signed me from Wealdstone and soon had me playing in the first team. It all happened so fast that I didn't know whether I was coming or going – but that's Harry! He's like a whirlwind who catches you up and takes you with him.

He is one of the best managers that I have ever worked with for giving players self-belief and motivation. You cannot feel low for long when he is your boss – he just won't let you. Harry was the originator of the Crazy Gang and the famous spirit of Wimbledon is a tribute to his years as manager. When we won the FA Cup not long after he left, I knew where he was sitting and I raised the trophy to him as a salute to the man who had done more than just lay the foundations.

Later, when I joined Sheffield United, I knew that I was going to a club whose manager I could relate to. He knows his job and does it very well. Harry says what he thinks and he stands by it. He is completely up-front, and players like and respect him for that.

If I am asked to pick any one influence on my career – it has to be Harry Bassett.

Vinnie Jones

1

Dave or Harry?

HAVE YOU EVER WONDERED what the caveman felt like when he finally invented the wheel? Suddenly a whole new world opened up to him – barrows, bikes, cars, roulette. The world was never going to be the same again. Just imagine what went through his mind, or what he said. Probably something like, 'Ugg!'

That's near enough what I said when I discovered the ball. I could hardly speak in those days – not like now when I never seem to know when to stop. Anyway, I was given this strangely-shaped parcel as a gift, probably on my first birthday.

In golf they tell you to address the ball. In my case I undressed the ball. I simply ripped off the wrapping-paper and there it was. A whole new world was before me and my joy could only be expressed through that simple word, 'Ugg!'

But let us go right back to the very beginning and, in so doing, answer a question that has plagued me all my life – 'Why Harry?'

Really it couldn't be more simple – it's my Dad's name. When I was a kid, just about everyone else that I knew was called either John or David. To avoid confusion among family friends I was first known as 'Harry's boy' and later as 'Young Harry'. Whether I liked it or not that name has stuck with me. People that I knew as a kid still call me Harry, when I was in my teens footballers called me Harry, and now the entire football world – with the possible exception of the Sheffield United fans – seems to call me Harry.

Harry junior arrived as part of the war effort on 4 September 1944, a day which is both historic and memorable. Historic because that was the day the Allies captured Brussels and Antwerp and marched into Holland. Somewhat less historic, but considerably more memorable, for Joyce and Harry Bassett since it marked the birth of their only son and heir. In any event, it is a matter of record that on that day I, David Thomas Bassett, squawked my first breath at Honeypot Lane Nursing Home, Kingsbury, no more than a couple of miles from Wembley Stadium. I weighed in at 7lb 3oz and within a few days was the centre of attention at the parental home, 224 Brentfield Road in north-west London, wedged between Neasden and Stonebridge Park.

Apparently, I revelled in near-retirement conditions until I reached the age of five when, in the week of my birthday, I was taken hand-in-hand with my mother to undergo the first great culture-shock of my life — school. Bewildered and bemused, I became a charge of the Brent Road School, Willesden, a great and noble seat of learning which failed miserably in its efforts to spark within me even the slightest interest in the wonders of the academic world. It did, however, introduce me to several equally-talented youngsters for whom the high-spot of the day was the lunch-time kickabout on the cracked and uneven rectangle of asphalt which passed for the school playground.

My commitment to these soccer sessions on such a perilous pitch was nothing less than total. There was no recognisable formation to the sides and I chased everything. It was always my ball — and I was going to get it regardless of which end of the 'pitch' it happened to be. Consequently I was always at the heart of the action whenever a master would cast a roving eye over us. Fortunately it must have been the right master on a few of those occasions because, when I was nine years old and still in my second year of the juniors, I was selected for training with the school Under-11s team. I soon got my chance, which was no mean achievement for a nine-year-old, and I was later selected to represent Willesden Schools at district level. In my final year at junior school we reached the Final of the Crisp Shield but lost 2–1 to West Ham Schools, which must rate as the first great disappointment of my soccer career. There would be many more to come.

Never being one to do things by mere halves, I failed my 11-plus quite dramatically and was therefore labelled as a 'thickhead' and condemned to the educational scrap-heap. Shortly after that my parents moved to High Wycombe, no doubt hoping, and possibly even praying, that my new school, Hatters Lane Secondary Modern, would enjoy greater success in promoting my classroom interests.

It was really no contest and my love affair with football grew more passionate with every passing day I walked straight into the school team and was again chosen to represent schools in the area but, compared to London, rural Wycombe was hardly a football hotbed and fewer fixtures meant fewer opportunities to play.

The rural peace and splendour of the Buckinghamshire countryside also proved a bit too quiet for my parents and after two years my father returned from work one day to discover that my mother had put the house on the market. Within a couple of months we were back in the hubbub of London's commuterland, this time opting for Eastcote.

Despite the benefits of private tuition, paid for by my long-suffering parents in the forlorn hope that it might help me scrape through an exam, I had blown my 13-plus. Undaunted, my parents smartened me up, brushed me down and gave me a finger-wagging on the benefits of education before packing me off to the new experience of

Roxeth Manor School in south Harrow. I would remain there for four years, studying sport and academic trivia until I was almost 17.

My curriculum was soccer, soccer and more soccer during the winter months and cricket during the summer, spiced up with an occasional venture into the athletics arena. I was also offered rugby, which I dismissed because it interfered with soccer, and swimming which I detested because I didn't like water. Much as it grieves me to expose a sporting flaw I might as well admit that I have never quite mastered the art of swimming and have now come to the conclusion that I probably never will.

I really regret that my academic pursuits were not more pleasing to my enthusiastic parents but, hopefully, my career has shown that it takes all sorts and all different ways to achieve something in life.

From the age of eight I can't remember a time when I didn't have a football at my feet. Kicking a ball was my life, my very existence, and everything else had to go by the board. If I wasn't playing I would either watch my Dad turn out for his local London Transport depot or, as a special weekend treat, go to one of the top matches in London with my grandfather.

Unlike most kids of my age, I didn't have an allegiance to any particular club – I just liked to watch a game of football. Neither did I have a favourite player to idolise, as most of my mates seemed to do. Instead, my appreciation was more widespread – although I do admit to a leaning toward the Busby Babes of the mid-1950s and, closer to home, the skills of players like Johnny Haynes, Jimmy Greaves and Graham Leggett. I even saw Jimmy Hill play.

Since football had dictated the course of my life so far, it seemed extremely unlikely that I would ever shine in any examination and so it was a complete surprise, even to myself, when I successfully passed an aptitude test for a commercial course at Roxeth Manor School. The alternatives were technical subjects such as woodwork or metalwork, neither of which held the slightest bit of interest for me.

I had briefly flirted with the idea of journalism as a career and told the tutors that I had applied for the course largely because it embraced shorthand and typing. Perhaps a more practical reason was the fact that, of 26 places available, 23 were occupied by girls. I found that it dovetailed nicely with the more interesting subjects like history and geography, and my parents, who had once again put their hands in their pockets to pay for the course, were particularly anxious that I should pass. In fact they were somewhat more than anxious and I had become the focal point of some pretty strong domestic threats.

Failure, I was led to believe, would disgrace the family and taint my name for ever. What could I do? I stayed in four nights a week, trying desperately to cram four years of wasted opportunity into just a few months and – surprise, surprise – I finished up with five 'O' Levels which included Commerce, English Literature and English Language.

Having saved the family's honour and dispelled the need for immediate emigration, it was time to find myself a job. I was nearly 17 and had somehow developed an aptitude for figures, so I applied for a number of clerical posts. Most of my prospective employers took one look at me and said, 'Thanks, but no thanks.' Even those who showed an interest finished up by putting me off in one way or another. Finally our careers master – a nice guy called Mr Lodge – drew my attention to an advertisement for a trainee with the Scottish Life Assurance Company. It sounded reasonable and so I went along for an interview. No one was more surprised than me when they offered me the job. I accepted immediately, not through any deep-rooted desire to work in the field of life assurance, but more because it was in Harrow and very handy.

And so it was that in August 1961, just before my 17th birthday and armed with a new suit and a freshly-ironed white shirt, I launched myself upon an unsuspecting commercial world. Surprisingly enough, it was fun. I started as an office boy and was promoted through the junior ranks until, at the age of 21, they gave me the title of inspector, presented me with a company car and sent me out on the road to sell insurance to accountants, banks and other financial institutions. It was all good experience and helped me gain enough knowledge of the business to enable me to eventually start my own insurance brokerage some years later.

Anyone who knows me now could be surprised to learn about my insurance connections. After all, I've never been what you might call prudent.

Job applications weren't the only thing on my mind when I was preparing to leave school. I was also trying to convince several Football League clubs that I was worth a trial. Most of all, I wanted to go to either Chelsea or Fulham, the West London neighbours whose regular First Division clashes had thrilled me back in the heady days when Fulham were last in the top flight. Many's the time that I queued for hours to get crammed into the Bridge or the Cottage. It was what football was all about and every moment of it strengthened my ambition to be a part of it.

Most clubs greeted my application with a thundering display of apathy but, as luck would have it, both Fulham and Chelsea showed an interest, albeit mild. First Fulham gave me a trial with their youth team which, in those days, included a talented unknown by the name of Rodney Marsh. They offered me a place too, but I wasn't very impressed by the set-up at Craven Cottage and I turned them down. Daft? Perhaps, but Ted Drake, the Chelsea manager, was knocking at the door offering me amateur forms at Stamford Bridge and I felt that this was a much better route for me.

I was soon to be disillusioned, discovering early on in our relationship that I wasn't seen as being a part of Chelsea's long-term plans. The regular games that I had hoped for just didn't materialise and eventually I got so fed up with the lack of competitive matches that I joined the amateur club Hayes, then competing in the Athenian League.

That was my first meeting with Geoff Taylor, the club skipper, who has since figured prominently in my managerial career. He was then 28 and a seasoned top amateur who played just about anywhere during his 12-year stint with Hayes, although he preferred to operate in defence. I was still 17 but I forced my way into their senior team before the end of that first season and it seemed that I had already made my mark with Geoff. He remembers me as a self-appointed high-flyer who wanted to do everything and be everywhere on the pitch at once. I was quite sturdily built and probably took too many chances in those days, but you can put that down to the arrogance of youth. I didn't mind a dust-up either and, to this day, Geoff still reminds me that he spent much of his time breaking up scuffles between myself and a legion of unknown opponents.

Somewhat surprisingly Ted Drake and Dickie Foss, the Chelsea youth-team coach, retained an interest in me and the following year I was invited to join the Stamford Bridge squad for a youth tournament at Augsburg in Germany, along with young players like Ron Harris and John Hollins who were later to make their marks as Chelsea stalwarts. The following year saw the departure of Drake and the arrival of Tommy Docherty, which also marked a sudden end to Bassett's brief and inglorious link with the Chelsea youth squad.

I continued playing for Hayes and found some

compensation in the fact that I was playing among grown men, which was an altogether tougher proposition than playing in sophisticated youth teams where the opposition was always around my own age. It was while on a brief tour of Switzerland with Hayes that I received my first – and only – offer to play abroad. It came from Basle, a Swiss First Division side. Although I was flattered by their approach, I was still anxious to make the grade in England.

I stayed with Hayes for another two seasons before I felt that I'd had enough. My pride had taken a bit of a hammering after getting the elbow from Docherty and I felt that I needed to play in a higher grade of football if I was ever going to prove myself. I had played for Wycombe Schools and so it was logical that I should move to Wycombe Wanderers of the Isthmian League, then probably the strongest amateur competition in the country, including top teams like Leytonstone, Walthamstow Avenue, Maidstone United and – should you need reminding – a club called Wimbledon.

Wycombe were then managed by Don Welsh, the former England international and Charlton Athletic player who had been manager of Liverpool in the early 1950s. I began in the 1963–64 season and it is interesting to note that we lost 1–0 at Wimbledon, but then beat them 2–0 at Wycombe. Despite this, however, the Dons won the championship by a clear margin of six points in the days when a win gained only two points. Although it was of little significance to me at the time, their ambitions were already being clearly signalled.

It was also Wimbledon's last season in the Isthmian League since they were to shed their official amateur status – if indeed there was such a thing in those days – and join the semi-professional Southern League. It was a sign of things to come that they finished as runners-up to Hereford United at their first attempt.

Strangely, I didn't settle at Wycombe and stayed at

Loakes Park for only six months before deciding to return to Hayes where I saw out the rest of the season. It was as though I had never been away and it was good to be back with Geoff Taylor and the team. There was a warm, homely feeling about the club and I knew that I was back where I belonged, possibly never to roam again.

I was already looking forward to starting the new season – and what a season it turned out to be for me. I was still a few weeks off my 20th birthday when we kicked-off our first match and, from the very first day of that 1964–65 season, everything seemed to go right for me. I was quite fast and revelled in my position as a forward, knocking in goals from every angle and from every conceivable position. I think I lived a charmed life. It seemed that I only had to hit the ball towards the goal for it to finish in the net. Even if it hit the woodwork it was sure to deflect into the net rather than away from it. Perhaps one of the more important goals that I scored that season was the extra-time winner in the semi-final of the London Charity Cup against Barnet – it certainly seemed pretty vital to my team-mates at the time. I honestly lost count of the number of goals I scored during that memorable season and, not surprisingly, one or two of the Football League scouts started to take notice and very soon the word was out that Hayes had a hot-shot who was worth looking at.

To say that I attracted the attentions of both the current England skipper and a future England manager during my time at Hayes might be overstating the case a bit – but I certainly got a real thrill playing against them. The occasion was the inauguration of Hayes' new floodlighting. To mark the event the board had persuaded Fulham, complete with Johnny Haynes and Bobby Robson, to give us a lesson in football. They did precisely that, trouncing us 9–1 with Robson scoring the second goal.

Toward the end of that 1964–65 season I was approached by Watford, then playing in the Third Division and managed by Ken Furphy. Cliff Holton, the former Arsenal favourite, had found a new lease of life at Vicarage Road, playing alongside such men as Keith Eddy, Terry Mancini, Tom Walley and Ricky George, who was later to join Hereford and score a famous FA Cup goal that defeated Newcastle. They also had a brilliant young inside-forward in Dennis Bond, who was later signed by Tottenham and then seemed to disappear into the wilderness until he rejoined Watford later and enjoyed the best run of his career.

I signed amateur forms and played regularly in their reserve team in the Football Combination, which was then of a similar standard to the Central League for clubs in the north. The Combination consisted primarily of League clubs' reserve teams and young unknowns like myself often found themselves facing legendary players from the old First Division, top performers who were having a run-out after injury, or were suffering a temporary loss of form. It was a great experience. On more than one occasion I found myself playing alongside Messrs Holton and Bond when they were having a run-out after an injury.

I must have impressed Ken Furphy because the following 1965–66 season, when I was barely 21, he offered me professional terms with Watford. To become a professional footballer was the realisation of a boyhood dream and I thought long and hard before turning Watford down – yes, down! Was I mad? All my soccer-crazy friends thought so, but I still had a career outside the game, in insurance, to consider. Scottish Life had been very good to me. I had just been promoted, the money was good and I had been given a company car. 'Why blow it?' I asked myself, when I could still have the security of a job as well as playing football. Besides, the deal offered by Watford was no better than the money I was already getting at Scottish Life and, to cap it all, I had serious doubts as to whether I could make the grade at top professional level. My confidence was always high – but not that high.

For me, life as an ordinary run-of-the-mill professional in the lower divisions would never have been good enough. True to my birth-sign – I'm a Virgo – it would have to be done the Bassett way. I would have to excel at it. The First Division was a must – with possibly a chance to play for England too.

I am nothing if not a realist and something inside me sounded a warning bell which told me that by choosing a career as a professional footballer, I would be bound to fall short of the target that I knew I would have to set for myself. There was, however, one fleeting moment of recognition when I was selected to play for an England Xl against Enfield, a game which was in effect a trial for the forthcoming amateur international against Wales.

I was barely halfway through my first season with Watford when I packed up my gear and turned my back on Vicarage Road, little realising that, over 20 years later, I would return to the club for a brief and unhappy spell as manager. I said goodbye to Ken Furphy who, coincidentally, was later to manage Sheffield United, and headed back to the more realistic world of the amateur leagues – choosing, this time, to join Hendon.

Hendon was an ambitious club. They reached the FA Amateur Cup Final for the first time in 1955 when a capacity 100,000 Wembley crowd saw them lose to the giants of the ameteur game, Bishop Auckland. However, they returned to lift the Cup in 1960 when they beat Kingstonian. Now they had switched from the Athenian League, after a remarkable League and Cup double in 1965, and had joined the ranks of the much more powerful Isthmian League. They seemed desperately keen to hang on to the Amateur Cup, too, and had been drawn to play my old mates from Wycombe Wanderers in the quarter-final.

Several days before the match was due to be played, I had gone down with a virus and so both the doctor and the manager ruled me out of the game. The team didn't seem to miss me too much and steamed through to the semi-final at Wycombe's expense. Our victory celebrations were marred by the fact that one of our players, Jimmy Quail, had broken his leg. That meant that, injury apart, I would definitely be playing in the semi-final and, if we were successful, at Wembley in the Final. I had felt frustrated at not playing against Wycombe and, that night, I dosed myself up with everything that I could find in order to shake off the virus and ensure that I would be fit enough for a Sunday league match for Thames FC, my local club, the following morning.

Most players in top amateur soccer just lived for the game and enjoyed turning out in the junior Sunday leagues. I was no exception. I would hate to give the impression that these Sunday matches were merely a showcase for our skills – far from it. We were playing against players who always gave 100 per cent effort but perhaps just lacked that necessary flair to make the top amateur grade. If they knew that you were a regular player with a senior amateur club, they'd always put that extra bit of bite into their tackles. On that particular Sunday morning after the Wycombe match, I was well and truly bitten. A defender came in with a crunching tackle and as I fell there was a sharp crack. As I looked down at the grotesque angle of my twisted leg, I knew that it was broken. End of Bassett's Cup run, end of Bassett at Hendon, and the end of Bassett's soccer career for the next 18 months.

I was off work for about three weeks and I was hobbling around on crutches with my leg in plaster for about 13 weeks in all. Both Jimmy Quail and myself were encased in our plaster cocoons, looking like a couple of alabaster flower-pot men, watching from the bench as Hendon lost the FA Amateur Cup Final to Wealdstone. Jimmy had played at Wembley before, but I had never reached a Final and I feared that I had blown my only chance. I cursed myself for having played in that Sunday morning match, but then logic told me that it could so easily have happened at any time, another day, another place.

Over the horizon loomed the World Cup of the 1966 summer which, for me and for thousands of my generation, was the benchmark for the English game. The year when the founders and masters of the game gave their pupils an admonishing slap on the wrist for their pretensions, reminding them all of just who was in charge.

I was out there on the pitch for every second of every match, making every pass, timing every tackle and firing every shot. Although still only 21, I desperately envied every member of the England squad – angry at myself for not having the necessary talent which would have enabled me to become one of them. I have been asked whether I would rather have been a successful player than a successful manager and the answer has to be a resounding 'yes'. To have been able to play the game at its highest level and entertain thousands with the skills of a top international player would have been the realisation of a precious dream harboured since childhood. I would willingly have sacrificed any managerial success to have achieved just that.

It was during my enforced 18-month break from football that I found time to pursue other interests, particularly in my social life. Until now girls and other diversions had always taken a back seat to football, but now my priorities were beginning to change. Particularly when a copper-haired bombshell called Christine Carpenter joined Scottish Life as my secretary. She already had a string of beauty titles to her credit and, although I did take her out occasionally, it was to be two years before we got together seriously.

I would meet other girls at lunchtime or occasionally in the evenings when I wasn't training, and I know that she thought I was messing her about. However, that wasn't really the case. I had just bought my first bachelor flat in Ruislip – it was the Swinging Sixties, an era of optimism, mini-skirts and flower-power – and we were all having the time of our lives.

The flat was always full of my mates and our girlfriends and there seemed to be a party happening every single night. Committing myself to one girl at that time was certainly the last thing on my mind. Apparently I led Christine something of a dance socially and, I have since discovered, she also found me very difficult to work for. Not surprising really since I would talk, think and dictate at 100 miles an hour, even in those days, and most of her time was spent in trying in vain to slow me down.

With the help of regular training and exercise, my leg strengthened and had completely recovered by the summer of 1967. The long lay-off had been almost unbearable but I had lost none of my appetite for the game and was raring to go by the time the new season was upon me. This time I had signed for St Albans City – but I soon realised that it was a mistake.

It was an unhappy experience which I suffered until Christmas before going back to start my third spell with Geoff Taylor and Co at Hayes. I was to remain with them for the rest of that term and for the following two seasons, during which time I was sent off twice.

The occasion of my first transgression was an Athenian League match against Dagenham and I felt that I was receiving rather too much attention from the opposing defence. Things became a bit heated and I was given a warning before being dispatched to the dressing-room. The result of my indiscretion was a £5 fine and a 14-day ban. I was informed of the findings of the FA Disciplinary Committee in a curt note signed by Dennis Follows, the Football Association secretary and the same man who had written in such courteous terms to invite me to represent England in an amateur XI just a couple of years earlier.

A year later it happened again. This time it was in an FA Cup match against Staines. Again I had been the focus of rather too much attention and things came to a head when I had been fouled for the umpteenth time and my assailant added insult to rule-breaking by following up with a kick in the backside. When the referee started to caution me, I suggested, perhaps a little too pointedly, that he must be 'rather blind' – or words to that effect. That culminated in that short route back to the dressing-room. It wasn't long before the standard communication came from Follows bearing the news that, in view of my previous misconduct, I had been fined £10 and banned for six weeks.

I was furious – particularly in view of a recent ruling by the FA to allow professional footballers to be paid during the periods of their suspension – and I rattled off a snorting reply. The gist of my letter was to remind the FA that amateurs were not paid (or at least they were not meant to be) and it was therefore grossly unfair to penalise them financially when professionals appeared to be getting off scot-free. Just for good measure I signed off with an accusation of hypocrisy and double standards – but they still refused to waive the financial penalty. I shouldn't think that the letter did me much good in the long term but it certainly helped to relieve my feelings at the time.

I have always been a great believer in fate. Occasionally a person can make a snap decision, or change direction on nothing more than a passing whim, and it has a major effect on his or her life. Mine came in the summer of 1970, shortly before my 26th birthday, when I joined Walton & Hersham who, like Hayes, were members of the Athenian League. It was a move which was to see my career accelerate and, ultimately, cause my entire life to change direction.

Walton & Hersham was managed by Allen Batsford who I'd met briefly while playing for Hayes. Allen was a deep thinker, a tactician, which was a rarity in the amateur game in those days. I could relate to him and wanted desperately to be involved in his set-up.

I approached him before the start of the 1970–71 season but he seemed to have a fairly cool attitude at first. He was aware that I had a reputation as being something of a hard-man and suggested that we both should take some time to think about it. Why didn't I call him when I returned from holiday in three weeks' time?

I did just that and, while I know that he certainly had some reservations about signing me at first, Allen has since gone on record as saying that he has never regretted it. It was the beginning of a long and rewarding relationship and I still regard Allen as my mentor and the man who, above all others, helped and inspired my career in the game.

He also did much for my performance on the pitch and it was while under Allen's wing at Walton & Hersham that I gained my representative and international honours. It had been a few years since my one and only international trial against Enfield and I believed that my chance to play for England had been long-buried, never to be resurrected. But all that changed under Allen.

First there came an invitation to play for the Surrey FA and then recognition at a higher level when I was invited to play in a handful of FA Amateur XIs in representative matches against the Army, the Navy and other august bodies. Then came the ultimate recognition for a player in the amateur game — an invitation to play for my country. The FA were organising a three-week tour of five games in Scandinavia and Iceland during the summer of 1971 ... and was I available to join the squad?

Was I available?

Can a duck swim?

I indicated that I was and, after a training get-together in Scotland, we flew to Stavanger for our first game. Also included in the party was my Walton & Hersham team-mate Roger Connell, who was later to play his part in the revitalisation of Wimbledon. I was named as substitute for our first match against Norway and I managed to get on for the last 20 minutes to win my first international cap. This was followed by full appearances against Denmark and Iceland to start a collection of ten caps. In all, I was in the squad for four years and substitute 16 times.

That brought me into contact with Charles Hughes, who was in charge of the squad at the time. He was a much-maligned man. He was a disciplinarian who did not suffer fools gladly and therefore did not endear himself much to the press. In truth, Gérard Houllier the Liverpool manager, reminds me of him.

I used to spend a lot of time training with Hughes during the England days, and I think he had a great influence on me. I learned a lot from him. I watched his coaching methods and the perception that he was a long-ball guru is total rubbish. We did not play long-ball tactics when I was in the England squad — quite the opposite. We played very good football. His tactics were based on pressurising the opposition to take possession. I still think he was one of the best coaches the British game has ever seen. He made many coaching films for the FA and I would say that they are still among the best that have been produced.

I enjoyed working with him, although he could be

demanding and even insulting. I remember on one occasion during an England coaching session he said he believed I was a one-eyed player and said that I could only play a one-touch game during our session. Just me – everybody else could play as normal. It improved my game and I used the same ploy some time later when I was coaching Dennis Wise and it worked for him as well.

Unfortunately, I believe Charles made one or two comments that were taken out of context. As an example, he once said that if Brazil knew about the POMO (position of maximum opportunity – at the back post, for example) they would be even better. Since they were world champions at the time, people took the mickey. Having said that, Charles was autocratic, he was ruthless in his football life and maybe that was his undoing with the FA because I have no doubt that he was a political animal as well, and that does not go down too well among the powers that be.

I have great respect for both Charles Hughes and Allen Batsford.

It was not only on the field that my fortunes had changed. Christine had been working with Scottish Life for a couple of years, during which time she won the Miss Wembley beauty title and also reached the finals of both the Miss England and Miss Great Britain contests. Hardly surprising then that she had a steady boyfriend. However, when he decided to emigrate to Australia, she declined to go with him and Bassett took it upon himself to ease her suffering at his departure. It started as nothing more than a friendly drink, all in the interests of staff relations. At least that is what I told myself. After all, she was my secretary.

Sufficient to say that, as our relationship developed, we both realised that work and romance don't mix and so Christine left to take another job outside Scottish Life. By this time I had developed a good grasp of the insurance business and, for some time, had nurtured ideas of starting my own brokerage. Strictly against the rules, I started laying the foundations of my own business while still on the staff of Scottish Life and started putting out feelers among my existing clients.

In 1970 I arranged to rent offices in Stanmore from a man called Ron Noades. I ran Manor Insurance Brokers for nearly two years while still an employee of Scottish Life. Hardly ethical perhaps, but it's the sort of thing that goes on all the time in business. Finally, however, someone somewhere must have blown the whistle. And when I was called into the manager's office for a little chat about business practice, I knew that, at last, judgement day had come. We parted amicably enough but I was now 28 and, after nearly 12 years as a company man, it was time to row my own boat on a full-time basis. The timing of that decision was prompted perhaps by the rebirth of my soccer career with Walton & Hersham and I felt that it would not be a bad thing to set myself up while still possessing a degree of influence.

It was not only in business that the Bassett pulling-power was proving its worth. Having offered succour and sympathy while Miss Christine Carpenter was getting over her broken romance, our relationship flourished and we finally became engaged. Women seem to have total recall over this sort of thing and I am constantly reprimanded for not proposing to her over a romantic candle-lit dinner. Apparently we were driving somewhere one evening when I said, 'Perhaps we should get engaged'. For all the feeling that went into it, according to Christine, I might just as well have been offering contractual terms to a player.

She must have agreed, though, because we were married at St Lawrence's Church, Eastcote, on 8 July 1972. We had already bought a house which I had found the previous year at Chalfont, in the Chilterns. It had at one time belonged to comedian Billy Dainty and, although the wedding was still a year away, I decided to sell my flat anyway and move in while the builders and decorators worked around me.

The wedding itself was a riot. It seemed that everyone that I had ever met, and dozens who I'm sure I'd never met before, were there, including the entire Walton & Hersham team who formed an archway of well-worn football boots as we came out of church. Mind you, I'm not sure that Christine was too impressed by the connotation of the old boot. After a two-week honeymoon in Majorca – everyone went there in those days – it was back to a hard training routine in readiness for my third season under Allen Batsford at Walton & Hersham. As captain I was glad to see that our squad was stronger than ever and, although unaware of it at the time, this season was going to prove to be a memorable one for me.

There were more England caps to come from games against France and the Republic of Ireland. Although it was such a great honour to be selected to play at international level, I have to say that the pinnacle of my amateur career came, not from any international match, but from leading Walton & Hersham to victory in the FA Amateur Cup at Wembley in April 1973. I was skippering the side from midfield and we had reached the semi-finals along with Highgate United from the West Midlands, Slough Town and Bishops Stortford. We beat Highgate 4–0 and Slough disposed of Bishops Stortford to face us in the Final.

It was a tough game, played in front of 46,000 fans at Wembley, and we won thanks to a goal from Roger Connell in the 88th minute. Up to then it was the greatest thrill of my life. No one can describe what it is like to lead your team up those steps to receive your trophy. Anyone who has experienced it will say that even Bobby Moore couldn't have felt more proud on that unforgettable day in the summer of 1966 when he led the victorious England World Cup team up that very same flight of steps.

I was particularly proud to receive it since the historic Amateur Cup competition was nearing the end of its days. The following year was to see the end of 'shamateurism'. The game was to go open at all levels and 1974 would see the FA Amateur Cup won for the very last time.

It was a decision which we all knew to be right. Top amateur clubs had been paying their players for over two decades and tales of inflated 'boot money' had abounded for much longer than that. I don't mind admitting that I was receiving £25 a week as an 'amateur' with Walton & Hersham and it was possible to line our pockets even more by collecting additional cash incentives structured to success in both League and Cup.

One of our more lucrative pot-hunting excursions came later that year when we had battled through four preliminary rounds of the FA Cup to be rewarded with a tie against Brighton & Hove Albion in the first round proper of the competition at our own ground, Stompond Lane. It was during Brian Clough's brief spell as manager at the Goldstone Ground following his very successful period with Derby County – and immediately prior to his brief 44-day reign at Leeds.

We were playing some good, direct football and fully deserved to hold Brighton to a goalless draw. We were delighted and, according to the press the following morning, Mr Clough was somewhat miffed and, albeit in the heat of the moment, likened us to a team of donkeys.

The replay at Brighton was arranged for an afternoon kick-off the following week because power cuts due to industrial action had prevented the use of floodlights. That we stuffed Cloughie's team 4–0 on their own ground is now history and anyone within earshot must have been puzzled by the strange sound of elated braying emanating from the visitors' dressing-room. Cloughie, however, was much more gracious in defeat and the following morning's *Daily Telegraph* quoted him thus: 'We were whacked by a team of very competent amateurs. They performed with more technique and more organisation than us in every aspect of the game. You name it – they did it.'

Whoever penned those immortal words, 'Pride cometh before a fall', certainly knew a thing or two. In the second round we were drawn away to Hereford United and lost.

I spent four seasons with Walton & Hersham. They were probably the happiest days of my playing career and I regard them as a real bonus after breaking my leg. Many players never recover from bad breaks and I remember having serious doubts myself as to whether I would ever be able to play top amateur soccer again. However, a man like Allen Batsford makes you believe in yourself and that is why it was him I turned to in order to help rekindle my flagging career. By helping me to gain international honours and an Amateur Cup winners' medal, he had achieved much more than I ever dared hope and it was all due to his influence that my fortunes had changed so dramatically. There was yet even more to come. In spite of all his success, Allen's relationship with the Walton & Hersham board was turning sour, but none of us had the slightest clue that his name had been among the 28 applicants for the vacant managerial seat in London SW19.

Wimbledon were going through an acute financial crisis and had just experienced one of their worst-ever seasons in the Southern League. Former Palace, Orient and Colchester manager, Dick Graham, had resigned after a brief and unsuccessful spell and, when Allen was offered the job in the summer of 1974, the club had just been saved from extinction by a cash injection of £2,500 from their supporters' club, coupled with a similar sum coming from club president Bernie Coleman.

Most of the playing staff, fearing the worst, had already flown the nest and when Allen took over, he inherited a 'squad' of only seven players and was given a budget of around £14 per man. Walton & Hersham was never a wealthy club, but when I tell you that Allen had to take a drop in salary to join Wimbledon, you will realise just how bad things were.

I was the first to learn of his decision. I won't pretend that I wasn't surprised but, when he looked at me and asked, 'Are you coming?' I only had to give a very brief thought to his offer before deciding to give it a go. I had been happy playing under Allen, and Wimbledon seemed to be as good place as any to end my career. Besides, I told myself, it probably wouldn't be much different from life at Walton & Hersham.

How wrong can you be?

2

Graduating to the Dons

WIMBLEDON ALWAYS REMIND ME of Hans Christian Anderson's *Ugly Duckling*. They have been criticised over the years and have at times been a little ungraceful – but they are still there among the achievers of football and should therefore be acknowledged for the fact that, not only have they survived among the big birds of English soccer, but they have also frightened most of them to death by the sheer honesty of their endeavour.

Many big scalps hang in their dressing-room and who is to say that there will not be many more? The Ugly Duckling has turned into a beautiful soccer swan which might have dipped out of the Premiership but is among the favourites to get back there.

It was not like that when I joined them. I made a bit of a joke that, despite doing so badly at school, I had nevertheless become a Don. Wimbledon were among the best clubs outside the Football League, but they were still at the Ugly Duckling stage and few people dreamed of the achievements that were to follow in years to come.

My time at Wimbledon was a crazy period which started in non-league football and was to finish, 13 years later, in sixth place in the First Division of the Football League, which was the game's top flight before the introduction of the Premiership concept. Allen Batsford's revival of the club was, to say the least, remarkable. He had asked three of us to come to Wimbledon from Walton and the team was further strengthened by the arrival of Roger Connell and Keiron Somers, both former colleagues who had left Walton a year earlier following a dispute over contracts. After a season with Hendon they jumped at the chance of rejoining their old boss to play in a higher standard of competition.

A 1–0 win over the Crystal Palace first team in a pre-season friendly was an early sign of things to come. We followed that by stringing together a run of 22 consecutive victories in all competitions, which soon shut the mouths of the minority who had been against Allen's appointment. Fixture congestion was something of a problem. Not only did we have a full programme of 42 Southern League games, but there were also other competitions like the Southern League Cup, the London Senior Cup, the FA Trophy and the glamour of the FA Cup itself – if you were good enough to make it through the qualifying rounds.

Including friendlies we played a total of 73 matches that season, while some of the top First Division teams, who had played probably 20 games less, were complaining about the pressure. Of those 73 games, we won 49 and drew ten, scoring 128 goals and conceding 52.

We won the Southern League championship that year – in fact we won it for three years on the trot as we moved toward our ultimate target of League status. However, it was the trophy that we didn't win which was to make my first season at Wimbledon so memorable. After battling through four qualifying rounds, we eventually made it to the first round of the FA Cup and were promptly rewarded with a home tie against Bath City, which we won 1–0. The second round gave us another home tie against Kettering, and 6,000 fans packed into Plough Lane to watch us win with ease, going on to reach the third round for the first time in the club's history.

We held our breath as we waited for the draw on the following Monday lunchtime. Liverpool? Everton?

Manchester City? Arsenal or Tottenham perhaps? We feared nobody and a third-round tie against one of the First Division's glamour clubs would have suited us just fine. Even a Second Division club would have been acceptable – provided it was Manchester United, then storming back to the top flight after a suprise relegation the year before. However, it was not to be. Instead we were rewarded with an away tie at Burnley, a club which had enjoyed fleeting success in the late 1950s and early 1960s. Although still in the First Division, Burnley operated on a tight budget and were soon to fall into a rapid decline. Indeed, only a few years ago the Turf Moor club were foundering at the bottom of the old Fourth Division and had to win their last match of the season to be certain of retaining Football League status.

At the time of the draw Burnley were third in the old First Division but, by the day of the match, they had slipped to seventh. Nevertheless, it was still an away tie against First Division opponents and over 1,000 Wimbledon fans journeyed to Turf Moor to see us pull off one of the biggest upsets in the history of the FA Cup. In front of 20,000 spectators and the TV cameras we won 1–0 to become the first non-League club to defeat a First Division team away from home.

The mood in the dressing-room and on the coach home was euphoric. The celebrations seemed to last all weekend and come Monday, when the FA Cup committee were due to make the draw for the fourth round at their Lancaster Gate headquarters, we were still hyped-up, knowing that far from being a pushover we were suddenly the team that everyone wanted to avoid. Then the reality of the draw – an away tie against mighty Leeds United – brought us back down to earth with a bump.

The result is now part of FA Cup folklore – how we held them to a goalless draw on their own ground in front of a 46,000 crowd, and how our goalkeeper, Dickie Guy, saved a Peter Lorimer penalty eight minutes from time after I was adjudged to have fouled Eddie Gray inside the box. If we celebrated after beating Burnley, then we went absolutely loopy after that draw at Elland Road. I only have to write down 11 names for any soccer fan of the 1970s to assess the level of our achievement. They are Harvey, Reaney, Frank Gray, Bremner, McQueen, Madeley, McKenzie, Clarke, Lorimer, Giles and Eddie Gray. No mean line-up with all but one of them winning full international honours.

The replay at Wimbledon was scheduled for three days later but, after being rained off, it actually took place a fortnight after the first game and fans queued all night for tickets. Unfortunately, since our Plough Lane ground could not accommodate even a quarter of the fans who wanted to see the match, a late decision was made to switch the venue to Crystal Palace. Again we contained Leeds well and the 45,000 crowd – most of them shouting for Wimbledon, the underdogs – were yelling themselves hoarse every time we got the ball. Weight-training had ensured that we were at peak fitness and had provided us with the extra stamina we needed to keep Leeds at bay.

The game had its moments of mayhem. There had been some press talk about us slagging off Leeds after that first game. It wasn't true, of course, but some of the Leeds players were understandably a bit wound-up about it and on occasions fists flailed in the air.

They were forced to shoot mostly from long range and a Johnny Giles effort appeared to be going well wide when I got in the way and deflected it past my own goalkeeper. It was the only goal and the end of a dream, but I shall never forget that Cup run. Having given away a penalty in the first match, and scoring an own-goal in the replay, I shouldn't think anyone will ever allow me to forget it. The boys took it well and nobody blamed me but, as you can imagine, I probably felt the disappointment more than most.

Sadly, our success in both Cup and League competitions carried little weight that summer when the Football League met for their annual meeting. We had thrown our hat into the ring hoping, as many had hoped before us, that success in the highest sphere of non-League football would secure our election to the ranks of the full-time professionals. However, despite having enjoyed the best season in the club's history, Wimbledon polled only four votes. Kettering Town were the most successful non-League applicants, gaining 20 votes but still being unsuccessful as the Foot-ball League clubs again closed ranks and opted to look after their own. We were bitterly disappointed but it made us all the more determined to ensure that we could not be ignored for much longer.

A word at this stage about our star goalkeeper Dickie Guy. He was always Mr Prim and Proper, the top man in the dressing room and when we arrived at Wimbledon we could not help but take the mickey out of him. When we arrived in Leeds for the first Cup tie, I got a couple of the lads to phone through to his room and pretend to be the BBC wanting to interview him as part of a match preview. He would have to put on a suit and meet them in the hotel foyer. There would be a fee, of course.

Sure enough, Dickie fell for it and Glen Aitken, Selwyn Rice and myself sitting in the reception. He looked around for the reporters, kept looking at his watch and then saw our faces. The penny dropped when we started making gestures at him. He nursed that wound for some time until, after a training session, he asked me into the kit room, put his fists up and said that it was time he and I sorted out our problem. He insisted that I was continually taking the mickey out of him and was undermining his position. I just laughed and the whole thing melted. He must have thought about it, because he then turned into a bigger lunatic than anyone at the club and was constantly playing jokes and taking the mickey out of everyone else. We have been good friends ever since and I am a godparent to one of his children.

The following season, the second under Allen Batsford, saw us reach the second round of the FA Cup, only to lose at home to Brentford. We retained the Southern League title as well as winning the Southern League Cup. Again Wimbledon applied for Football League status, only to be rejected once more after polling a paltry three votes.

Wimbledon have a bit of a reputation for being the paupers of the Premiership and it was no different in the club's non-League days. In spite of all our successes on the pitch, the club's finances were again in tatters, having managed somehow to lose £20,000 during the year. Our supporters' club raised £4,000 to enable us to compete that summer in the Anglo–Italian tournament for non-League clubs and, although we reached the Final, we lost 1–0 to Monza. We were a fairly tough side but the Italians we faced were like animals and even Allen Batsford, not one given to airing extreme views, complained that we had been kicked from one end of Italy to the other.

Wimbledon's president and major shareholder was Bernie Coleman and he eventually stood down, making way for a new board under the chairmanship of Ron Noades. Although Ron and I go back a long way, we've never been particularly close. He is about five years older than me but it was his brother Colin, who was in my class at Roxeth Manor, who was a good mate of mine.

Ron had always shown a keen interest in football and ran Roxeth Manor Old Boys before becoming chairman of Southall, then managed by my former Hayes skipper, Geoff Taylor. He had worked for an estate agent before starting his own property company and a series of successful deals considerably improved his lifestyle. I had been responsible for introducing him to Bernie Coleman, little realising the extent of his ambition or that the meeting would herald his eventual takeover at Wimbledon.

The arrival of Noades at Wimbledon brought sweeping changes. He wanted to make the club work and, in order to achieve this, it needed a strong financial base. Cutbacks meant the enforced departure of four top players including Kieron Somers and Mick Mahon. New players came in but the priority for Ron Noades was Wimbledon's election to the Football League and he launched himself on an intensive public relations campaign, supported by heavy canvassing of League club chairmen, to achieve his aim.

It was important that we were successful on the field, too, and we realised that we would have to win the Southern League championship for a third successive year if we were to stand any chance of making it into the Football League. Our keenness to win got us into trouble when players were sent off for what I can most fairly describe as incidents caused by a mixture of over-enthusiasm and frustration. I was a culprit in a match at Maidstone United when I was given my marching orders, along with Selwyn Rice, for what was the most trivial of offences. It is a tribute to our nine team-mates that they were still able to win 2–0 without us.

That 1976–77 season was to bring us another successful FA Cup run and we again reached the third round, although the draw had again been kind and given us non-League opponents, Woking and Leatherhead, in rounds one and two. Again we prayed for a money-spinning tie with one of the glamour clubs, and again our prayers were only partially answered, this time with a home draw against Middlesbrough. It was during Jack Charlton's regime at Ayresome Park (their ground before the Riverside) and, although they presented formidable

First Division opposition, they didn't have the buzz of Arsenal, Manchester United or Liverpool.

I remember that the build-up to the game was intensified by a row about low ticket sales. Middlesbrough accused Wimbledon of pitching the prices too high, while the Dons alleged that it was 'Boro's own dour reputation and style which had deterred many of their fans from making the long journey from Teesside to see the match.

The pitch was a nightmare. The mud had frozen solid the previous week and didn't thaw until the day before the game. Jack Charlton reckoned we had hosed it down and it certainly wasn't an easy surface for either side. In the event, it was a fairly uninspiring goalless draw and the following Tuesday we lost the replay 1–0 to a dodgy penalty. Not my fault this time.

On the 'Boro side were players like Graeme Souness, Terry Cooper and Dave Armstrong. They were on a run of three months without a defeat so we weren't too upset at going out to them.

With our FA Cup success and extended runs in various other competitions, we completed a remarkable 75 fixtures that season. So many games had to be rearranged that the pressure became very intense towards the end and in the 32 days from 16 April to 17 May we played 11 matches – nine of them League games. We eventually won the championship by five points from Minehead and we also collected the London Senior Cup for the last time. I didn't actually get a medal for my appearance against Staines in the London Senior Cup Final. At one stage I suggested to the referee that his sight was failing and he sent me off. I'm not sure if it was what I had told him or the four-letter word with which I embellished it!

We had done all we could and now it was up to the representatives of the Football League clubs.

The date of 17 June 1977 is the most momentous day in Wimbledon FC's history. It was on that blazing summer's day in the Queen's Jubilee year that the Football League held its annual meeting at London's Café Royal, with much interest being focused on the four clubs applying for re-election to the Fourth Division – Halifax, Hartlepool, Southport and Workington. In the wings waiting, hoping, perhaps even praying for their chance were Altrincham, the nominees of the Northern Premier League, and Wimbledon. Each of the 92 clubs had two votes to cast among the six clubs – and only four of them would be playing League football the following season.

The tension was unbearable as the Football League president, Lord Westwood, announced the result of the ballot in almost alphabetical order: Altrincham polled 12 votes (much to the relief of the Wimbledon contingent), Halifax 44, Hartlepool 43, Southport 37, Workington 21 and Wimbledon 27. The hard-nosed canvassing tactics of Ron Noades, the Wimbledon chairman, and the vice-chairman, Jimmy Rose, had paid off. Wimbledon were at last in the Football League and poor Workington, forced to apply for re-election for the fourth year running, were out.

The fact that I was soon to become captain of a Football League club without ever having kicked a ball in League competition was difficult to swallow and took a little time to sink in. I was also forced to face the reality that, when the season opened, I would be making my Football League debut just a couple of weeks short of my 33rd birthday. Perhaps a little late to realise my childhood dream?

Remarkably, Allen Batsford had steered the club from the brink of disaster to the Football League in only three seasons as a part-time manager. It had seemed logical that the club should have put him on the full-time payroll, particularly in that last season when we were making a serious bid for election to the League but, for some reason, Ron Noades appeared reluctant to make a commitment. I remember thinking how ridiculous it must have appeared to outsiders when a supposedly ambitious club – the most successful part-timers in the game – wouldn't appoint a full-time manager.

Noades realised he had no choice when we joined the League and at last he offered Allen a new contract. The chain of events, however, was made even more bizarre by the fact that Dario Gradi had been appointed as Allen's assistant – on a higher salary! Dario, who had come to Plough Lane at the instigation of Ron Noades, had been a player with Sutton United and later had spells as youth-team coach at Chelsea and assistant manager at Derby County.

So at the start of our first season in the League, we had a captain – me – who had never played League football before and a manager who had never been full-time before. In addition to playing I was brought in as unofficial coach to the first team. We also had a squad of players who were mostly part-timers and who wouldn't train more than twice a week because the club refused to compensate them for loss of earnings at work.

I felt sorry for Allen. By refusing him a full-time contract for so long and then appointing an assistant manager on better terms, Ron Noades was surely undermining his authority. After everything that Allen had achieved it was like a kick in the teeth, a massive vote of no-confidence which affected the team's performances. It took eight games to register our first League win. We suffered an ignominious defeat in the first round of the FA Cup against Enfield and we won only four games before Christmas.

That Yuletide was an easily forgettable period which culminated in a round trip to Rochdale on Boxing Day. The Fourth Division fixtures had already been drawn-up before the League's annual meeting and because we had replaced Workington we automatically inherited their fixtures. Boxing Day was then traditionally a time for local derby matches and while a trip to Rochdale may have suited Workington (it was about as near as they could get to a derby, being situated way up in the North-West) it was not good news for us. It was made all the more difficult by the board's decision not to provide a coach for the team. Noades argued that because it was Christmas a coach would cost more and the club could not afford it. In the event we all had to drive to Lancashire in our own cars – little wonder then that we lost 3–0.

None of this did anything to help Allen's situation and he felt that he was getting little help from Gradi. The following week he went to the chairman and said that he didn't want Dario to continue, suggesting instead that I should become his assistant. This led to a row and, in Allen's own words, he 'blew his top with frustration', which was quite uncharacteristic. He admitted later that he regretted what he had done, but at the time he felt that he was being forced into a corner and so decided to go for the jugular. A 2–0 defeat at Swansea on 2 January was the prelude to Allen's resignation, but I have always felt that he took the gentleman's option. There is no doubt in my mind that he was manoeuvred into an impossible position and, had he not jumped himself, he would most certainly have been pushed. I think that he was treated disgracefully.

I was pleased that Allen was eventually awarded a testimonial and, for his dinner in London in July 2001, I donated a number of my own medals and awards to the Wimbledon trophy room in return for a £500 contribution to Allen's fund. I think a total of about £6,000 was raised and he thoroughly deserved it.

Several years after his departure, when we reached Division Two, Allen had returned to the club as chief executive for a short period. Perhaps to soften the blow Ron Noades had promised Allen a testimonial match – 'sometime in the future' – in recognition of his achievements. It was a long time in coming. Hardly surprisingly, the man who realised Wimbledon's ambition of League football, only to be rewarded by employment for half a season, rarely goes to see them these days. It hurts too much.

Batsford's departure left the way clear for Dario Gradi to take over the managerial seat. Or did it? The next day I was somewhat surprised to be summoned from the training ground for a meeting in the chairman's office.

'How would you like to be manager of Wimbledon Football Club?' he asked. It was a bolt out of the blue and I looked at him blankly, not really believing what I'd just heard.

When it penetrated, I needed only a few seconds to make up my mind and the answer was short and sweet: 'No, thank you.' My refusal – a gut reaction – was partly because I was still smarting over the manner of Allen's departure, but also because some sixth sense told me that it would be a mistake. I had ideas of my own, certainly, and enjoyed taking coaching and training sessions, but I felt that I wasn't yet ready for the full responsibility of management. I held a full FA coaching badge but management was something for which I was completely unprepared.

Dario was given the position and I was offered the job of assistant manager. At the same time I was to continue as captain at an all-in figure of 90 quid a week. I thought about it overnight and decided to ask the only man whose judgement I could trust. I telephoned Allen.

'Should I take it?' I asked.

'Go for it,' was his reply. He added, 'Your playing days are nearly over but you've still got plenty to offer.' I wasn't at all sure if I liked that last bit.

Full-time involvement at Wimbledon would mean taking a back-seat in my insurance business and I discussed this at great length with my partner, Gary

Poland, before accepting the job as Dario's assistant. Shortly after the Gradi–Bassett partnership became operational we began to see an improvement in our results, but not before our poor run had extended to 26 games with only four wins, leaving us foundering at the foot of the table.

Ten victories in our remaining 20 fixtures saw us scramble to a respectable halfway position in the table. For the record, the Fourth Division championship was won by Watford as they started their impressive push to Division One under the guidance of Elton John and new manager Graham Taylor. Conversely, Rochdale, who had stuffed us 3–0 on Boxing Day, finished bottom. On a more personal note, that season marked the end of my brief playing career in the Football League. I had played 35 games, a handful of Cup matches and scored the only League goal of my life. That was against Gillingham when we won 3–1 at Plough Lane. Of such things are boyhood dreams made.

I was becoming aware that age was taking its toll. The legs were not as fast as they had once been and Dario was anxious to introduce some promising youngsters into the side. He told me quite bluntly that I didn't figure in his first-team plans any more, but I was happy enough to turn out for the reserve side which was now under my control, and I continued playing at this level for another couple of years.

Our second season in Division Four started with a run of 13 unbeaten League games before we ran out of steam at Huddersfield. However, the team kept the momentum going and won promotion by finishing in third place on goal-average. Alan Cork, who had joined us from Derby without ever having played in the Rams' first team, helped our success with 24 goals. The season had also seen the debut of Wally Downes, surely one of the craziest practical jokers of his day. Wally, like Cork, would later play an important role in our rise to Division One.

Our life in the Third Division was to be terminated after only one season. We finished at the foot of the table and started the 1980–81 campaign back among the broken dreams of football's bargain basement. Yet there had been some bright signs which gave us a little hope for the future. We had been able to blood some of our promising youngsters and that relegation season saw the first appearance of a tall young goalkeeper who Brian Hall spotted playing for Edgeware Town. He had played well in the reserves and had merited his two first-team games when Ray Goddard, our regular 'keeper, was injured. His name was Dave Beasant and we had paid just £1,000 for him.

Motivation is a rare quality when you've just been relegated to the Fourth Division after a solitary year in the Third. You have to climb the mountain again. Yet the excitement of your original achievement is missing. It's a hard slog which calls for a professional attitude and this was lacking as Dario Gradi tried to recover the team's fortunes. It was hard going and, by early December, we had accumulated only 22 points from 23 games.

The chairman promptly turned his attention to another area of South London and led a consortium to buy out Crystal Palace. The deal was completed in January 1981 and, before he left, he told me he was taking Dario with him. Then, for the second time, he asked me if I would like to become manager of Wimbledon.

There were still 19 games to go at this stage. I did not hesitate. This time I was ready. 'Yes please,' I said, and that was that. It was, to use an old sporting cliché', originally from baseball I think, the start of a whole new ball-game. I thought that I'd been around a bit and had sampled many of the varied wines of life ... but somebody should have told me:

'You ain't seen nuthin' yet, 'Arry.'

I was the boss of the Ugly Duckling!

3

I'm In Charge

NO MATTER HOW LONG YOU HAVE BEEN PLAYING FOOTBALL, no matter how many times you have been on the subs' bench, no matter how much time you have spent as a physio or coach, nothing prepares you for the day in which you become manager of a football club. It can be the loneliest job in town, the most fulfilling and the most frustrating – all in one 90-minute spell.

Most managers shout themselves hoarse from the touchline, knowing full well that their players are able to hear very little – and of what they do hear they take very little notice. You can spend all week preparing for a match, but once that whistle starts the game the manager might just as well be locked inside his office for all the good that he can do.

Perhaps that is why there is such a camaraderie among managers. When we play against one another, of course, we do our level best to put one over on our opposite numbers. But that apart, most managers are very supportive of one another. We all know what it's like to have a trust betrayed, a vote of no-confidence from the board, or a newspaper story that you have sold a vital player, when in fact it was the board who sold him – against your wishes.

I was thrilled to bits when I became manager of Wimbledon. It was a bit like going to Alton Towers and buying tickets for a giant rollercoaster. It's great until the car starts to move and you realise that you are going on a journey that will have your heart in your mouth, your stomach several yards behind you and no such thing as constipation.

I faced my first match as manager on 31 January 1981. At the time Wimbledon were placed 13th. We won 3–2 away at Port Vale and started a run of eight matches during which we dropped only three points. It certainly helped to rebuild the confidence of the team and we lost only three of our last 19 games. It was enough to see us sneak into fourth place and win promotion back to Division Three.

It was a great feeling to gain promotion after only three months of becoming manager, but it was won as much in the dressing-room as on the field. I've always been a great believer in fostering team-spirit. Players can slag each other off as much as they like, but it is mostly done in a spirit of fun and I have never seen anything wrong in a few practical jokes. That is just as well really when you consider the bunch of jokers we had at Wimbledon.

It is not surprising that they were known as the Crazy Gang of football. Some of the tricks that they got up to, both on and off the pitch, were so outrageous that they made the legendary pranks of the real Crazy Gang seem pretty tame. Nobody was safe and no reputation was held sacred as the real characters started to emerge. There were the court jesters like Cork and Downes, who would play it hard both on the pitch and in the dressing-room, and there were young and talented players like Glyn Hodges, Kevin Gage and Mark Morris who were just emerging from the junior sides to be fed to them as cannon-fodder – that is, before they learned the first rule of survival at Plough Lane: 'Always give as good as you get.'

One of my first tasks as manager was to appoint Alan Gillett, the youth-team coach, as my assistant manager and I then brought in Geoff Taylor to run the youth operation. Since he retired from playing, Geoff had taken over as manager of Ruislip Manor from Phil McKnight, the former Orient and Chelsea player. I had tried to get Geoff involved in the Wimbledon operation the previous year but, although he came to discuss it with Dario, no concrete offer had been made and the idea seemed to fizzle out. Now I had the chance to build my own team and saw both Gillett and Taylor as a vital part of the coaching set-up.

Our return to Division Three was greeted by a remarkable display of apathy on the part of the Wimbledon fans. The club's permanent financial crisis meant that we had to sell players to survive and I started the season with a depleted squad rather than the stronger one that I would need to survive in the Third Division.

I lost two particularly important players when Dario Gradi took Steve Galliers with him to Crystal Palace for £70,000, and when our captain, Tommy Cunningham, went to Orient for £34,000. We still kept our chins up, though, and went into the new season full of optimism. We still had Alan Cork to score the goals. He had hit 26 in 50 games the previous season, so I knew that if we kept feeding him he would keep on banging them in the net.

Our opening match saw us on the wrong end of a 4–1 thumping at Swindon. We were a goal down at half-time and caved in to three more in the second half. Our confidence dipped a little but there was yet more to come. Our first home League match was against Millwall and we were beaten 3–1. We gained a point at Huddersfield but then lost 3–1 at home to Aldershot in the League Cup. Doncaster then beat us at home and Fulham did a job on us a few days later, beating us 3–1 at Plough Lane.

We had played seven League and League Cup games and lost all but two of them – and they were drawn. We had scored five goals and conceded 15. Also we had a growing casualty department. Things could not get any worse ... could they? Yes, they could ... and they did. Following the defeat by Fulham, we were away to Walsall and Alan Cork was carried off with a broken leg that was to keep him out for the rest of that season. Not long before Corky broke his leg, I had said to him, 'Well, nothing else can go wrong.' He has reminded me of that ever since and warned me never to say such a thing again.

Walsall beat us 1–0. We drew 2–2 with Bristol Rovers, lost 2–0 at home against Gillingham and then travelled to Lincoln where we were given a 5–1 hiding. Things were getting serious. We were desperate to get our first win under our belts. Our opening sequence of 11 games had proved to be a nightmare and, even allowing for our horrendous injury situation, there could be no excuse. We were playing for pride by this time. Our supporters were becoming disillusioned and only 1,659 turned up to see us play Chester at Plough Lane on 22 October 1981. Those that did back us were rewarded at last when Paul Lazarus found the net in the first half and at last we had a victory.

Poor results can drain confidence very quickly and the Wimbledon players' morale reached rock-bottom shortly before Christmas when we were beaten 4–1 by Enfield in the second round of the FA Cup. It was the second time in four years that Enfield had dumped us out of the FA Cup. I was reminded of the way that Walton & Hersham had disposed of Brian Clough's Brighton team in a similar manner in 1973, and I came to realise just how humiliating it is to be stuffed by a non-League side. At the time I was quoted as saying that our Cup match against Enfield was men against boys — and we were the boys.

By Christmas we had scratched together a miserable 13 points from 18 League games, a record which is even worse when you consider that this was the first season when three, rather than two, points were awarded for a win. Come the festive period, our record was three wins and four draws with 11 defeats. We had an unexpected breather during Christmas because bad weather caused havoc to the fixture schedule. The traditional seasonal elbow-bending must have worked wonders because things picked up in the New Year and we registered three wins and one draw from our next four games.

That sequence didn't last, though, and it seemed likely that we were once again doomed to relegation as the end of the season approached. Our only possible life-line was the fact that four of our last five games were at home and there was the faintest chance that we could survive if only we took maximum points. The trouble with that hope was that, even if we were able to achieve this unlikely target, we would still have to rely on poor results from other relegation candidates to assure our survival. As it happened, we won four and drew one of those last five matches to take 13 points which lifted us away from the foot of the table. We considered ourselves more than a little unfortunate to be condemned to the fourth relegation spot on goal-difference.

We scored 61 goals that season – only five less than Burnley, who won the Third Division championship, and four less than Carlisle who came second. Our main problem was a leaky defence which conceded 75 goals in 46 League games.

Believe me, they weren't all the fault of the goalkeeper, Dave Beasant. He had made his mark the previous season, emerging as first choice over Ray Goddard and also collecting the Dons' Player of the Year award for the first time. Despite the 75 goals conceded, he had been ever-present during this relegation season and it was to start his incredible run of consistency which saw him play in every League match for six seasons. Only in their Cup-winning year – 1987–88 when I had left Wimbledon – did he miss two League matches. That's not a bad record for a goalkeeper who cost £1,000 and then went on to play for England. He is still supremely fit and playing top-class football, and is a credit to his profession.

As though the results weren't bad enough that season, the club was also rocked by a tragedy off the pitch. With mounting injury problems early on in the programme, I had signed former England defender, Dave Clement, on a free transfer from Queen's Park Rangers. He played nine games for us before he also became an injury victim, suffering a broken leg at Doncaster in January 1982.

Dave's injury seemed to compound several personal worries and problems and he gradually became more and more depressed as he wondered what he was going to do with his life. Two months later, Dave accompanied Geoff Taylor to a reserve match as a spectator and Geoff remembers that he seemed very agitated. At half-time he wanted to have a private chat in the dressing-room but Geoff's services were required elsewhere.

The following morning, while preparing for our pre-match lunch at Chester, we heard the news that Dave Clement had taken his own life the previous night. It had a deep effect on all of us who had known him and had played with him. I was devastated and poor Geoff Taylor has never forgotten how lonely Dave looked on that last day, and has often reproached himself for not being there to help him with his problems. However, I am convinced that, had Geoff managed to spend time with him, it would only have served to delay the inevitable. Once a depressive (which Dave Clement apparently was) has decided to end his problems and his life, it is rare that he ever deviates from his chosen route. The affair is all the more tragic because, with his broad experience, I am certain that he still had so much more to offer the game in a coaching capacity – and that would surely have meant so much to him.

Wimbledon were now poised to start their sixth year in the Football League. Despite having been promoted to the Third Division twice, we had failed to make the grade on each occasion and now found ourselves right back where we had started. I also felt that the board, now headed by chairman Sam Hammam, were taking a close look at the future managerial prospects of Harry Bassett and, if I valued my job, we'd have to make it back into Division Three yet again.

After relegation to the Fourth Division in the summer of 1982, we were joined by a new club physiotherapist, Derek French, a man who was born to be part of the crazy, zany, almost surrealistic rise of Wimbledon over the next four years.

When I found him, Derek was dividing his life between working as a part-time physio at Barnet and driving a mini-cab. We were certainly no wealthier than Barnet and when 'Frenchie', as he was always known to us, came to us, we told him not to give up his mini-cabbing.

He has been the club fall-guy and the butt of several cruel jokes – but he's taken most of them well. He wasn't too impressed, though, when Wally Downes almost drowned him during the club's first pre-season tour of Finland. All the boys had gone for a swim in the lake and it seemed quite important to Wally that he should discover just how long Frenchie could survive under water. He went to the limit.

On a later occasion, a couple of the younger members of the team dangled him over the side of a boat by his ankles in a Finnish port. There was a heavy swell and Frenchie was screaming for his life as money and personal belongings cascaded from his pockets into the murky sea before they eventually hauled him back to safety. He will also claim that Mark Morris, quite wilfully, attempted to decapitate him during pre-season training. I was illustrating a tactical point from a free-kick position and had used Frenchie as part of the defensive 'wall'. On the word 'go', he was to take off like a rocket and charge the ball. He did exactly that but, as he charged forward, Morris' arm shot out and karate-chopped him straight across the windpipe.

Frenchie also dines out on the tale of the League match during which he rushed on to the pitch to attend a minor injury. Wally Downes – who else? – thought he looked a bit hot and so picked up the bucket and emptied it over Frenchie's head, much to the surprise and delight of the crowd. Frenchie has only been close to committing murder on one occasion. He had injured his foot during a training incident and one of the players, Steve Galliers, at first showing a great deal of mock concern over the injury, suddenly jumped on it. Frenchie's scream of agony must have been heard throughout South London. Everyone who witnessed the incident has an abiding memory of our revered physio hobbling after a somewhat fitter Mr Galliers, screaming: 'I'll kill you, you *****, I'll kill you.'

But even Frenchie cringed at Wimbledon's infamous 'turd-in-the-shoe' incident, when one of the players decided – probably for a bet – to defecate in a team-mate's footwear. I was never quite certain of the identity of the culprit but I have my suspicions. The poor victim was forced to go home in trainers after committing an otherwise perfectly good pair of shoes to the incinerator.

Newcomers were always regarded as fair game and Dave Beasant still remembers his inauguration at Wimbledon. Dave arrived on a motorcycle for his first training session after signing from Edgeware. Some jokers filled his helmet with talcum powder and, when he put it on, it covered the top half of his body. He looked like the original Homepride flour grader.

Fortunately, I've always been in favour of high spirits and, with a bunch like Wimbledon's Crazy Gang, the worst thing that I could have done would have been to interfere, or take any form of disciplinary action. As far as

I am concerned, players who work hard are entitled to play hard – but every one of them knows the penalty if they allow that play time to affect their performance on the pitch.

Boosted by our death-or-glory charge at the end of the previous season, we kicked-off with a run of 11 League games without defeat and were top of the table by early October. Then, typically, came a duff run during which we lost four out of five League games in addition to making a swift exit from the Cup. By Christmas I was beginning to doubt that we would ever get it together again. The New Year saw us beaten 2–1 at home by high-flying Hull City and, after the game, I gave the players the rollocking of their lives, threatening to drop seven of them.

I must have touched a raw nerve somewhere because, from that moment on, every man in the squad gave me his blood as we embarked on a run of 22 games without defeat, during which we took 54 points from a possible total of 66. We clinched promotion with four games still to go but, ever true to the Wimbledon make-or-break philosophy, we wanted to go up as champions. We eventually achieved that target, finishing eight clear points ahead of Hull who were in second place. We scored 96 goals that season with Stewart Evans (24) and John Leslie (23) heading the list. I wonder how many more we might have scored if only Alan Cork hadn't missed most of the season – still suffering from that broken leg which kept him out of the game for 18 months.

Even when we had the championship in the bag, I did not want to see my players just going through the motions, so at half-time in a match away to Halifax, I decided to tell them what I thought of them. We were a goal down and I thought my players were taking liberties, playing well below par because they had already achieved the title.

I was furious. I shouted and said that the way we

were playing we couldn't tackle a paper bag. As it happened, there was an empty sweets bag on the floor and I swung my foot at it. My slip-on shoe flew off and disappeared somewhere in the showers and toilet area. I could see that the players wanted to laugh but I just ignored it and carried on raving. When I had finished, Frenchie retrieved my shoe and I put it back on, only to find that he had filled it with water. This time there was a roar of laughter and I had to join in.

Before the players went out for the second half, I reminded them that they had forgotten everything we had done on the training ground and especially in set play. I told them that if they scored from a set-play move, I would give them £100, but if they didn't, they would have to give me £100. Well, of course, they did score, and Wally Downes ran over to the dugout and held his hand out for the money. We drew 1–1.

The final match of that season – a 3–1 win at Bury – is a night which will live for ever in my memory. We had already clinched the title and the television cameras were at Gigg Lane to record highlights of the game. They would have recorded better footage if they had been with us on the train back to London that night.

Not surprisingly, spirits were running high and I knew that we were sure to be in for a spot of bother when a group of players – led by Wally Downes wearing an inane grin – peered into the compartment where I was sitting with Derek French. We stood no chance at all. In less than a minute we had been stripped down to our underclothes and our shirts, shoes and trousers had disappeared through the window to adorn the countryside somewhere in the Midlands. Worse still, the players prevented us from leaving the train at Watford Junction, close to where we both lived, and we finished up at Euston.

Fortunately I still had my jacket, but we both felt pretty stupid and those late-night revellers must have wondered what fate had befallen us as, shirtless, trouserless and shoeless, we made our way across the station to board another train bound for Watford. We took a taxi from Watford station to my home in nearby Northwood and I dare not repeat the welcome I got from Christine when she opened the front door to be confronted by her semi-naked husband pleading for money for the cab fare.

Our success that season enabled the club to buy out the pre-emption clause on the Plough Lane ground from Merton Council and that just about emptied the bucket. I was informed by chairman Sam Hammam that there would be no money available for players, but he did seem happier now that the future of the club appeared settled after getting the council off our backs.

Sam is Lebanese by nationality and had joined the board under the chairmanship of Ron Noades. He had been on the point of joining the mass exodus to Selhurst Park but changed his mind, opting instead to buy out Noades' shares and remain at Plough Lane where, I assume, he felt that there was more chance of running things in his own way. His rise at Wimbledon has been nothing short of remarkable since he walked in, practically off the street, and secured his place on the board on the strength of a loan to the club. He had previously tried Chelsea, but had received a much better welcome at Plough Lane. Sam owned the club outright and in 1990 Merton Council agreed that the Plough Lane site could be developed, paving the way for a new stadium and sports complex a few miles away. Many millionaires pump money into football clubs hoping that investment will bring success. It appears to have been the other way around with Sam – the club seems to have made him a wealthy man.

I remember, in 1981, Sam telling me that there was no money available for players because he had no assets in this country. In my naive enthusiasm to help the club I agreed to put my house up as a guarantee for a bank loan of £100,000. Any problem and the bailiffs would be round to Chez Bassett like lightning. I now realise what a stupid move I had made but, not surprisingly, Sam seemed quite happy to sit back and let me take the risk. The evening after signing I realised the full impact of my commitment and, to some extent, my vulnerability compared to Sam's.

By the time that Peter Cork, a banker and director of the club, found out what was going on it was too late. He pointed out that I had left myself wide open by signing the 'joint and several' clauses governing the loan and explained that, in the event of a default in repayment, the bank could come down on me for the lot. I remember how sternly Peter looked at me, not unlike a schoolmaster rebuking a wayward pupil, as he asked, 'Do you know exactly what you have let yourself in for?'

Another director and former club chairman, and still my oldest and dearest friend, Joe McElligot commented, 'You must be raving mad.'

But these were mild rebukes when compared to what Christine had to say to me after she discovered that I had effectively hocked the family silver. If you really want to know the details of her reaction and what she said to me, I'll have to send them to you – preferably in a plain brown envelope.

Peter Cork's finger-wagging had sent a cold draught whistling up my trouser-leg and, next morning, I asked for a meeting with Sam. I was worried that I had left my home and family vulnerable. Together we went to see his lawyer, Peter Cooper, who later became a director of the club.

I found Peter to be most sympathetic to my situation. He offered me good advice but also pointed out that the deed had been done – or in my case, almost signed away – and Sam appeared none too keen to have my name – or my house – removed from the guarantee documents, a move which, he thought, would be bound to upset the bank. In the end, with Peter Cooper's help, we drew up an agreement ensuring that I would receive shares in the club in the event of the bank chasing me for the money.

This did give me a little more peace of mind and a certain feeling of security but, in reality, the shares were virtually worthless anyway. At least they were worthless then. If only I could have looked into a crystal ball and seen what would happen 20 years later when Sam sold out to the Norwegians for about £30 million. But back then, my name remained on the loan agreement for almost another year before the directors eventually took over the guarantee. There was even talk of me becoming a director of the club at this time, but nothing ever happened — Sam saw to that.

Sam always maintained that his reason for having involved me was so that I had a greater incentive as manager. He felt that I would probably work longer and harder if I had a financial interest in whether the club tasted delight or disaster.

In fairness to Sam Hammam, I was totally unaware of how wealthy he was and, at the time when all this happened, I had known him for only three months. In the euphoria of my new role as a manager — and the thrill of promotion — I had completely forgotten about the volatile nature of football. Had this sequence of events taken place in 1982 instead of 1981, my head might have had a little more control over my heart. Well, it might.

We started the 1983–84 season as Third Division new boys for the third time. By now we had been up-down-up-down-up in successive years and were gaining the reputation of being the classic yo-yo club. This time I was determined that we were not going to go down again and I had my eye on Steve Hatter, a central-defender from Fulham. The board had again insisted that there were no funds available and so at our first home game of the season, against Newport County, we organised a blanket collection among the crowd to help us raise the money.

John Leslie had left us to join Gillingham and in so doing had severed the last link with players from Wimbledon's non-League days. We got £15,000 for him and we were just able to scrape together enough to secure Hatter's signature. Alan Cork was fit again at last and I was able to strengthen the squad with a few next-to-nothing signings including a young full-back called Nigel Winterburn, who came to us from Oxford and who later became such a big star for Arsenal and for England. I had actually wanted to sign Brian Sparrow from Arsenal but Terry Neill, then the Gunners' manager, wouldn't let him go to us for £10,000. As it happens, we signed Nigel at no cost at all.

We welcomed back Steve Galliers from Crystal Palace, paying a bargain £15,000 for him, and he reflected the mood at the time when he told the press: 'I wouldn't have come back if I didn't think that Wimbledon were capable of going places. 'While Francis Joseph had been lost to Brentford for £40,000, we signed Gary Peters as captain from Fulham and also enlisted Chris Dibble and Tony Tagg from Millwall.

The blanket collection for Steve Hatter had been successful. It was quite a day actually because it was our first home League match of the new season and we beat Newport 6–0, with Alan Cork hitting a great hat-trick. It was the start of something big.

Our season started brightly enough and we picked up a useful First Division scalp when we put Nottingham Forest – yes, Cloughie again – out of the Milk Cup, winning the home leg 2–0 and then holding them to a 1–1 draw at the City Ground.

After the game away to Forest, I made a classic

blunder. You can imagine what the mood was like after the final whistle. In my wisdom I decided that we should have a night out in Nottingham to celebrate. Big mistake. And a lesson learned the hard way as I flirted with alcoholic poisoning for the next few days. I was not the only one either as was shown by our next game just three days later. We were thrashed 5–1 by Scunthorpe. It taught me never to stop in town after a great result.

Even Stanley Reed, our chairman, said that the good people of Nottingham had been incredibly hospitable to us. Actually I think he said, 'The women of Nottingham were wonderful to us.' But don't quote me on that as my memory is a little blurred.

We hit the top of the division in February with a 6–2 win at Orient and, as the end of the season approached, it became clear that we were together with Oxford, Sheffield United and Hull in the scrap for promotion. Then came the most critical match of the season – away at Bramall Lane – which seemed certain to put the winners just a stride away from promotion.

A crowd of 23,000 packed into the ground to see Wimbledon win 2–1 with goals from our consistent double-act, 'Good Evans' and 'Champagne Cork'. All we had to do was beat Gillingham at Plough Lane two days later and promotion would be ours – but we thought we had blown it when we went down 3–1.

Then came the news that Sheffield United had also lost at Bolton and therefore we were assured of one of the three promotion places.

We won our last match, at Burnley, to finish second to champions Oxford United and four points clear of Sheffield United who had sneaked in just ahead of Hull City on goal-difference. The yo-yo team had done it again – the sixth move in six successive seasons – but this time it was up to the unknown fields of the old Second Division. I shook hands with my players, thanked them for their efforts – and then told them that I would not be with them for the following season.

Silence is not something normally associated with the Wimbledon dressing-room but, at that moment, you could have heard a mouse belch. It was all down to that man Noades again. Crystal Palace had not enjoyed the best of fortunes and Alan Mullery, who had himself replaced Dario Gradi, had been given the elbow. For the third time in our lives, Ron had offered me a job of manager, this time at Selhurst Park, and I was immediately interested. I saw it as an opportunity to work with a larger club which had better facilities, more support and more money available. It was also a chance to break free from the penny-pinching attitude of the Wimbledon board and from the overall austerity of the Plough Lane set-up which, despite all our success, was still not much better than several of the non-League clubs.

I agreed to go to Palace and, in so doing, wrote myself into the record books as having had the briefest managerial appointment of all time. Four days was all it took for me to realise that I had made the biggest mistake of my life so far. I kept asking myself what the hell I was doing at Selhurst Park when something inside me was screaming that I really belonged to Wimbledon. I could also see that the squad I had left behind contained much more talent and promise than the gang which I had inherited at Palace. I'm sure that was the first time that I realised that Wimbledon – the team that I had cobbled together for almost nothing – had the potential to reach the top flight of English football.

My heart told me that this was the wrong time to be leaving. I couldn't sleep, I couldn't eat and I lost weight worrying about it. By the fourth day I could stand it no more. I had spoken to Stanley Reed, the Wimbledon chairman, several times during the four days of my departure and he had indicated to me that, while the Dons door had been closed behind me, it had not been bolted. I telephoned Stanley and Sam Hammam to see if they would have me back. Fortunately they had not filled the vacancy and so I went to break the news to Ron Noades.

Ron wasn't too delighted about my decision, but he and I have always understood one another and he must have realised that hanging on to an unhappy manager would be even worse than retaining a disgruntled player. He didn't stand in my way but, when we announced the parting of the ways after a spell of just 96 hours, the press had a field day. Some of them even tried to suggest that I was returning to Wimbledon because Ron had tucked me up.

I think that it is fair to say that we both finished up with traces of egg on our faces, but I would like to go on record as saying that none of it was his fault. The entire episode can be put down as an error of judgement on the part of yours truly. Later, when the season had started, my fears about the Palace team's shortcomings were confirmed. We beat them 3–2 at home and then 5–0 away – which emphasised to me just how right I had been not to sever my links with football's Crazy Gang.

I was glad that it turned out all right for Ron and Palace, though. He appointed Steve Coppell and success followed. Nobody was happier about that than me.

My possible departure had been a close shave – but I was still manager of Wimbledon and together we were still 'on the up'.

4

Serving Uncle Sam

THEY SAY THAT YOU SHOULD NEVER GO BACK – but I had no regrets about returning to Wimbledon. Well, of course, it is not true to say that I had no regrets at all. There were no stars at Plough Lane – and precious few stripes – but we still had Uncle Sam.

Sam Hammam made it quite clear that, although I had returned to Wimbledon, our relationship had been tarnished and he indicated that it would never be the same again. This proved to be more true than I could possibly have realised at the time.

In retrospect I suppose I should have been rather more annoyed at Sam's attitude. I had been truthful about my thoughts and feelings and, had it not been for Ron Noades, I would never have contemplated leaving Wimbledon in the first place. However, I was to realise that Sam would not forgive – or forget – my possible move to Palace. He did not like coming second to anyone and, as time passed, he made that more and more obvious.

Sam's stance struck me as being a little strange. After all, had he not been on the verge of doing exactly the same thing himself when Ron Noades led the exodus from Plough Lane across South London to Selhurst Park in January 1981? As I saw it, the only difference was that he changed his mind before he put on his hat and coat. It just took me a little while longer.

However, he seemed quite happy to have me in charge of the team again and immediately started to discuss terms for a new three-year contract. Since it was the Wimbledon chairman, Stanley Reed, who had left the door open for me, we just got on with it, even though there was a definite 'atmosphere' between Sam and myself.

It took time to reach a mutually-satisfactory agreement and I signed a new deal just before the start of the new season. The contract was to bind me to Plough Lane for three more years and equalled the Crystal Palace deal – which was more than he was offering before I left for Selhurst Park. I was anxious to avoid any unnecessary acrimony and left the dust to settle as we prepared for our first-ever season in Division Two.

I went shopping on a shoe-string, this time picking up Lawrie Sanchez from Reading for £29,000 and defender John Kay from Arsenal for £25,000. I also wasted £40,000 buying a player called Dave Martin from Millwall. It wasn't one of my better decisions and 18 months later, I moved him on to Southend at a loss of £15,000 which we could ill afford.

The fixture computer had been kind to us, providing a home curtain-raiser against Manchester City. The confidence provided by that strong finish to the previous season was evident from the kick-off and it looked like a dream start as we went two goals up in the first 13 minutes. City, however, were nobody's fools and they fought back strongly for a 2–2 draw We had a fair start to the season, but then an indifferent spell emphasised some of our weaknesses.

I was just grateful that Geoff Taylor's youth team was coming up with youngsters like Andy Thorn and Brian Gayle, who would be ready to break into the reckoning for first-team places before the end of the season. Off the park, the Crazy Gang continued to live up to their dubious reputation with some pretty wild times – more of that later.

The FA Cup also threw up a couple of cherished memories, starting with a third-round home tie against

Burnley who were now also in the Second Division. We won 3–1 and who should come out of the hat for round four? None other than Cloughie again. We didn't fear an away tie at Forest and held them to a goalless draw; winning the replay 1–0 with a goal from Paul Fishenden. Our reward was a fifth-round tie at home against fellow Londoners, West Ham United, a club we had met in neither League nor Cup competition since our breakthrough in 1977. We held them at home, 1–1, but were annihilated 5–1 in the replay. As we kissed goodbye to the FA Cup for another year, I remember thinking that it wouldn't bother me if we never met the Hammers again.

Our main objective that year was to consolidate our position in Division Two and we were able to achieve this with a strong run towards the end of the season which saw us finish in mid-table. It is interesting to note that the efficiency of the Second Division defences that season can be measured by the fact that we scored only 71 goals – 25 less than the previous season – albeit with four fewer games. We also conceded an astonishing 75 League goals, the third worst in the division and only four fewer than Cardiff and Wolves, both of whom were relegated.

For the record, Oxford won the Second Division title – their second successive championship year to take them into the top flight for the first time. I remember thinking how unfamiliar it felt to be going neither up nor down. It had happened for the first time in my five seasons as manager and was only Wimbledon's second static year since joining the Football League eight seasons earlier. Nevertheless, I was fairly happy with the team's League performance that season and the additional benefit of a reasonable Cup run had boosted the players' confidence. Now we knew what to expect from Division Two and looked forward to making our mark in the 1985–86 season.

By now we were beginning to get the reputation as

long-ball specialists and, in many respects, it was this that had proved to be our salvation in the Second Division. I have been pilloried in the press for using this tactic and certain journalists have even suggested that it is the only one I know. They are talking through their backsides. I believe I have a full range of tactics to suit all occasions, but that was what was necessary at the time. Opponents couldn't cope with it and we were there to win matches. It brought us success.

Like most managers, I plan each game according to the strengths and weaknesses of the opposition. I'd hardly be doing my players justice if I insisted that they played the long-ball game week in and week out, regardless of who we were playing. However, that is the way that some of my critics see it – or perhaps it is the way in which they want to see it.

It is a little ironic that I have found myself having to defend being successful while others have to defend their failures. Anyway, having defended my reasons for employing the long-ball game at Wimbledon, perhaps it is time to return to the club's second season in the old Division Two. It was the year when we were destined to upset the football hierarchy by achieving the impossible – promotion to join the élite of the football world in Division One.

We went to Harrogate army camp which was probably a mistake because the facilities were poor and did not make for the best preparation. It was done on the cheap but we should have stayed in a decent hotel.

We opened confidently with a 3–0 win at home against Middlesbrough followed by a goalless draw at Leeds. Then Sheffield United beat us 4–0 to bring us down with a bump. We recovered sufficiently to win each of the next three matches by a single goal to nil. Our first ten League games yielded 17 points from a possible 30 – which is hardly promotion form – and the next 11 provided only 16 to give us a total of 33 points by the halfway stage of the season.

That put us in touch with the promotion candidates but, if I'm honest, I didn't give much for our chances of catching them. Then, all at once, we seemed to click and the goal famine which had been bothering me came to an end.

We celebrated Christmas a few days early with a 5–0 revenge over Sheffield United at Plough Lane and then went on to beat Crystal Palace and Barnsley to take nine points from three games. Then someone forgot to say 'Happy New Year' and we were beaten 3–1 at home by promotion rivals Portsmouth. Three days later we were booted out of the FA Cup by Millwall, and Oldham added to our misery by beating us 2–1 at Boundary Park to record their first win in 11 matches.

A few choice words from yours truly, some fierce training and a juggled line-up saw us get things back together with a convincing 3–0 win against Grimsby — and our performance gave me a great deal of confidence. We were still in with a shout for promotion and I remember thinking that, if only we could maintain the impetus, Division One could become less of a wild dream and much more of a possibility. Then Mother Nature stepped in with snowstorms and a freeze-up that was to kick the game into touch for over a month. I cursed our luck, fearing that an enforced lengthy lay-off would totally destroy our momentum.

I need not have worried. When hostilities resumed five weeks later, we were held to a goalless draw at home against Brighton and then beat leaders Norwich 2–1 with goals from those old reliables, Evans and Cork. Millwall and Fulham went the same way, but I was a little perturbed when we dropped valuable points at home to Blackburn. I knew that if we were to maintain our promotion push then we needed more fire-power up front. I went to the directors with my begging bowl and – perhaps carried away by the prospect of First Division football at Wimbledon – they dug deep into their pockets and even deeper into the club's overdraft. The man I wanted was John Fashanu, the Millwall striker who had impressed me so much earlier in the season. George Graham, then managing Millwall, valued the player at £155,000, around four times the figure that we had spent on any other player. The club came up with the money thanks, I believe, to a massive loan from Sam Hammam.

'Fash' made his debut the following week, coming on as a substitute in a heated clash at Portsmouth, who were also among the leading contenders for promotion. We came away with a point from a 1–1 draw and although he didn't score, I was extremely pleased with Fashanu's performance in what was an ugly game. He played the full 90 minutes against Palace, when he fooled their defence with a powerful header to score his first goal for us in another 1–1 draw.

Fash scored again the following week, in a 3–2 win at Carlisle which put us right back in the promotion race. The drive back from Cumbria that night is particularly memorable for me and full-back Nigel Winterburn, who was now attracting attention from several top clubs. Nigel had been called up as a late replacement for the England Under-21 squad, due to leave the following morning for a vital European Championship match against Italy. We eventually reached the team's hotel at 2am – but it was worth it. Nigel was selected to play and became Wimbledon's first professional international. As often seems to happen with internationals, Nigel was played out of position at left midfield but he still gave a good account of himself.

The win at Carlisle ensured that we were still in the promotion hunt – but we were just one of five other clubs scrapping for the two runner-up places. Norwich, the leaders, were already ten points clear and virtually home and dry. Alan Ball's Portsmouth team were in second place with 66 points from 36 games, and we were third – five points adrift of Portsmouth but with a game in hand. Hot on our heels was Charlton, with both Hull and Crystal Palace also still in the race.

It was imperative that we should win our next match at home to Sunderland, after which we had four away fixtures in our last six games. I pondered deeply on the team selection. Glyn Hodges had suffered a loss of form and had been unable to command a regular first-team place, but I decided to take a gamble on his flair which was long overdue for an airing. It paid off with Glyn banging in a second-half hat-trick to give us three more vital points.

The disappointment of a 1–1 draw at Shrewsbury was soon forgotten with home wins over Hull and Stoke coming just four days apart. Then Portsmouth started to crack under the pressure and, suddenly, the equation was there for all to see. With three away matches remaining, at Huddersfield, Charlton and Bradford, we needed only three points to be assured of promotion.

It was a drab afternoon at Huddersfield. The rain lashed down, punctuated by thunder and lightning, and it was as though the gods themselves were showing their disapproval of Wimbledon's impertinent bid to reach the First Division. The rain seemed to be blowing horizontally across the pitch and visibility was extremely poor. Through these near-impossible conditions came the figure of Lawrie Sanchez, one of only two players who were ever-present that season, to fasten on to a short free-kick and blast the ball into the net. It was a classic improvisation as we had never practised that move from a free-kick.

It was the only goal of the match and it saw Wimbledon into the First Division just nine seasons after being elected to join the Football League's Fourth Division. Almost exactly two years later, Lawrie was to write himself into another chapter of glory when he scored the goal which won the FA Cup for Wimbledon and which deprived Liverpool of the double. I know which of those two goals gave me the most pleasure.

The scenes at Huddersfield that night were amazing as the players rushed to throw their shirts to their drenched, but deliriously happy supporters. Dave Beasant went one step further and even threw his shorts on to the terraces. Who could blame him? He had played in every one of the matches during our remarkable rise from the Fourth Division.

The spirit of camaraderie was wonderful. Most of the players had been together for years. They had grown up together and they had gone to war together – and they had prevailed! Of that promotion-winning side only one, John Fashanu, had cost serious money – and what a bargain he turned out to be. Of the others, Morris, Gage, Hodges, Thorn, Gayle, Sayer and Fishenden had come up through the youth team. Winterburn, Cork and Evans had joined us on free transfers. Beasant had cost £1,000, Galliers £1,500, Fairweather £7,500, Smith £15,000, Kay £25,000, Sanchez £29,000 and Holloway £40,000. It was a team cobbled together for less than £275,000, but it had made it to the First Division with two matches to spare. With the heat off we drew both of the last two games, allowing Charlton to slip into second place ahead of us. I didn't mind. I was pleased for Charlton manager, Lennie Lawrence. He was pleased for me – and we were both delighted for our fans. Lennie developed into a good friend and confidant. I have often found him to be the voice of reason.

It was some time before it dawned on me that during our promotion season we had scored only 58 goals – 26 fewer than Norwich and 20 fewer than Charlton, both of who finished ahead of us. We also scored fewer goals than six of the teams who finished behind us and, perhaps even more pertinently our tally was 13 short of the previous season when we had finished in mid-table. Thank God for a strong defence which conceded only 37 goals, the same total as Norwich.

After its summer slumbers the football world eventually awoke, pinched itself and realised that it wasn't just a bad dream – Wimbledon really were up there in the First Division.

'Cuckoos, perhaps – squatting in someone else's nest,' suggested the pundits while assuring each other that it was merely a temporary aberration and that normal service would be resumed upon Wimbledon's imminent demise at the end of the season. It was simply a bad year for the soccer grape, one wag suggested.

The big clubs did not like it one little bit. They would much rather visit Sunderland, Middlesbrough or Sheffield United, where the facilities were better and the crowds were larger, than experience the spartan set-up where the average attendance was little more than for a Liverpool reserve match.

I could understand their view of course – but I didn't agree with it. Top clubs have long campaigned for a closed shop – or Super-League –which would provide protection against the worries of relegation and it has upset them in recent years that such unfashionable clubs as Watford, Oxford and Wimbledon have not only crashed their party, but have also done it with a certain measure of success. Even smaller clubs like Orient, Northampton, Carlisle and Swansea have been there too – albeit, not for long – but who can deny them the right of a crack at the big boys if their form and results have warranted it?

For me, one of the delights of the restructured English game is the fact that you can set out as Raggedy-arsed Rovers and work your way through the system to the top level – providing, of course, that your facilities meet the required criteria.

It wasn't just the top clubs who were po-faced at Wimbledon's successful arrival in Division One. Certain sectors of the press, who saw it as an affront to the national game, prejudged us unfairly – wailing that the Dons' style of play would sour the renaissance which soccer was currently enjoying. Our physical approach toward our opponents, they claimed, was more suited to Twickenham than Old Trafford – and all this before a ball had even been kicked in anger.

I felt that this criticism was extremely unfair. The press were promoting Wimbledon as some sort of ogre whose presence was both unjustified and unwelcome. However, their venom served only to bring us closer together, like any persecuted minority group, and the players became even more determined to show some of the bulldog spirit of the underdog and to fight that much harder to prove that they were worthy of their new position. Consequently, by the start of the season, we believed that we were equally as good as Liverpool and Manchester United. It no longer seemed to matter that nobody wanted us to be that good.

We went on a pre-season tour of Finland and it was then that I decided that Dennis Wise would play a more regular role in the side. His appearances had been spasmodic up to then, but I decided that he was now ready. The players had moaned a bit about the accommodation on our Finland trip so when we headed for Helsinki for our last game you can imagine that they were thrilled when we turned into a road leading to a beautiful lakeside hotel. They all cheered and there were shouts of 'Well done, Harry', until we went straight past the hotel and and finally stopped at some kind of a hostel in which the players had to share about ten to a room and had paper sheets for bedding. I have never seen Fash look so disgusted. I called it character-building but the players used other phrases!

We stumbled badly at the first hurdle. Our First Division debut was at Manchester City and we went down 3–1 after Andy Thorn had put us in front with the club's first goal in Division One. The prophets of doom nodded knowingly at each other and mentally reserved space for our obituary. They had barely finished telling each other 'I told you so' when, three days later, we beat Aston Villa 3–2 in front of only 6,372 fans who had bothered to turn up at Plough Lane for our historic home debut. This was followed by a 1–0 home win against Leicester, then another, and another, as both Charlton and Watford were beaten on their own grounds.

Four wins in our opening five matches put us at the top of Division One by early September – suddenly, Wimbledon was news. Not necessarily good news among those same sectors of the press who seemed totally unable, or perhaps unwilling, to come to terms with our success but it was news nonetheless. Then came a disastrous spell and it was almost as though the players had allowed themselves to become convinced that their moment of triumph had been some sort of freak accident – as unlikely and undeserved as a tornado or a lottery win. We stumbled to one draw and five defeats in our next six matches and also made a swift exit from the League Cup at the hands of Cambridge United.

One player who didn't come into the side through our youth policy was one Mr Vincent Jones, an occasional builder's labourer and a part-time player with Wealdstone. He was first brought to my attention by Derek French, who had known him since their days together at Bedmond. Vinnie would accept that he perhaps lacks one or two of the game's more subtle skills, but in him I saw an honest player, tall and strong, who would be able to bridge one or two worrying gaps which had started to appear in our defences.

I paid Wealdstone £15,000 – about the price of a stack of bricks and a dumper truck – for him and he leaped straight from the Vauxhall Conference to the First Division, where he retained his place for the rest of the season, playing 22 League games for us. In only his second game for us he scored the winner against Manchester United.

Fortunately, the changes worked and we broke our poor run with a home win against Norwich, followed by the sweet away defeat of Tottenham. Spurs were later to inflict their revenge by defeating us 2–0 at Plough Lane to deprive us of a place in the semi-final of the FA Cup, before a crowd of 16,000 fans. It was, at that time, Wimbledon's best-ever Cup-run and we had ended the interests of Sunderland, Portsmouth and Everton on the way to the sixth round.

Everton were the Cup holders at the time and to prepare for the match we went to Bournemouth for a few days. It worked as we took the FA Cup out of their hands with a 3–1 victory.

Before facing Tottenham in the sixth round, we went to Spain for our preparations. Unfortunately, the press came with us and there was so much hype that I think we all lost our focus; I certainly lost mine and, as a result, the trip to Spain proved to be a negative rather than a positive influence. It was a lesson to be learned.

Among other cherished memories of that season was the League double over Manchester United and our sensational 2–1 win at Liverpool which is about as close as any side can come to achieving the impossible. Howard Kendall was Everton manager at the time, and raised a glass of champagne to us as he believed that our success at Anfield was a major help to his side on their way to the Championship.

We won each of our last four matches to finish in a highly creditable sixth place that season and, to put it into perspective, it would have brought European soccer to Plough Lane had it not been for the tragedy of the Heysel Stadium disaster and the subsequent ban on English clubs.

I shall never forget after our last match, a 2–0 win at Sheffield Wednesday, Derek French reeled off a few names including Downes, Jones, Cork, Wise and Morris.

'They're all hooligans' he said. 'But if I was going to war, I'd feel a bloody lot safer with that lot.'

I knew just what he meant.

I had decided to let them have a night out in Sheffield on the eve of the match on the understanding that they would not let me down. I trusted them to get to bed at a sensible time and not do anything that would make for a poor performance the following day at Hillsborough. Some of them actually returned earlier than normal and I must say that I was probably the last one to return to the hotel. I had been out at a restaurant with some friends.

When the lift arrived to take me up to our floor, I noticed that it was full of furniture. It looked remarkably like the furniture from my room. When I opened the wardrobe, my worst fears were confirmed when I found my clothes, shoes and everything else. They had completely turned my room out and I had to go to reception and ask for another room.

Also at the end of that season, I received a phonecall from a bloke with a Spanish accent. He told me he was representing a Spanish club and had heard that I might be leaving Wimbledon. He invited me to meet him. I was not so daft as to actually fall for it. I knew straight away that it was a wind-up from the boys, but I decided to go along with the joke. I arranged to meet him a few days after the last match of the season at the Post House near Heathrow Airport. I went along with it because I assumed that it was their idea of getting us all together for a drink and a few laughs before we all went on holiday. I turned up in shorts and a tee-shirt and eventually this bloke came towards me. He looked quite like Lawrie Sanchez and I thought it was him at first. He handed me a card and told me he was representative of Athletico Bilbao. I laughed and got him round the neck and started to wrestle him, asking where the others were hiding. Suddenly, I realised by his reaction that I had got it all wrong and that he really *was* a representative of the famous Spanish club. I had to apologise and explain what it was like to be manager of Wimbledon. I looked at the way I was dressed and thought to myself that this job was going out of the window very rapidly. It turned out that he was a nice guy, very understanding. I didn't get the job, though; it went to Howard Kendall, so Bassett did not do himself any good at all that day.

My three-year contract with Wimbledon was nearing its end. Sam Hammam had become owner of the club and I believe that he was more than a little envious of the publicity accorded to myself and the team during that successful first year in Division One.

Sam felt that he should be getting more of the attention and more of the applause. This became increasingly evident when he started to discuss the terms of a new contract in September – and at various other times before the season had finished. When he eventually came up with a draft document, I was appalled to see that, apart from offering totally unsatisfactory financial terms, he was also attempting to dilute my powers. Then my anger gave way to amusement and I remember laughing out loud at the clause which would give him overall control of team selection if he disagreed with my choice. Sam Hammam had broken his promise to increase my pay by a significant amount, and now he wanted to pick the team too. Hardly surprising then, that even before the season had ended, I knew that we had finally reached the parting of the ways.

5

What's Elton John Doing in My House?

I HAD NO REGRETS ABOUT CHANGING MY MIND and going back to Wimbledon after mistakenly thinking that it would be a good move to take over as manager of Palace. However, as I neared the end of my contract, I knew deep inside that the real parting of the ways between me and the Dons was only a matter of time.

During the season I had started talking to Sam Hammam about a new contract. It was almost like play-acting because we never did settle anything. I thought that we had succeeded on a number of occasions but, each time we had another meeting I discovered that something else had been added or removed.

The months went by and, looking back, I am convinced that we were simply going through the motions without any real likelihood of ever reaching agreement. The simple fact was that Sam Hammam wanted me to leave. Even when I was named as Manager of the Year, he failed to be impressed. With the benefit of hindsight I can understand it all now but, at the time, I was probably still a bit naïve – and I certainly had no experience of negotiating Lebanese-style.

The truth of the matter is that Sam wanted to be 'Mr Wimbledon'. There was precious little chance of that with me being there because I had such wonderful rapport with the supporters. They had known me as a non-League player with the club and then as the manager who had taken them into the top division in English soccer. To them, I really was 'Mr Wimbledon'. We had come a long way together.

Sam just didn't like being number two – and to achieve his ambition to be the main man, I had to go. That was the reason why my new contract kept dragging on. When he finally added the clause which could give him the right to pick the team if he felt like it, there was no possible way that I could agree. A manager picks his own team – nobody else. Sam must have known that I could never go along with a clause like that. In fairness to him, I think that he has had that same clause put in every manager's contract since I left – and, as far as I am aware, he has never yet invoked it – but I could never agree to it in the first place.

At the end of that 1987 season, on 11 May, I resigned. That clause, and Sam's continual way of letting you know who was really the boss, was unacceptable to me. It was no longer 'Harry's Wimbledon'. This time I really meant it. There was another twist in the story too – there was another clause in the original contract which meant that I had to work another six months from the end of my term. Since that would have meant that it would be well into the following season before I was free, it provided obvious complications in getting a new job.

I have to say that I left Wimbledon, partly because I felt that it was time for a change – both for the club and for myself – but also because I felt that Sam was contriving an impossible situation. There is no way that I would want to stay where I wasn't wanted – and so I cleared my desk.

Manchester City were looking for a new manager. Billy McNeill had been in charge before moving on to Aston Villa in September 1986, and Jimmy Frizzell had taken over from him. However, it had been a difficult season for the Maine Road club. They had debts of nearly

£5 million, announced a loss of nearly £300,000 on the year and finished bottom-but-one – which meant relegation. Ironically, Aston Villa were the club below them, so it just wasn't Billy McNeill's year, was it?

City moved Jimmy Frizzell upstairs and wanted a new backside in the manager's chair. I was a candidate for the job and had several meetings with the then chairman, Peter Swales, who I found to be a very pleasant man. When I went to his house in Cheshire I had to chuckle when I saw it for the first time – it was painted sky-blue. I knew there and then that I was dealing with a man who was not only chairman of Manchester City, but a huge fan of his own club too.

That same day I was taking Wimbledon to Scarborough for a friendly. Scarborough were confirmed winners of the GM Vauxhall Conference and would be playing in the Football League the following season. Neil Warnock was their manager then and he wanted a celebration game. Who better than the last non-League side to get into the League – Wimbledon?

I travelled to Manchester on the same day and met Peter Swales and a fellow director, Freddy Pye, who is well-known in football circles. I am pretty sure that they wanted me for the job but we had a sticking point. If I was going to move from London to the unknown territory of a big club in Manchester, then I wanted my own back-room staff. Mr Swales wanted me to keep the existing staff. It was certainly to his credit that he was trying to be as loyal as possible to his employees – but I knew who I wanted around me.

'Think about it and get back to me,' he said.

It was left open and we shook hands and parted. I did think about it – in fact I don't think I thought about anything else – and it was quite a welcome break to go to Wembley on 16 May to watch Coventry City win the FA Cup with a surprise, but well-deserved, 3–2 win over Tottenham Hotspur.

It's not every day that you come home from a Cup Final and find your wife sitting in the lounge enjoying a cup of tea and a chat with a man wearing a scarlet-sequinned jacket, a pair of tights and a silly hat. But let's go back to the beginning of this strange encounter in my lounge.

Christine had watched on television as Coventry lifted the Cup at the expense of Spurs, and she'd then gone on to bathe our two daughters, Carly and Kimberley, when the telephone rang. She was up to her armpits in soap, shampoo and suds and the last thing she needed, at that precise moment, was a telephone conversation.

'Hello,' said a male voice. 'Is Dave there?'

Christine apologised, explaining that I'd gone to Wembley and wasn't expected home before seven. The voice then asked her if she had watched the game, what she thought of it and was she pleased with the result? The answers were yes, great, and yes, in that order. Then the voice asked, 'Is that Dave's wife?' Christine immediately went on the defensive. Just who is this guy who phones up, establishes that her husband was out of town and only then begins a conversation and asks her name?

'Er . . . yes.' Tentatively. 'This is Christine Bassett.' A pause. 'Who is that?'

'Hi, Chris,' said the voice cheerfully. 'My name is Elton John.'

To be absolutely fair, Christine did not begin laughing hysterically, or even begin to shake. She certainly felt like it, but she didn't. Instead – she froze.

'Perhaps you could take my number and ask him to give me a call?' suggested the voice, after a brief pause.

Christine managed to get her vocal cords working again. 'I've got two children in the bath, I'm up to my armpits in bubbles and there isn't a pencil in sight,' she gabbled. 'Can you phone back later?'

'Yes ... all right.' The voice sounded more than a little deflated and hung up.

Women don't swear as much as men but, when the penny dropped with Christine, she admits to a quiet 'Oh ****. . . What have I done?' She guessed it must be something to do with an offer of a job at Watford and she also guessed, quite rightly, that Elton John does not go around offering his phone number to everybody. She spent the next hour wondering if she had blown everything and how to break it to me that the chairman of Watford Football Club, and pop mega-star, had asked me to call him – and she hadn't taken the number. She need not have worried. At seven o'clock on the dot, the telephone rang again.

'Hi, Christine – it's Elton again. Is he home yet?'

I wasn't and she apologised again.

'That's a shame,' said Elton, 'because I'm just five minutes away from you.' There was a long pause – then he repeated, 'Only five minutes away.'

In times of crisis, women can display the most remarkable initiative. 'It is a shame,' she agreed when, all at once, the message sent shock-waves through her head.

God! He wants to come here ... He actually wants to come here!'

Then came total calmness. 'I'm sure he won't be long now – you could always come over here and wait.'

'Thanks, Chris – I thought you were never going to ask. See you in five.'

Exactly five minutes later Christine answered the door to find Elton John accompanied by Muff Winwood, a director of Watford Football Club, standing next to the empty milkbottles. She ushered them into the lounge and offered them everything in the house. They both settled for a cup of tea. Christine remembers that Elton executed a perfect twirl in front of the television for the benefit of the freshly-scrubbed children who were now ready for bed. Kimberley, then aged five, was singularly unimpressed and asked him to move because she was watching her favourite programme.

There followed an unforgettable half-hour for Christine as she and Elton found common ground – he had been born in Pinner and knew it well. She had been a Watford fan all her life, her father had even played for the club and she had been taken to almost every home game as a child. Afterwards, Christine said that it all became a little surreal as they explored each other's taste in music, literature, cars and holidays and then – she remembers this very clearly – as they heard my car pull up, it was Elton who suddenly began showing signs of nervousness about meeting me. It was almost as though he was frightened that I might reject the offer that he had come to put on the table. In my case, I'm sure that Christine was more than a little apprehensive about my reaction to being confronted by one of the all-time greats of the music world right there in my own front room.

She need not have worried. I meet thousands of new faces every year and I greeted this one in the time-honoured manner reserved for friendly people who I don't really know.

'Hello, son,' I said. 'All right?' Even Christine would have sworn that I had known him for years.

'Hello,' he replied. 'I'm Elton John.' Not many surprises there and we shook hands.

He told me that Graham Taylor was leaving Watford to take up the post of manager with Aston Villa and that news of his move would be made public on Monday. Then he made his offer. 'How would you like to manage Watford for me?'

I said that it would suit me just fine. We shook hands again and that was it. There would have to be a meeting the next day to tie up any loose ends and later I would have to meet chief executive, Eddie Plumley, to finalise the details and rubber-stamp the deal. Elton assured me that there would be no problems. He was bubbling with excitement, probably because it was the first time that he had been able to achieve something for Watford entirely on his own initiative. I was to discover later that his unilateral decision was not necessarily a good thing – but, at that moment, it didn't matter. I was now manager of Watford and everything in the garden was rosy. It was a snap decision. I did not weigh up the situation properly and, on reflection, I should have taken more time to give it full consideration. But it just seemed to fit *perfectly* into my life at that time.

Nothing, in fact, could have been more handy. I was living in Northwood, a pleasant commuter parish on the Metropolitan Line and only about three miles from Vicarage Road. My daughters were at a local school and I still had my insurance interests at nearby Eastcote. Christine and I had often said that if the opportunity ever presented itself, nothing could suit us more than a job with Watford. It was, in fact, Taylor-made!

I had already promised that I would telephone Alan Gillett, Geoff Taylor and Derek French on the Sunday morning to update them on the Manchester City situation – which had developed no further since my meeting with Peter Swales. When I finally contacted them and said forget all about Manchester City we were all going to Watford, their reaction was mostly positive. Alan Gillett said he preferred to go north, but the others, who all lived much closer to Vicarage Road than Maine Road, seemed fairly happy to accept the fact that I had made the decision for all of them. There was still the minor hiccup about the remaining extra months of my existing contract with Wimbledon, but I didn't anticipate any real problems there. I had already officially resigned and it would give the Dons ample time to seek and appoint a new man in readiness for the following season. Which shows just how wrong you can be!

I felt that I had achieved much for Wimbledon and I had remained there until the end of the season. There seemed to be no point in hanging around until early September when my contract officially expired. That would have been no good to me, no good for Watford, and no good for Wimbledon, Again, I was being a little naive in assessing the attitude of Sam Hammam. I could hardly believe my ears when he started talking about receiving compensation from Watford and I urged Elton not to pay him a penny.

The negotiations were delayed because the Watford players were going on a trip to China and Elton was going with them. I was off to Switzerland for a coaching seminar, followed by a holiday in Spain. My first day in my new job would be 13 June.

I was stunned when I heard what Sam Hammam was asking in compensation for agreeing to let me go. He maintained that I was still under contract to the Dons and that it was a blow to lose me. A figure of £150,000 was thrown into the ring – about six times my annual salary. Previously £70,000 had been asked – Sam was conducting business in his own inimitable style.

The meeting between each club's representatives became heated, to say the least. With Sam was another Wimbledon director, Jim Lelliot. Elton became so enraged at one stage that he described them both as 'a couple of clinkers that needed cutting out'. Eventually a deal was struck but, to this day, I still feel that Watford should not have had to pay a penny – especially since my leaving Wimbledon was inevitable and had already been decided long before Watford appeared on the scene. If I had gone on the dole, I really believe that Sam Hammam would have expected compensation from the DSS!

That was not the only bit of controversy. Tony Stenson of the *Daily Mirror* seemed to be under the impression that I should let him know every time I wiped my backside. He knew on the weekend of the Cup Final that something was in the wind and he tried to get me to give him the details. Elton had asked me to say nothing to the media until there could be a full press conference, so I kept my mouth shut. Putting two and two together, Stenson decided for himself that I was going to Aston Villa – and he was furious when it was announced that I was joining Watford.

The result was that the *Daily Mirror* carried a full-page piece of poison about me, written by Stenson and entitled 'Dirty Harry'. In it I was called 'a hooligan in £400 suits', as well as 'the spoiled son of a London Transport driving instructor'. It also contained such wonderful literary prose as, 'When he's had a few drinks, Dirty Harry's favourite party piece is to drop his strides and show his Womble manhood.'

It got even better than that when I was accused of being a Male Chauvinist Pig, ruining meals more often than not and upsetting Christine with my terrible time-keeping. So it went on. Discerning readers would have guessed the reason for this unwarranted attack when Stenson wrote, 'Think you're his friend and be ready for a shock.'

Very often the general public think that the press are unfairly treated by people who are newsworthy I can say with all honesty that it is very rare for me not to co-operate unless there is some very good reason. When you read the sort of garbage that Stenson cobbled together in a pique of petulance, it makes you want to shut up shop. Christine and I read all the newspapers in bed – and most were pretty good – but we were brought down to earth with a bump by that piece. It was not that we took it seriously at all, but it showed how you could be torn apart on the whim of a reporter, just for carrying out the instructions of your new boss.

There was no lasting adverse effect from that so-called piece of journalism, but I wanted to give it a mention so that supporters and young, up-and-coming managers can see how certain elements of the press operate. Hopefully it will encourage younger players to keep their wits about them when they are 'befriended' by some journalists. Some of the profession are great – but there are quite a few who are friends to nobody but themselves.

With my future seemingly assured, Christine and I were able to relax with our young daughters in Spain for three weeks. When we returned we were delighted to receive an invitation to attend a pre-season garden party at Elton's house in Windsor. It was an annual event thrown for everyone, from his fellow directors to the laundry ladies, at Watford Football Club, together with their families. The word was that these parties were becoming more lavish with each year that went by.

This year the theme was nursery rhymes – and to say that it was stupendous would be selling it well short. The giant marquee was the old woman's shoe, all the waiters and waitresses were dressed as nursery-rhyme characters, there was an artistic gingerbread house on each table and, at the end of the marquee, a huge Humpty-Dumpty had been sculpted from ice. On top of all that, there was Hansel and Gretel's cottage – jam-packed with presents for every child at the party. The food and drink was wonderfully extravagant and gave everyone a taste of the millionaire lifestyle. It must have cost a fortune but it was just Elton's way of saying 'thank you' to everyone at the club – and a grand introduction for new members.

At the end, when most people were drifting away, he asked us to hang on – and that was when the real party started. There were about six couples and he invited us into his luxurious home through a hall covered in gold and silver discs, to the inner sanctum of his private world. He showed us his endless wardrobes with cupboards full of platform shoes, and he looked on good-naturedly as Frenchie insisted on trying some of them on.

Next he unlocked another room and led us into a vast wardrobe filled with furs. He selected a magnificent full-length coat and insisted that Christine try it on for size. Mouth agape, she slid into it – and it fitted her perfectly and might have been made for her. 'It's yours,' he said simply. I've never known Christine to be speechless for quite so long. In fairness to Elton, I know that he is now a keen conservationist and no longer buys real furs.

Then it was to the bar downstairs where we were served with more drinks before Elton insisted that we all draped ourselves decadently around the baby grand piano and joined him in a sing-song. Christine appeared hypnotised as he went through half a dozen of his favourite rock numbers for us – including 'This Song's For You'. I remember that he was wearing a red and black all-in-one leisure suit with platform shoes and, during a break in the singing, I was marched away and dressed in an identical ouffit – much to the amusement of everyone else. I was perched on the piano stool next to Elton, looking every bit his twin as he led us in a medley of cockney songs and it is a source of considerable regret for me – though not to everyone else – that we never made a recording of 'Shirley' Bassett singing with Elton John.

It's just as well that we had a good holiday that summer because my batteries needed to be fully charged in order to face the turmoil, emotional stress and disappointments which lay ahead. Elton and Graham Taylor had achieved wonders with Watford during their ten-year reign together, guiding them from the Fourth Division to the First, their first Wembley Final and a subsequent taste of European competition in 1987. I knew that there was a tough job for me ahead.

6

What a Disappointment

GRAHAM TAYLOR HAD LEFT BEHIND HIM A CREAKING SIDE which was well past its best, and one of his last acts had been to negotiate the transfer of Watford's lone remaining star, John Barnes, to Liverpool. That was the scenario which I inherited when I rolled up my sleeves and began life as manager at Vicarage Road.

Without Barnes, the shortcomings of my Watford inheritance were woefully obvious. From the start I had assumed that they were all good professionals of course – but I was soon to find out that some were well past their best and others not as good as they thought they were. After years of playing Graham Taylor's brand of football I found them both reluctant and, in many cases, incapable of change. Now, many of you may say that my methods and Graham's were the same but I like to think that, although we were both advocates of the long-ball game, given the players at our disposal, mine was a more positive approach.

It is interesting to note here that, while I was criticised for introducing the long-ball game to Wimbledon – and the game's purists were voicing their discontent with our methods – it was a style of play pioneered at Watford under Graham Taylor. I don't recall too many people wanting to string him up for this direct and supposedly unsubtle approach to the game. Graham, of course, has always been something of an establishment figure, while I have been much more obvious fodder for the national soccer hacks, most of who love nothing better than taking down someone's trousers and giving their backsides a good kicking in public.

From the start things did not go well at Watford. I even became a natural target for the local weekly, the *Watford Observer*. Their soccer writer faithfully followed in the footsteps of his Fleet Street mentors by using my back as a dartboard, bemoaning the departure of Steve Harrison – Taylor's assistant – who he clearly thought should have been Graham's automatic heir.

The flak started the week I joined, when he ran a story about the short-comings of Hills FC, a Watford Sunday League side, which I had run 21 years earlier. We had something of a reputation as an aggressive team and he had been thumbing through the archives to discover that we had been expelled from the competition. Of course, he omitted to mention that our expulsion had nothing to do with our enthusiastic style of play – it was enforced simply because we had failed to complete a Watford Sunday League registration form by the required date. A stupid and embarrassing oversight certainly, but hardly enough to justify the muck-raking campaign which he appeared to conduct from the day I arrived at Vicarage Road.

Perhaps there was another reason for all his hostility. Our local scribe had apparently won the ear of my predecessor – who was notoriously reluctant to speak with the national press at that time – and had built up a nice little side-line selling Watford stories to Fleet Street. My arrival on the scene saw this lucrative source of income suddenly run dry. Not that I did this intentionally, of course, after all I've always been very willing to talk to the press. If I've got something to say I would much rather it came straight from me than from a third party who is lining his own pockets simply by being my mouthpiece. After all, I'd only moved a few miles from Wimbledon where I was hardly known as one of the game's silent diplomats and it would have been unreal – as well as unfair – to change. Despite this journalist's early attitude, I was keen to help the local press and when that same reporter asked to join our pre-season tour of Sweden – something which Graham Taylor had never allowed – I relented and agreed that he could join the party. In retrospect it was a mistake and he never changed his aggressive stance and went on to become one of the more vociferous anti-Bassett lobbyists.

My first day at Watford did not exactly accord what you would call a warm welcome. It appeared that in his enthusiasm to get me to Watford, Elton had omitted to consult certain members of the board about my appointment and, perhaps with some justification, they felt a bit miffed. Obviously, with an anti-Bassett faction in the boardroom from day one, it did not take long to filter down to the staff and players. Not that they needed a lot of encouragement.

There was already apprehension in the dressing-room. It was almost as though many of them knew that they had reached the end of the line and, facing a new season without their mentor, Graham Taylor, had left them listless – and in some cases, bloody nearly helpless. The arrival of the Plough Lane gang in the shape of Messrs Bassett, Gillett, Taylor and French did little to suggest that their cossetted and protected lifestyle would continue.

Graham had run Watford in every respect, but I thought he had run it almost like a Billy Graham evangelism with him as the chief minister. It seems to have worked for him, the preaching approach to his players. If it works, then you cannot knock it, but it was not my style at all and I felt that it had done something to the players' thinking which would be difficult to repair. When Graham left, the players were looking for a new minister. In fact, one paper suggested that Watford were expecting me to be a Graham Taylor clone, but I turned out to be a clown.

That's quite insulting really, but you get used to stupid things like that. No way was I ever going to be a Graham Taylor clone – we are poles apart in our thinking and our approach to the game.

Christine recalls that first day. Having followed Watford as a kid and now being nuts about Elton and everything that he stood for – and owned – she was anxious to know how I'd got on. Apparently I was uncharacteristically quiet.

'Funny place,' I said. 'There's almost a religious type of atmosphere there – not much enthusiasm either.'

It's easy to be wise after the event but, in retrospect, I started to suspect that I had made a wrong move even before the season started. Taylor was a hard act to follow certainly, but I didn't expect that everything I did would be compared with my predecessor.

Even my secretary would eye me coldly and say, 'Graham didn't do it that way.'

My biggest problem, though, was the attitude of the players. I know now that, as the new man coming in, I afforded many of them far more respect than they deserved. To say that the players I had inherited were set in their ways is an understatement. I realised as soon as we started the early training sessions that it was going to be an uphill shove. They had been taught one form of existence to which they adhered rigidly, both on and off the pitch and, in my opinion, they were totally inflexible. They made it obvious that they didn't know me, didn't even want to know me, and that they didn't believe in my methods.

While the long-ball strategy that I had used at Wimbledon wasn't far removed from the tactics previously employed at Watford, every manager has his own ideas as to positioning and other tactical variations. Quite frankly, some of them couldn't – or wouldn't – adopt, or even try, new ideas. It didn't take long to decide that things could not go on like this.

I saw our pre-season tour of Sweden as an ideal chance to assess the players and see how they reacted away from their Vicarage Road womb. It was a strange experience after those hair-raising trips abroad with Wimbledon, when the rule-book spent most of the time hanging out of the window.

This time there was no togetherness, no sense of belonging and very little laughter. Instead of a football team preparing for the challenge of a new season they were more like nameless, faceless delegates attending a boring business conference. True, there were small cliques of players who would always hang around together – but that's only to be expected. There was no over-all team spirit – only a bunch of rather worried-looking players, wondering what the future held in store for them. Some seemed to have adopted their own new agendas. Even Derek French, whose humour I have found to be such an asset on any tour, failed to crack some of those stone-like masks.

I now accept that I made an error by unloading too many players too soon at Watford. However, that was fairly typical of me – once I make up my mind to do something, I get on with it immediately and nothing short of an earthquake can make me change my mind. This was another example of the old Bassett 'shit-or-bust' philosophy coming into play – but I now realise, with the benefit of that wonderful thing called hindsight, that this speedy exodus of players was neither in the best interest of the club nor myself. It left the rest of the established players even more unsettled and, in some cases, the replacements that I had bought were not yet ready for First Division football.

In my haste to get things right by ridding myself of the disruptive elements in the side, I had broken my own golden rule. Instead of reacting to the problem I had over-reacted and I had to face the consequences as fans demanded to know why supposedly talented players like Richard Hill and David Bardsley had been sold to Oxford, Mark Falco to Glasgow Rangers and Kevin Richardson had been allowed to go to Arsenal.

I had gambled on Trevor Senior to solve our goal-scoring problem. He had enjoyed a very successful time with Reading and was an honest player always giving 100 per cent effort. Unfortunately for everyone, Trevor had difficulty translating that effort into goals at Watford. In fact, the word 'disaster' springs to mind, which gave the fans even more anti-Bassett ammunition.

They had also seen me sign former Wimbledon favourite Glyn Hodges from Newcastle United and pick up defender Mark Morris, who had signed schoolboy forms for Wimbledon in 1978 when Dario Gradi was manager. He had made his debut in 1981 after signing apprentice forms when I selected him to play in a Third Division game against Exeter City. He went on to play more than 200 games for Wimbledon in all four divisions, including 27 in the club's first year in Division One. He is a good defender, excellent in the air, a solid tackler and more intelligent than he cares to let on – and I saw him as an ideal addition to the Watford squad.

Unfortunately, most of the fans and some of the senior players saw him as another of the 'Bassett boys' and gave him a hard time at first. His playing ability was obvious, though, and he was soon to become – and remain – an established member of the Watford side long after my departure.

It isn't widely known that I also tried to get Vinnie Jones to join me at Watford. Ironically, he was born in Shrodell's Hospital – now part of Watford General – less than a goal-kick away from the ground and he followed them enthusiastically as a kid. He had played less than a season of League football after I had given him his chance at Wimbledon and, to use one of his own colourful phrases, he nearly 'messed' himself when he heard that I was leaving, fearing that my departure would mark the end of his brief and, thus far, inglorious career.

I thought that Vinnie could do a job for Watford but, unfortunately, the board were scared of his reputation. I told him to try to improve his image on the field and I would come for him later but, sadly, we ran into deep trouble before I was able to sign him. The compensation for him was an FA Cup winners' medal with Wimbledon – so I don't think he was too upset.

After Watford beat Wimbledon, Elton, Frenchie, myself and one or two others went to The Bell at Bedmond which was Vinnie's local. There were about half-a-dozen people in there when we arrived, but word went round the village like lightning and the whole population turned up to take a look at Elton. Alan Bentley, the landlord of The Bell, asked if we could bring Elton every week. It showed the Chairman's spirit, though, that he was prepared to come to the pub with us after the game. He was a good lad, a down-to-earth bloke.

Signing Mark Morris was probably the only thing that the fans applauded during my spell at Watford. Mostly, they were just happy to hurl insults at me – particularly later in the season when I was to commit the cardinal sin of dropping long-time favourite Luther Blissett, who had returned to Watford after his brief flirtation with continental football. Luther had lost form and I replaced him with a black player that nobody had ever heard of – his name was Tony Agana.

Like many youngsters, Tony had harboured dreams of becoming a full-time professional but, after a few false starts, he decided that it would be more realistic to settle for life as a part-time player with a non-League club and earn his living outside the game. He had spent a term with Weymouth in the Alliance League – as the GM Conference was then known – and was working through that summer of 1987 as an insurance agent while contemplating a move to Wycombe Wanderers, who were about the same standard.

I had heard good reports about him. It seemed that he was fast, could beat his man and could score goals too. I decided to give him a chance – which is more than most of the players did. It was more than Steve Harrison did, too, for when he returned to Vicarage Road as my replacement in January 1988, he gave poor Tony half a game in his first game in charge – an FA Cup replay at Hull – and then completely ignored him as Watford continued their slide down towards the Second Division.

Tony played his heart out for me – as did many of the other new players – but the results just weren't coming. Then, at the worst possible time, Elton dropped a bombshell by announcing that he was selling the club. Psychologically, it was like a kick in the crotch to everyone – perhaps to me more than most – and it dented the players' confidence still further. I could tell that Elton's impending departure was giving them even more to worry about and, on more than one occasion, club captain John McClelland telephoned me – waking me up after midnight – to tell me he couldn't sleep.

They were difficult days. I had dispirited players, an anti-Bassett faction on the board and the fans were howling for my head. Now it seemed that Elton – the Mr Watford who had supported me to the hilt – was kissing it all goodbye. He was involved in litigation with the *Sun* newspaper at the time and had now adopted a low profile. He rarely appeared at the club and the timing of his announcement could hardly have been worse.

I remember feeling very sick about the whole thing and more than once I have asked myself how long Elton had considered selling Watford before he made that announcement. There had been some earlier talk about the sale of the club and it is possible that this, together with

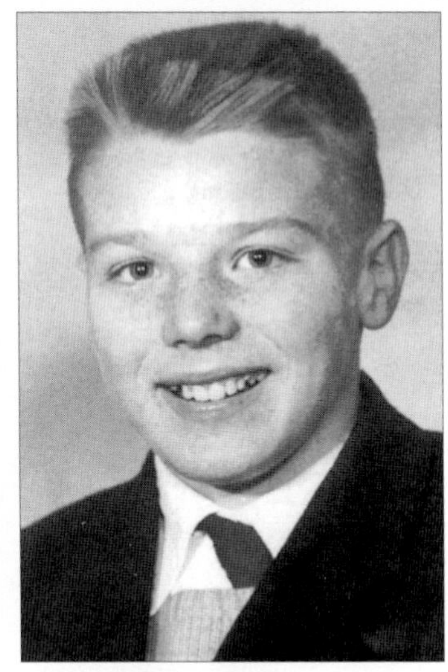

Above left: Always prepared, even from an early age! Me as a cub.

Above right: As a schoolboy, my dedication in the classroom may have been lacking but I made up for it during lunchtime kickarounds.

Below: Ready for action! In my Bridge Road School kit, aged 10.

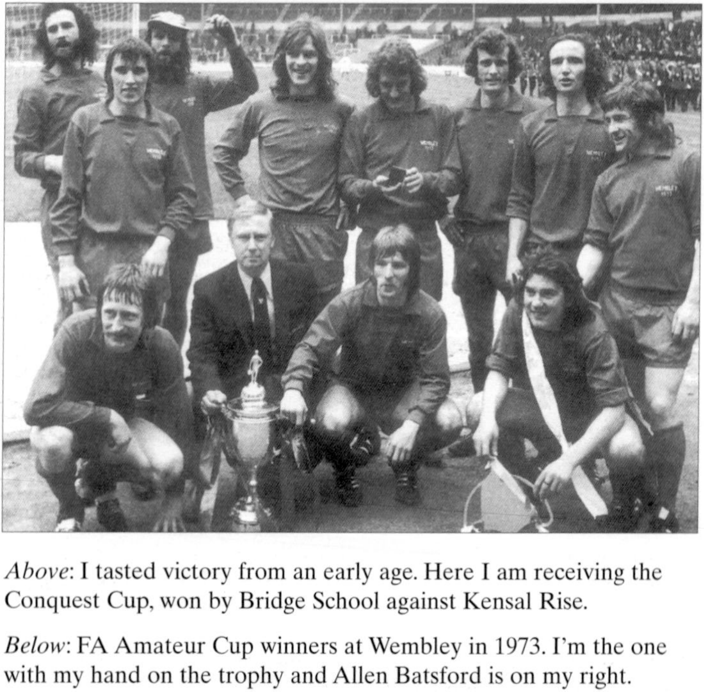

Above: I tasted victory from an early age. Here I am receiving the Conquest Cup, won by Bridge School against Kensal Rise.

Below: FA Amateur Cup winners at Wembley in 1973. I'm the one with my hand on the trophy and Allen Batsford is on my right.

Above: Walton play Hereford in the second round of the FA Cup in 1973. Unfortunately, they beat us 3-0, and then went on to beat West Ham in the next round.

Below: We are the champions! Celebrating with Wimbledon in 1976, the year we did the Southern League 'Double'.

In action for Wimbledon against Maidstone, in our last non-League season.

My days at Watford. *Above*: Attending to my paperwork.

Below left: With Elton John the day I joined the club.

Below right: Elton gives my wife, Chris, a hug at his garden party.

Bassett the Blade. Here I'm demonstrating techniques to John Gannon at the Sheffield United training ground.

Above: Pulling a cracker at Christmas with my friend Trevor Francis. Back then, we were in charge of great rivals: I was at United and he was at Wednesday.

Below: Happy days, celebrating a promotion with the Blades fans.

Proudly holding my Manager of the Year Award in 1992.

the knowledge that his playing side was past its best, was what influenced Graham Taylor to leave with two years of his contract still remaining. Not that it would have altered my decision to join Watford in the first place – but it would have been nice to have started the job in possession of all the facts. A lesson for me to learn.

On the pitch we had started the season with a 1–0 home win – ironically, against Wimbledon – another of those fixture computer creations that make you wonder if computers actually have an inbuilt, wicked sense of humour. Luther Blissett got the goal and the fans went home almost happy. We lost three of our next four games – Nottingham Forest and Manchester United beating us away, and Norwich at home.

A home draw with Spurs and a 3–2 win at Sheffield Wednesday made things look a bit more optimistic – but then we went seven games in which we scored only once in reply to a total of nine from such opponents as Chelsea, Everton, Coventry, Southampton and Queen's Park Rangers. We bounced back from a 4–0 defeat at Liverpool to beat Arsenal 2–0 – so we did have our moments – but it was a struggle every single day.

I was contacted by Robert Maxwell after the Liverpool defeat. It was around that time that Elton had declared that he would be selling his interest in Watford. Maxwell phoned me and said that he was interested in buying the club.

'I have checked you out, Bassett,' he told me. 'You'll be given your chance.'

Sensing the anti-Bassett faction, which was now growing both within the club and on the terraces, some of the senior players started to cut themselves off from the newer 'Bassett boys' – perhaps feeling that salvation wasn't too far away in the form of Steve Harrison – especially since the press and public alike had already somewhat prematurely, appointed him as my 'heir apparent'.

I recall returning from the 1–0 defeat at Coventry to fulfil a social obligation at the Supporters' Club. They had asked several weeks earlier if I would present their darts trophy and when I arrived with Derek French we could actually sense the hostility in the air. As Frenchie said – we'd have been made more welcome in a 'blacks only' club in the middle of Harlem.

As for the board, they were as divided as ever and I had little opportunity to discuss the problem with any of the senior directors. Watford has this unique second-level board, comprising the former Arsenal Svengali, the late Bertie Mee, a club director, and Eddie Plumley the club secretary, who acts as a sort of minister-without-portfolio. Between them they seem to run the club and to form a pretty effective barrier in preventing anyone – including me – from taking problems to a higher authority.

It was finding friends and sympathetic ears harder and harder to come by. Soon, things got so bad that I could not even trust my own secretary. The strain of failure was beginning to affect our domestic life, too. I'm not a moody person but the pressures were beginning to get to me and both Christine and I know that it was the worst time in our lives together. Not that there was any threat to our marriage – we both knew that we would come through it all in the end – but it was such a bloody awful experience, living with failure and so much unpopularity.

It even got to the stage where we were afraid to go into a restaurant in Watford for fear of encountering some hostile reaction. Christine even experienced some venom from parents at the local school. She would cross the road to avoid people rather than run the risk of embarrassment at some snide remark which might possibly be overheard by our two daughters.

It wasn't only the fans – she actually experienced open hostility from the boardroom too. During the home game against Sheffield Wednesday on Boxing Day – probably our worst Christmas ever – our daughter Carly was taken ill and Christine was summoned from the directors' box to care for her in the boardroom, where she was able to watch the rest of the match on closed-circuit television.

Watford then had a director called Muir Stratford – who Christine still rates as one of the rudest men that she has ever met. After what was admittedly an inept performance by Watford, in which we lost 3–1, he stormed into the boardroom, pointedly turned his back on my wife and sick daughter and screamed, 'Give me a bloody double – I've never seen so much rubbish!'

Christine was bitterly upset by the treatment – it only exacerbated the nightmare and, although I was furious when I heard about it, I realised that one could expect little more from a man like Stratford. On the other hand, there were those who cared and who tried to keep Christine's spirits buoyant during that difficult period. Among them were Zena Winwood and Fran Plumley, to both of whom I shall always be grateful. However, even their support couldn't ease the pain that Christine felt about our treatment at this so-called 'family club'. To her, Watford Football Club had been very special ever since childhood – and it hurt her unimaginably to have that special dream so cruelly and comprehensively shattered.

If I look back at the chain of events which precipitated my departure from Watford, I would immediately stab my finger at that hectic Christmas and New Year programme which saw my last vestige of hope evaporate. We had been well beaten by Sheffield Wednesday at home on Boxing Day and so I decided to make more sweeping changes to the side for the match at Portsmouth two days later.

This time, however, I would be committing Hari-Kari in the eyes of the fans by dropping two long-term favourites – neither of whom had been playing well nor, in my opinion, giving 100 per cent. However, as a common courtesy and also to convince people that this wasn't purely a panic measure, I felt that it might be a good idea to flush the idea through the chairman first.

I met Elton and Muff Winwood at John Reid's home after the Sheffield Wednesday game to tell him what I planned to do, and to ask if he would support me. He said that he would and consequently striker Luther Blissett and goalkeeper Tony Coton were both dropped for the match at Fratton Park. We had a drink and for the first time in weeks I began to relax. The more I drank the more relaxed I became and, by late that evening, I was so relaxed that they had to send me home in a chauffeur-driven car. It was gone 11 o'clock, I had blown the Boxing Day supper with the in-laws and I could hardly speak. Not surprisingly, for the first – and only – time in our entire married life, I was condemned to sleep on the couch.

Strangely enough, from the start of that game at Portsmouth there seemed to be a new spirit in the team. We drew 1–1 with our goal coming from Tony Agana, but we felt a little aggrieved because we had the better of the game and knew we should have won. The same enthusiasm and tenacity was evident in our next match, at Tottenham on 1 January and we were mortified to lose 2–1 when a 1–1 draw – even the papers agreed – would have been a much fairer result.

Derek French, our physio, was sent off in this game for verbal abuse while we were substituting a player. It crowned a miserable Christmas period for him – he had been breathalysed just a few days earlier. The fact that one of my backroom boys was facing two possible bans provided more ammunition for the anti-Bassett faction on the board.

The big one – against Manchester United at home – was to come on the following day, 2 January. At last I felt that we could be turning the corner.

'Just show the same commitment as in the two previous games,' I told the team and then we'd be able to send our success-starved supporters home with something to cheer about.

Came the day and we absolutely murdered them on the field. We were all over them and lost 1–0 to a Brian McClair goal. I was mortified. Instead of picking up seven points from our last three games, we finished up with one. I had done everything that I could and, in those vitally important matches, the team had given me everything too. To lose to Manchester United after outplaying them in every department left me feeling cold and empty. Still the fans weren't satisfied and they turned towards the directors' box where Christine was sitting.

'Bassett out! Bassett out!' they chanted — and if she could have dug a hole at that moment she would willingly have buried herself. It was the end and we both knew it.

Fate took a hand the following day. It came in the form of a telephone call from Ron Noades, the Crystal Palace chairman, who has always made a habit — or is it a hobby? — of featuring in my life. Ron had heard the jungle drums at Watford and knew that the directors felt that they had made a mistake in appointing me. Sheffield United were having a rough ride in the Second Division and had parted with their manager, Billy McEwan, who had been in charge for less than two years. Ron knew the chairman, Reg Brealey — Ron knows everybody — and felt sure that he could get me the job. Was I interested?

Knowing now, more than ever, that my Watford days were numbered, I decided to go for it. Watford still had 16 League games to go — which I felt was plenty for someone else to pull them out of trouble. By the same token, it would also give me enough time to save Sheffield United from the drop to Division Three. All things considered, this was probably a good time for me to leave London.

The following Saturday, Watford were due to play Hull City at home in the FA Cup. That morning I went into Eddie Plumley's office and offered my resignation, knowing that if the board felt it was in everyone's best interests that we should part company, the Sheffield United job was virtually mine for the taking. Eddie told me that he would discuss the matter with Bertie Mee and they would decide whether to go to the board.

We drew with Hull City and had a replay on our hands – a replay in which I was not to be involved.

The following Monday morning I received a telephone call to say that the board had considered the matter and would be prepared to accept my resignation. I met Elton and Bertie Mee at the home of John Reid and we all agreed that it was the end of the road. Watford, to their credit, gave me a decent pay-off, even though Elton and I had never got around to actually signing a contract.

That afternoon I returned to Vicarage Road to conduct my last training session before telling the rest of my staff not to bother to turn up for work the following morning. Then I called the players together and told them that I had resigned. Some were sorry, others were extremely diffident – but none of them were surprised. From the following day their future would be in the hands of coach Tom Walley and Steve Harrison, who the board would be recalling from Aston Villa – much to the delight of the players and most of the fans.

I'm not one to bear a grudge, but I do feel very strongly about the taunting and the insults which were hurled at me and my family. Such action was both ugly and childish, and so very unnecessary. They drove me away, but deep down inside I know that I could have done a good job at Watford if they had given me a free hand. That would have meant rebuilding with younger players, but neither the club nor the fans seemed to be prepared to take one step back to ensure that they could move forward. For that blindness alone they deserved exactly what they then got – football in the lower divisions!

With hindsight, it is fair to say I was a square peg in a round hole. Watford is a parochial town north of London but nothing like the big city. Graham Taylor had elevated the club above its station, but could not sustain it, which is probably why he left. He returned in the late 1990s to give them one more season of Premiership football during season 1998/99 and that was it. Vialli came in to lift expectations and hopes once again, but where does a club go when that hasn't worked? At best, it can hold its own in the First Division, but if that is not possible there is only realistically one direction. Vialli did not live up to his 'designer' manager image and he was sacked after only one year. Graham had decided to retire and concentrate on TV work and at the same time became a director of Aston Villa at the request of Doug Ellis. When John Gregory resigned, Graham could not resist the call and the challenge to have one last go in the top flight and is now once again Aston Villa's manager.

That evening I went out for a curry with my loyal staff. The occasion was largely one of commiseration.

'What do we all do now?' they wanted to know.

'God knows!' I answered them knowing that the start of a new Bassett challenge was only a few days away.

[illegible]

[illegible]

[illegible]

[illegible]

7

Flashing Blades

AS A LONDONER GOING NORTH OF WATFORD, I knew that I had to do a bit of homework. Blindfold me and drop me in any street in London and I know immediately where I am. When I thought about going to Sheffield United I knew that I would be going as a foreigner – and I also knew that if I wanted any sort of street cred, I would need to do some homework. So I did.

To the uninitiated, Sheffield is perhaps nothing more than a bleak steel city in South Yorkshire – a haunting reminder of the days of the Industrial Revolution, choked over the years with the soot from factory smoke and coal-dust. In reality, nothing could be further from the truth. The years of austerity are all in the past and the city is really buzzing. The 19th-century brick relics still remaining serve only to camouflage the true spirit and heart of a city which is as vibrant today as were London and Liverpool in the Sixties.

A note for those who revel in sporting trivia is that on 14 October 1878, a football match was played at Bramall Lane – 'with the assistance of electric light' – between two teams selected by the Sheffield Football Association. The game attracted 12,000 paying customers and it is estimated that at least another 8,000 gained access free of charge. However, it does seem that this early attempt at floodlit soccer was only partially successful. It was all right when the ball was on the ground, but it was impossible to follow its trajectory in the gloom when a player gave it a long, high punt up-field ... I'm sure there's a message there somewhere!

My first meeting with the Sheffield United board came within a week of my departure from Watford and followed a phone call out of the blue from Michael Morgan, a soccer writer on the *Sun*. I'd only met Mike once – at the end of Watford's 3-1 home defeat by Sheffield Wednesday the previous Boxing Day.

So I was somewhat surprised that he had managed to get hold of my home telephone number and track me down. He told me that he had taken the liberty of mentioning my name to Derek Dooley, with regard to the Bramall Lane vacancy. Mike told me that when he'd asked Derek if he fancied me for the job, Derek replied, 'He wouldn't come here, would he?' Mike told him he'd give me a ring, find out and let him know. So I told Mike to pass on my number and let them know that I would be happy to talk to them. The next thing I knew, Reg Brealey telephoned me a few days before United's League match at Bournemouth and suggested that we meet on the Saturday morning prior to the game. I agreed and it also provided an ideal opportunity to celebrate Christine's birthday. On Friday we drove to Chewton Glen, a particular favourite haunt of Christine and I, deep in the New Forest. That evening as we came down for dinner we saw another couple standing by the large open log fire. The man looked at me and, in a 'whisper' which echoed all around the room and must have been heard by everybody, he said to his wife, 'That's Dave Bassett – he's just been elbowed from Watford!'

Even in this delightful backwater there seemed to be no respite from the penalty of failure.

On Saturday morning we had a leisurely breakfast – and then there was nothing. No team talk, no worries about late fitness tests, no confidence-boosting chats with players and no adrenalin pumping through the body in anticipation of a much-needed win. Instead I found myself passing time before what really amounted to a job interview – something that I had not experienced since I applied to Scottish Life as a 16-year-old schoolboy

The Sheffield United directors had suggested that we should meet at our hotel and, at the appointed time, I found myself face-to-face with chairman Reg Brealey and three of his board colleagues – Paul Woolhouse, Michael Wragg and Derek Dooley, the club's managing director. Nobody who loves the game of football could be unaware of this tall, genial Yorkshireman, who set the game alight in 1951–52 by scoring 47 goals in 31 League and Cup matches as his team, Sheffield Wednesday, cruised to the Second Division championship. Neither could anyone ever forget the numbness which swept through players and fans alike as that glittering career came to a sudden and tragic end on 14 February 1953 when, after breaking his right leg in a League match at Preston North End, surgeons were compelled to perform an amputation after gangrene set in.

After nine weeks in hospital, Derek Dooley returned to Hillsborough where his contract was paid until the end of the season. Then he went home to face Sylvia, his bride of only a few months, with two crutches, one leg and no job – and he was just 23 years old. In 1955, Sheffield Wednesday awarded him a benefit match – Hillsborough's first game under floodlights. A crowd of 58,000 turned up to pay their tribute to that talent and the gate receipts of £,7,000 enabled him to buy the house where he still lives today.

Ten years later he returned as Wednesday's development fund organiser and in January 1971 he was appointed team manager. He held the job for almost three years before being fired, somewhat callously on Christmas Eve 1973. For years, Derek refused to return to Hillsborough, and I guess it's easy to understand his reasons why. But thankfully, time has proved to be a great healer. Derek and Sheffield Wednesday are now happily reconciled. So much so, that they even named a restaurant after him at Hillsborough. Wednesday's loss, however, proved to be United's gain and Derek crossed the great emotional divide between Hillsborough and Bramall Lane to become Sheffield United's commercial manager in 1974. Seven years later he was elevated to the board as one of soccer's first full-time paid directors and he played a major role in plotting United's revival.

That Saturday morning in Bournemouth was the first time that I had met Derek and I was impressed by the enthusiasm which he and the other directors showed. Their team was struggling at the foot of the Second Division but I could sense immediately their total commitment to the restoration of First Division football to Bramall Lane. Within minutes they had convinced me that Sheffield United was a sleeping giant – a big club which had fallen on hard times. Moreover, they emphasised that Sheffield, like Liverpool and Manchester, was quite capable of supporting more than one First Division team. It was, they told me, a city with a deep-rooted passion for football – something I had been unable to experience with either Wimbledon or Watford – and something which told me instinctively that my future now lay at Bramall Lane.

There were drawbacks of course – not the least of which was money. The club was not only broke but also heavily in debt. Echoes of Wimbledon here, I thought to myself. Most of the playing staff were either not going to make the grade or were well past their sell-by date – which seemed to mirror the situation that I had inherited at Watford. Another problem for me was the fact that – apart from having a reputation for fish and chips and decent beer – I knew precious little about Yorkshire, its people or its culture. I'd never exactly earned a reputation for diplomacy within the game and that posed a question in itself. Would they see me as just another cocky

Londoner who just thought he could run a football team?

Reg Brealey, Derek and the others asked me some pretty searching questions about my views on the game and I must have come up with the right answers because, after going into a little huddle for a short time, they eventually came up smiling and offered me the job. I learned later that the decision had been unanimous. Meanwhile, Christine had been introduced to the wives of Messrs Woolhouse and Wragg who were busily trying to convince her that the Londoner's impression of Sheffield was entirely wrong and that it really wasn't all steel, smoke and grime. She didn't need too much convincing anyway – I knew already that part of her was desperate to get away from London so that we could make a fresh start.

I didn't accept the job immediately – even though something inside me was screaming 'yes' at the top of its voice. I had learned the folly of making snap decisions at Watford and there were also other things to consider. Major issues like the prospect of Christine and I moving so far north to Yorkshire – leaving an area where we had both grown up and where our daughters, now six and eight, had recently settled into new schools.

Several people I knew in Sheffield – Emlyn Hughes and Howard Wilkinson among them – tried to dissuade me from taking the job.

'The club's broke,' they said. 'It can only do more damage to your reputation.'

There was also the question of salary to consider. Sheffield United had offered me approximately half the figure that I was getting at Watford. In fairness to them, I was told that the contract would be laced with incentives linked to promotion, League position and Cup success, which is probably the fairest way of determining a manager's worth. It's like investing in a company – the more successful it becomes, the higher your returns.

Besides that, I have always argued against enormous salaries being paid simply on a man's reputation – it takes away the incentive and the club can suffer while the manager gets fat.

I discussed the move with Christine. She knew I fancied it – I had likened it to a dormant volcano – and we agreed that I should take the job but that we shouldn't move up to Sheffield until, at least, the end of the season. In effect, we were really hedging our bets because we knew it might not work. Sheffield United might finish in Division Three and then I might have a 'not required on voyage' ticket slapped on me for next season.

I informed Reg Brealey of my decision after the weekend and the board seemed genuinely pleased. Derek Dooley went on record as saying, 'I thought he'd want to stay in London – I didn't think we had a chance.'

He later told the press: 'I was completely swept away with his enthusiasm from the first meeting. He's more than a breath of fresh air – he's more like a hurricane. He could have even got me playing for him and I've only got one leg.'

It was only after I had accepted the position that I learned there had been 49 written applications for the job, including several from 'top-flight' managers who had fallen from grace and were desperately trying to claw their way back into the game. Mine was the 50th name in the ring – and I was the only one who hadn't applied. It was agreed that I should sign an 18-month contract and this suited me fine. With 16 League matches still to play I felt that we were well able to get out of trouble, even though the board told me that there was no more money available and that all deals would have to be self-financing.

'If a club has millions they send for Ron Atkinson – if they are skint they send for Dave Bassett,' I said at the time.

I drove to Sheffield for a press conference to

announce my appointment the following Thursday and I was anxious to get involved as quickly as possible before Saturday's home match against Plymouth Argyle. Then, after all the hype, came the inevitable anti-climax when the game was snowed-off. A week later came my first competitive game – and we lost 2–1 to Portsmouth in the FA Cup after being a goal up after just 20 seconds.

Within a few days of taking over at Bramall Lane, I had returned to Wimbledon to sign Wally Downes on a free transfer. Wally had been with me for ten years and, although he was approaching the end of his playing career, he still had much to offer a club like Sheffield United – both on and off the pitch. He was a great dressing-room character and, perhaps even more important, he was someone who I could trust.

Wally made his debut against Stoke within a couple of days of signing and, although we lost 1–0, it was an improvement. At least we weren't conceding three, four or even five goals – which had been the case in the couple of weeks prior to my arrival. Then, a week later, we lost 1–0 at home to Shrewsbury and heads, which were already low, sank even further as it was realised that Bassett's arrival at Bramall Lane wasn't the 'second coming', and that I didn't have the power to weave instant miracles.

For the first time I became aware of the sense of hopelessness which was enveloping, not only the players, but also the staff and fans. I don't think anything could have put a smile on their faces that winter. The place was dead – the players had lost faith in themselves and there was not a corner in the club which hadn't succumbed to an aura of impending doom. There was no atmosphere, no life, and no laughter and, while I consciously set out to change the mood off the pitch, I was becoming increasingly aware of the problems which faced the club on it. It was almost a parody of the problems I had encountered at Watford and I knew that if I was to achieve anything at all, I would need some new players immediately. That much was blatantly obvious.

It had been made very plain to me that there was no money available and that I would have to sell in order to buy. I started by going back to Watford for Tony Agana. Steve Harrison had replaced me at Vicarage Road and, although I had got on well enough with him in his days as assistant manager to Graham Taylor, he had criticised everything I had done since he returned to Watford. Not only was it unnecessary it was also very unprofessional and smacked of the actions of an inexperienced manager. However, I knew that he fancied one of our players, Martin Kuhl, who I valued at around £120,000. Steve agreed to a part-exchange deal but insisted that, if I wanted Agana, I would have to take Peter Hetherston too — at a joint cost of £85,000. Hetherston had not been a part of my plans but I agreed as I was keen to get Agana. I also took the opportunity to pick up another of my Watford players, Cliff Powell, who was available on a free transfer — a price I considered to be a bargain.

It seems that I was only just in time to get Agana. He had played in only half a game since I left Watford and had been condemned to the reserves — which appeared to me to be a chronic waste of talent. He had been planning to buy a house and went to Harrison to ask him to sign some mortgage documents, a harmless enough request. Harrison's reaction came as a shock to poor Tony.

'I wouldn't buy a house here if I were you,' he said. 'I'm selling you to Bournemouth — go down there and sign.'

The player hadn't even been consulted about the move and it was almost a fait accompli — who said that the days of soccer slavery were over?

Both Agana and Hetherston made their home debut in the derby match against Barnsley — and it was Agana who saved my face and gave the fans something to cheer about when he scored the winner in the 89th minute. A win at last – after three successive defeats. We won the next one too, away at Hull City, but this was followed by three more defeats, including a 5–0 drubbing at Leeds during which Wally Downes was sent off. He was given his marching orders again a fortnight later – this time against Bradford City – so there's definitely something about West Yorkshire clubs which brings out the worst in our Walter.

I wasn't very happy with Wally after the second sending off, but I had agreed to drive him back to London as I was going there myself. I had the hump with him and didn't speak to him as we set off in the car, so I put the radio on to listen to *Praise and Grumble*. A Blades fan came on to say that Wally Downes was probably the most hated man in South Yorkshire. He then paused and said, 'No, he's the second most hated man after the Yorkshire Ripper.' Wally's mouth dropped open, and for once in his life he was speechless! I had a really good laugh about that one.

Part of the agreement at Sheffield was that I should work with the existing back-room staff and I had not realised just how much this would hamper progress. I had been prevented from bringing Geoff Taylor and Derek French with me as I would have wished, but Alan Gillett – who had been a valued and trusted member of my set-up at Wimbledon and Watford – had already decided to look for new horizons. He subsequently spent two years coaching in Japan before returning to Britain to become assistant manager at Plymouth Argyle and now works for the Football Association.

I had been used to working with Geoff Taylor as my right arm and I won't pretend that it wasn't difficult inheriting someone else's staff. Geoff and I were a team and we worked in a certain way. He would know exactly what I wanted him to do and he could be relied upon to make constructive suggestions. We would argue too – but that's part and parcel of the game – and the flare-ups were soon forgotten. Most important, Geoff knew me very well and could handle me in most situations.

It was Geoff who invented my 'heads' – the contract head for sorting out terms with players, the financial head when they failed to con me into buying a round of drinks, the coaching head when I was talking tactics, the joker's head when I needed a laugh and, perhaps most pertinently, the hump-head when I was in a bad mood and it was wise to leave me alone. Geoff was my 'right-head' man and that, in a nut-shell, illustrates just how well Geoff Taylor knew me – my strengths and my weaknesses – and it was proving more than a little difficult working with a stand-in backroom staff which was already partially responsible for Sheffield United's dire position.

I was soon to discover that these 'colleagues' had the knives out for me from day one, and I shall be forever grateful to the well-known manager who took the trouble to telephone and advise me that one of these inherited staff had visited his club and spent half-an-hour in their treatment room, bitching about me and my methods. If I had any lingering doubts about their ability or loyalty, that single piece of information was all I needed. Come the end of the season and heads would roll!

The anticipated soccer miracle failed to materialise and, as the weeks rolled by, I found things going from bad to worse. Eventually I summoned Geoff Taylor on a part-time basis, paying his salary and hotel expenses myself in the hope that together we could halt the slide towards Division Three.

It is now a matter of record that I failed to keep Sheffield United in Division Two. We finished in 21st place, just one point behind Ron Atkinson's West Bromwich Albion who had held us to a goalless draw on our own ground in late April. Victory in that match would have saved us. Instead it saved them. Subsequently we lost away to Reading and won our final match at Huddersfield to qualify for the lifeline of a Play-off. We failed to seize the chance, however, and were condemned to Division Three by failing to win either of the two legs against Bristol City. Watford also went down, losing their First Division status. I can assure you that it was quite a kick in the guts to have been associated with two relegated teams in one season. It was certainly a time for self-assessment and any reflections that I had were brought into sharp focus by the knowledge that, a mere 24 hours before that defeat by Bristol City had sent us spiralling down to the Third Division, 'my' Wimbledon team had achieved the impossible and won the FA Cup. More than half the Dons who did the business that day were previously my players and I was very proud of them.

I have never been able to live with failure, but the inescapable fact was there for all to see – I had failed the club and the people of Sheffield and I could see only one way out. I went to Derek Dooley and offered my resignation – adding that I would not be expecting any form of financial compensation because, quite simply in my book, I hadn't earned it. At the back of my mind, too, was the fact that Christine and the girls would be preparing to come up to Yorkshire during the summer and I didn't want to bring them north only to find that I was out of a job inside two months.

Derek's reaction was typical of a man who has always backed his own judgement.

'We hired you to do a job for us,' he said quietly. 'I suggest that you go back to your office and get on with it.'

It was a terse message, brief and to the point – yet I saw it as a vote of confidence and it provided a much-needed boost to my sagging spirits. I knew that if I were to do the job properly then I would need my own team around me and I got the go-ahead to bring in Geoff Taylor as my full-time assistant, and also Derek French who had temporarily abandoned the physio's couch and was working on a building site while he patiently awaited the call to Sheffield.

It was obvious, too, that the existing youth-team policy was not working and so, later, I brought in Keith Mincher to start again from scratch. I have always been a great believer in catching them young and I like to think that the youngsters we took on board at Wimbledon have played their part in keeping First Division football at the club in recent years – at a time when the club would not have been in a position to dive into the transfer market to buy players of the necessary calibre.

I started to plan the rebuilding of the team on a budget and again scoured the lower divisions for prospective talent. I also kept a beady eye on the free-transfer market for experienced players who might be able to do a good short-term job for me. Fortunately I had a tower of strength in Paul Stancliffe who had already skippered the side for five seasons. I think he was a bit stunned when I was appointed manager – he knew that I had experienced a few problems at Watford – but he was also very much aware of what I had achieved at Wimbledon. I believe that he was confident that, together, we could do the business at Sheffield United. He was also aware that, if the team were to succeed, they would have to adopt a different type of football. I shall never forget my first day at the club, when the chairman took me into the changing room to meet the players and Paul led them in a chorus of Maybe it's Because I'm a Londoner. It was one of the very few high-spots in those early days and I warmed to him immediately.

Through Paul I soon learned that some of the players were worried about their futures – particularly since the reputation of 'Clear 'em out Bassett' that I had gained at

Watford had preceded my arrival. However, we had just been relegated and changes were inevitable if we were to stand any chance of regaining our Second Division place the following season.

Again it was emphasised that there was no cash available – particularly now that Third Division gates could be expected. I was able to raise some much-needed funds by selling Peter Beagrie to Stoke for £215,000 – although we received only £160,000 owing to the fact that Middlesbrough had a one-third 'sell-on' clause in the contract which gave his former club a third of any profit made by transferring him on. In addition, Tony Philliskirk went to Oldham for £25,000, and Clive Mendonca to Rotherham for £15,000. These deals enabled me to buy more players – notably, Brian Deane from Doncaster and Ian Bryson from Kilmarnock at £40,000 each. Alan Roberts came from Darlington for £15,000 and goalkeeper Graham Benstead, who had joined us on loan from Norwich towards the end of the previous season, for £35,000. I also signed a former Wimbledon man, Francis Joseph, on a free transfer from Reading.

Our first warm-up match was a friendly against Skegness Town, which is notable only because it marked the first appearance together of Agana and Deane – both of whom were on the scoresheet in an easy 8–1 win. This was followed by a four-match tour of Sweden during which we scored 32 goals while conceding only two, thereby proving that my newly-assembled squad at least knew where the net was.

Meanwhile, one or two players were scoring off the field in Sweden as well as on it. They tended to see any female as fair game and, while they don't always win, they get 'A' for effort. The lads didn't have to try too hard during one of their fabled 'corridor parties' which marked the end of this particular tour. Because drink is so expensive in Swedish bars, most of the touring players buy their own supplies at a local supermarket and have room parties – which tend to spill out into the hotel corridors. This particular hotel had been the venue for a wedding reception and the bride, who was about 35, was not a bad looker. She and her bridesmaid seemed 'game for a laugh', as they say, and spent a short while with the boys before the bride retired to her room and her groom. Fifteen minutes later, both girls returned in full party spirit, having left the poor bloke in bed on his own. They appeared to be a couple of soccer groupies and a good time was had by all – and an even better time by at least two of the squad. In the interests of good taste I shall reveal no more – but I've often wondered just how long that marriage lasted. This doesn't mean, of course, that all soccer tours are trails of drunkenness and debauchery – but there is no point in denying that it does sometimes happen.

It was interesting that, during a pre-season friendly with Doncaster Rovers in which we drew 0–0, Reg Brealey remarked that he wondered where the goals were going to come from. It was more of a statement about my choice of players than a question. Little did he know that the deadly duo of Deane and Agana were going to score 66 between them that season. Derek Dooley had predicted that they would be a powerful scoring combination and I was glad that both he and I were vindicated and that Reg's limited knowledge of the game was revealed.

During the summer we had managed to cultivate a good spirit in the side, thanks largely to the influence of Paul Stancliffe and the former Wimbledon clowns, Joseph, Downes and French. In fact, Wally Downes achieved far more for me off the field than on it, since he broke his ankle in a pre-season friendly against Sheffield Wednesday and never played for the club again. He was released at the end of the season and became a coach at Crystal Palace, later to join me at Bramall Lane and more recently to become manager at Brentford.

Our season started with a 3–1 win at Reading, which included goals from both Brian Deane and Francis Joseph in their first game for the club. This was followed by a 4–1 home victory over Bristol Rovers which saw two more of my summer signings – Bryson with two goals and Roberts – appear on the scoresheet. By mid-September the spirit in the club was unrecognisable from the place which had been shrouded in depression only six months earlier. When both Agana and Deane scored hat-tricks in our 6–1 demolition of Chester, it gave our supporters more than a mere hint that the Bramall Lane revival had begun. That pair of hat-tricks also signalled the arrival of a potent striking partnership which was to score so many goals in all competitions that season. It was a duo which had cost less than £100,000 to bring together and yet, by the end of the season, I knew of at least one First Division club prepared to pay £1 million to secure their signatures. The person waving his cheque-book around was none other than Sam Hammam, the owner of Wimbledon. Funny old world – as someone once said.

In addition to the deadly finishing of Deane and Agana, both Roberts and Bryson were figuring regularly on the scoresheet. We won nine and drew one of our opening 12 games and there was a strong feeling of confidence and camaraderie about the side. We were setting the Third Division pace along with Wolves, who had come up from Division Four, and Port Vale.

We had already beaten Wolves at home and drawn 3–3 away in the Potteries, so we knew we were there on merit. Then, perhaps predictably the 13th game proved to be our undoing, heralding a run of three successive away defeats – two in the League and Manchester City in the League Cup which was then sponsored by Littlewoods. These defeats proved to be just a temporary aberration, however, and we were able to get our act back together immediately but then fate kicked us in the face when Simon Webster broke a leg in the first round of the FA Cup at Mansfield Town – and only a superb equalising goal from Brian Deane earned us a replay.

I have always made it my business to keep abreast of players' availability and my years in London had served me well. I needed a replacement for Webster and I knew that I need look no further than Bob Booker, a Brentford stalwart of some ten years' standing, who I was able to sign on a free transfer as a short-term solution to the problem.

Did I say short-term?

He made his debut immediately slotting into the side for the home match against Bristol City. After a shaky start he won the crowd over – and he was still holding his place when we returned to the First Division – two seasons later. Bob was to become, and remains, a real Blades folk hero. In fact, he was the first 'Ooh, aah' before Cantona – 'Ooh, aah, Bobbookar ... Say ooh, aah, Bobbookar ...'

We lost our momentum again over Christmas, collecting only one point from three successive home games, culminating in a 3–1 defeat at the hands of neighbouring Chesterfield in front of nearly 16,000 fans – our largest crowd of the season so far. Diplomacy was never my strong point and I tend not to be slow in imparting criticism when I feel that it is deserved. Suffice it to say that, after that Chesterfield game, I tore into my players with a torrent of short, sharp words which described their shortcomings exactly – and yet which I dare not reproduce on the written page. The rebuke appeared to have the desired effect and we revitalised our promotion bid, recording seven wins and three draws in our next ten games. Ironically, just as Chesterfield had motivated our latest unbeaten run, they also brought it to an end – beating us 2–1 on their own ground to become one of only two teams to record the double over us that season.

That winning run coincided with the arrival of Steve Thompson from Leicester City. I actually signed him in mid-November as cover. He was a big defensive player whose career had started with Boston United and then taken in Lincoln City and Charlton Athletic. He had been popular at both clubs but later moved to Filbert Street where he had been languishing in the reserves.

I decided to give him a first-team chance at home to Gillingham on 21 January 1989. We needed a win and we beat them 4–2 which sparked off a run. He was an honest player and stayed in the side for near enough the rest of the season. At the very least he had proved to be a lucky mascot. Later he returned to Lincoln and was manager at Sincil Bank for a while. He also later returned to Bramall Lane and was caretaker manager when Nigel Spackman left. While he was in charge, the Blades reached the semi-finals of the FA Cup before losing to Newcastle. He had a good run, but still didn't get the job permanently.

Meanwhile, we had also fared pretty well in the FA Cup. After beating Mansfield Town in the replay we went on to dispose of Doncaster Rovers away Huddersfield Town away and Colchester United in an away replay to reach the fifth round for the first time in 21 years. Our reward was yet another away tie – this time to Norwich City. Anyone who was there, or who witnessed the highlights on television, must have had a certain sympathy for a team so able to ruffle First Division opponents as we did, and then come away having lost the match 3–2. Our scorers? Deane and Agana of course.

Although it was sad to go out of the Cup after such a strong performance, our clear priority was success in the League. The eight games following the second defeat by Chesterfield gave us four wins and two draws. Chesterfield were managed by Paul Hart, who I later took to

Nottingham Forest as youth supremo. More recently, he was appointed manager and is certainly adding to his credentials all the time.

Now with only two certain promotion places, we were neck and neck with Port Vale and just behind were Wolves – all ready for that final sprint to the line.

One of those eight matches was at Northampton Town where we had won 2–1 and were feeling pretty pleased with ourselves as the final whistle sounded. Then, as we trooped back into the dressing-room, news filtered through about the Hillsborough tragedy during the FA Cup semi-final between Liverpool and Nottingham Forest and, all at once, our promotion charge seemed that little less important. The players were all shocked.

Sheffield Wednesday had not been involved in the match, but the chances were that many Sheffield people had been there among the Liverpool and Forest fans. It was another Heysel Stadium, another Bradford City, with the emotions running that much deeper this time because it was even closer to home. This time it had happened in our own city and we were all deeply affected by the news. It was a sombre coach journey back to Bramall Lane that night.

I've never been governed by logic. Instead, I tend to put a great deal of store in my gut feelings – and it was this sort of abdominal nudge which persuaded me, with just six vital games to go, to drop goalkeeper Graham Benstead who had been a part of almost every game that season. Many people thought that I was mad but I felt that it was time to put my faith – and the club's future – in the hands of a young and inexperienced player by the name of Simon Tracey.

I had picked up Simon from Wimbledon earlier in the season for a mere £12,000. He had been discovered as a junior, playing for a Sunday-morning side in a Croydon park, and had joined us at Plough Lane on a youth training scheme. After two years we gave him a contract, but he was forever in the shadow of Dave Beasant who didn't miss a League game for Wimbledon in seven consecutive seasons.

In 1988, after helping Wimbledon win the FA Cup with that famous penalty save, Beasant went to Newcastle United, and Simon finally got his chance. He was selected to make his first-team debut in the FA Charity Shield at Wembley, a game which Liverpool won 2–1. Then, on the opening day of the season, came his League debut at home to Arsenal. His dream turned into a nightmare as he conceded five goals to the team which would eventually win the championship with virtually the last kick of the season at Anfield. Each of those five goals were to prove vital to Arsenal. One less and the title would have gone to Liverpool. In the event, both teams finished level on both points and goal-difference – but the title went to the Gunners by virtue of their higher goal aggregate.

Simon was dropped and he never played again for Wimbledon's first team. However, I had always considered him to be a young player of great potential and so jumped at the chance of signing him as cover for Graham Benstead as we fought our way back towards the Second Division. He had played in only one League game, the 5–1 victory over Huddersfield. Now, with six crucial games to go, he was in the team on merit for our home game against Mansfield, who we had already beaten in both the League and FA Cup.

We lost 2–1 but I had seen enough of Simon to decide that he should hold his place for the remainder of the season. We had no idea then, of course, that he would still be at Sheffield United so many years later and receiving a well-deserved testimonial. His confidence grew visibly as we drew at Fulham and then beat Swansea and Aldershot at home. Then, with only two games remaining, came the big one against promotion rivals Wolverhampton Wanderers.

Our largest home crowd of the season had been 18,000 when Port Vale held us to a goalless draw in late

February – which, incidentally was one of only two home League matches in which we failed to score. That figure was well short of the 24,000 who turned up at Molineux to watch two famous clubs settle the Third Division promotion issue in the penultimate match of the season. Skipper Paul Stancliffe and Tony Agana scored in a 2–2 draw and, at the final whistle, there were celebrations for both teams, their supporters and their directors.

It could have had a very different ending though. With only a few seconds to go, the referee blew his whistle for a free-kick in Wolves' favour. Many of the Sheffield United team believed it was the signal for the end of the match. As Wolves prepared to take the kick, our goalkeeper and two key defenders were climbing the railings to celebrate with the ecstatic United fans. Messrs Bassett and Taylor shot out of the dug-out, waving their arms like madmen and, for a few seconds, loo rolls were a high priority on the Sheffield shopping list.

For Wolverhampton Wanderers and Sheffield United, the Second Division beckoned – while Port Vale would have to go through the nail-biting process of qualifying through the Play-offs if they were to join us for the season ahead.

At this point I would like to go on record as saying that I am very much against the end-of-season Play-off farce. This has nothing to do with the fact that Sheffield United lost their Second Division status through this mini-competition. On the contrary, if a team finishes next to bottom on merit – or lack of it – they have qualified for the drop.

My concern is for the team which has had a good season and might miss automatic promotion on goal-difference. They have already proved their worth over, say 46 matches and are clearly disappointed at missing out. On the other hand, a team languishing in mid-table might finish strongly and sneak into sixth or seventh place.

Elated by their success, but several points behind the team which finished third, they are thrown into the pool with the other hopefuls and are automatically at an advantage because their spirits are so high.

The situation is made all the more farcical by the fact that the winners of the Play-offs receive the bonus of additional gate money and a trophy while the team which has really earned promotion on merit gets nothing at all. However, having said all that, the Play-offs are now very much part of the commercial merry-go-round and no opinion of mine will change that.

While Port Vale and the other Play-off sides were sweating it out for their future in Division Two, we were off to Magaluf in Majorca to celebrate our success and to join many other clubs in what has become an unofficial end-of-season players' convention.

It was an 'interesting' break – although the party spirit I encouraged among my own players was not always shared, or appreciated, by other managers present. More of that later, for now it was enough that we were happy – and we were also pleased to hear that Port Vale had made it through the Play-offs. Justice had, after all, been done.

When I joined Sheffield United in the first place I had accepted an 18-month contract. In that time we had suffered the depression of going down – but now we were on the high of going back up again. Bramall Lane was beginning to feel more like Plough Lane with every passing day.

8

Going Up – Again

EVEN BEFORE THE NEW SEASON HAD STARTED, many self-appointed prophets of the game had condemned Sheffield United to a swift return to Division Three. Had their predictions proved to be true, I am sure that it would not have saddened some members of the press who had delighted in knocking our performance and belittling our achievements at every opportunity. However, I accept that they all have a job to do and, because they consider me to be among the more colourful – if less diplomatic – managers in the game, I have been a natural target for many tabloid reporters.

No, I do not have a persecution complex – but there are some things that managers and players have to put up with that the public do not fully comprehend. Kicking Bassett's backside started just under two decades ago, shortly after Wimbledon started their rise from the oblivion of non-League football, and I would be less than honest if I didn't admit that, at first, I found it to be a new and enjoyable experience. Prior to that, the only occasions when I had been of any interest to the national press was when leading Walton & Hersham to success in the FA Amateur Cup Final, and scoring the own-goal which was to decide Wimbledon's epic battle against Leeds United.

It worked very well at first when the media were treating Wimbledon as a novelty. We were a true Cinderella side then which, against all the odds, not only crashed the Football League but even threatened to hold its own against soccer's big boys. I was grateful for the attention too, for we needed all the publicity that we could get to encourage people through the turnstiles and get bums on seats. Actually, it was more a case of getting feet on terraces in those days.

The novelty seemed to wear a bit thin very quickly as we were seen not only to survive but to succeed in the sphere of more sophisticated competition. We weren't performing to the pre-ordained rules of the media. We weren't suffering defeat and humiliation wherever we went – and some of those hacks didn't like it. They felt that we didn't belong in the higher divisions, and some – the same ones who had patronised our 'plucky little efforts' in the early years – now regarded the club as something of a precocious child who had finally overstepped the mark.

When Wimbledon joined the Football League they had come in as the 12th London club, and many posed the question: Does football really need another struggling side? Particularly so as there were five other London clubs – Chelsea, Fulham, QPR, Brentford and Crystal Palace – all within a few miles radius. Then, even when we had finally proved ourselves, it seemed that the big clubs themselves didn't want Wimbledon in the First Division – and the newspapers started to echo their views. What, in fact, had been a fairy tale for the Dons had turned out to be harsh reality for the major clubs and they didn't appear to like it one little bit.

Because the press seemed to favour the larger and more established clubs, they were not slow in criticising our playing style, our facilities and our meagre crowds. Fortunately this did nothing to dampen the spirits or to dilute the dedication of the players. In fact it all tended to have the opposite effect, binding them together and strengthening their resolve – which is so often the case with any persecuted minority group.

I have never seen myself as a particularly controversial

character, but some newspapers – especially the tabloids – seem to think that they can get a story out of me which they could never get out of other managers. On a slow news day they seem to have a very simple maxim – 'if you're struggling for a story then give Bassett a ring – something will develop'.

A classic example was the screaming headline 'Gazza's a Buffoon' over a piece which appeared in the *Sun* on the morning of a Sheffield United match at White Hart Lane.

It has always been my contention that the more talented ball-players – particularly characters like Paul Gascoigne – are treated with unfair leniency on the pitch, while someone like Vinnie Jones would get his name taken just for sneezing at the wrong time. I was merely pointing out to the reporter that, just because Gazza might ruffle a player's hair after nearly decapitating him, it doesn't lessen the gravity of the offence. Referees should be more consistent in their interpretation of the rules of the game, rather than let themselves be influenced by the persuasive buffoonery of players like Gascoigne. Sadly, though, it seems that the 'boo-hoo' boy of the World Cup took it all too seriously and spent a large proportion of the game glaring or making silly faces and gestures at me behind the referee's back. I suppose he had the last laugh as well – we lost 4–0.

I know that the titles of the tabloid press are locked into a circulation war and I also understand that the journalists who have to deliver a story and sub-editors who write most of the headlines are working under immense pressure. That's why I am always prepared to give them as much time as they want. After all, if you are the manager of a football club you are, to a certain extent, public property. They have a knock sometimes, of course, but I don't take too much notice of it. It's all a huge game.

We are victims of a marketing and sales war and

therefore we're as vulnerable as any other public figure – but if there's one thing that really gets up my nose it is being misquoted. I have to protect myself and the club from bad publicity and I tend to react only when I feel that a reporter has been extremely unfair in his criticism.

I can take most of it in my stride, and I rarely become incensed by their views, but on occasions I have found myself writing letters to the editor – or even the reporter himself – when I felt that the journalist's code of factual reporting has been bent beyond acceptable limits. These missives, apart from relieving my own immediate feelings, have achieved little, of course – the journalistic profession is notorious for closing ranks and guarding each other's back whenever their victim dares to snap back them. Do those who make a living in criticising others really believe that they are above criticism themselves?

I can work quite happily alongside most sports writers – but I no longer include any of them among my closest friends. I did once, and unfortunately that friendship turned very sour – proving to me that the old adage about mixing business with pleasure, in football circles at least, really is true. I'm talking, of course, about Tony Stenson of whom I have already written. In my early days at Wimbledon he was one of the most supportive of the press corps and we became good friends. My wife Christine also grew close to Carol Stenson, which was a bonus for Tony and me, and the four of us would frequently spend our time together in off-duty hours. Stenson, however, turned out to be a real Brutus. As well as stabbing me in the back, it hurt so very much to think that a so-called friend could do what he did to me – and the article reduced Christine to tears. Neither of us could really believe it and we were particularly upset by the snide reference to our villa in Spain in which – he carefully omitted to mention – both he and his wife had been our guests. Sadly, it seemed that he was quite prepared to sacrifice our entire relationship for the sake of that one article.

Later he blamed his sports editor and he also said that he wanted to write a book about me. Sorry, Tony, I'm not that naive – not any more.

I was also the victim of the Watford mole syndrome. A couple of players and even some of the office staff had been primed by their Fleet Street friends to tip them off about any off-the-field incidents which might provide a juicy snippet and make my life at Vicarage Road even more uncomfortable than it already was. I know very well who were involved but they are completely unworthy of any mention in this book.

On one occasion, however, someone really screwed it up after seeing Tony Coton walk off the practice ground. Tony was a first-class goalkeeper, but he did tend to show a touch of petulance from time to time. As he walked from the field one of the moles wrongly assumed that I had banished him to the dressing-room. The story appeared and I can only hope that the 'mole' concerned received the due ear-bashing that he deserved from his contact for imparting duff gen.

In common with many others in the sporting limelight I am sometimes asked to speak at functions. Sometimes it is for companies or charities or, on other occasions, by players and football clubs who are organising benefit events. However, two of these male-only functions have landed me in the mire and attracted some most unwelcome publicity. The more recent of these was Lawrie Madden's benefit dinner in Sheffield when I told a mildly racist joke about our striker, Brian Deane. Among the guests at the function was Councillor Clive Betts, the left-wing leader of Sheffield City Council. He walked out during my speech and later complained so vehemently to the *Star*, the local evening newspaper, about my so-called racist remarks that they made an issue out of it in their editorial column. Brian Deane wasn't offended and I thought that Betts was only proving how very narrow-minded he was. Sadly the *Star* indulged him and even Lawrie Madden himself described the incident as 'unfortunate' when, really, he should have stepped forward to defend me. After all, I was there at his request – and I was there for free.

However, it was an earlier indiscretion at a testimonial dinner for Wimbledon stalwart Wally Downes which really landed me in the brown stuff up to my neck. It was an all-male occasion held at the Grosvenor House Hotel and, during my speech, I dropped my trousers simply to illustrate a point – and there is no pun intended.

Within 48 hours the *Sun* was on to me. Had I exposed myself during an after-dinner speech they wanted to know and, if so, what were the circumstances? I denied it vigorously, of course, insisting that I had merely poked my thumb through my underpants, and they seemed to accept that – albeit, reluctantly. 'It wasn't my thingy – it was my thumby!' screamed the headlines the following morning, following that with the sordid details of a joke that went wrong. It is for this very reason that the press are not invited to these functions – so how did they find out? A man at the party told a mate at work whose wife just happened to be a friend of an employee at the *Sun* ... and so it goes on.

Perhaps whoever it was will derive some satisfaction from the disclosure that it wasn't my thumb at all – it really was my thingy. The adverse publicity that the incident created made me realise for the first time that Dave Bassett was news even away from the football field. I found it more than a little unnerving. It also made me very aware of just how I should conduct myself in future. Until then I had been a keen mooner and used any excuse to drop my trousers at parties or dances just to get a cheap laugh. Christine hated it, of course. She would get very embarrassed and we had many rows about it. Now I realise how stupid and degrading it is – but it is still news to some sectors of the press.

In August 1989 it was Sheffield United who were in the media spotlight, not me. The seers of the game all agreed that Wolves would relish the challenge of Division Two and that even Port Vale had a better chance of survival than the 'no-hopers' at Bramall Lane. Within two months our detractors discovered that they had seriously under-estimated both our team-spirit and the calibre of the players who had comprised my summer shopping-list.

Mark Morris, who had first come to Wimbledon as a schoolboy before joining me at Watford, was a high priority. He cost what was then a club record fee of £175,000, good value for a talented centre-back and a man whom I've always felt possessed strong leadership qualities. I also picked up former Arsenal midfielder Colin Hill from Colchester United for £85,000, defender David Barnes for £52,000 from Aldershot, and I bought Julian Winter from Huddersfield Town for £50,000 – pushing my expenditure up to just over £350,000.

Earlier, I had returned to Wimbledon for the signature of John Gannon – who had spent some time on loan at Bramall Lane towards the end of the previous season. His training with Wimbledon had started at 12 years of age, resulting in him signing schoolboy forms at age 14 when the Dons were still in the Fourth Division. For him, perhaps more than most, the bright lights and big names of Division One must have seemed a lifetime away. However, by the time he had finished his apprenticeship we were up there among them and I remember his astonishment at the sheer speed of that remarkable rise.

John had started to challenge for a regular first-team place at Wimbledon and marked his debut in the senior side with a goal during the promotion season from

Division Two. He played a couple of games in the First Division the following season but fell from favour under Bobby Gould and his career appeared to be going nowhere when I signed him on loan. He performed well enough for me to be able to offer him a more permanent deal now that we were back in the Second Division. It was a good career move for him and, thanks to some of his former Wimbledon team-mates, he was able to fit in well – both at the club and also in the unfamiliar Yorkshire environment.

I have mentioned our brief trip to Magaluf. One night – or early morning – in the bar, I was getting a lot of earache from two other managers – namely, Brian Talbot of West Brom and Harry Redknapp, at that time manager of Bournemouth. Brian made it quite clear that they didn't like the way I operated. They didn't like the way my players conducted themselves and they didn't like the style of football that we played. I fully expected them to tell me that they didn't like the way I brushed my teeth in the mornings, the colour of my socks, or the way I tied my shoe-laces. Brian was by far the worst – but Harry nodded along with him.

The more they went on the more I grinned. The more I grinned the more they went on. I had heard it all before – too many times to let it spoil my holiday with the lads.

The computer had the last laugh, though, giving us what appeared to be a tough opening fixture against none other than West Bromwich Albion at The Hawthorns. Three of my close-season signings – Morris, Hill and Barnes were included in that opening match, as were Gannon and Tracey – who was ever-present during the season and was to be elected Blade of the Year by the supporters.

Only one player – Paul Stancliffe – had been part of the first-team squad which I had inherited some 18 months earlier. Apart from him, the team had cost under

£400,000 to assemble and time was to prove that these were the boys who would restore Sheffield United to the First Division for the first time in 14 years. Not bad when you consider that this sum included even the substitutes for that opening match – John Francis (£5,000) and Dane Whitehouse, who had been promoted from the youth squad.

The team oozed confidence as they cruised to a 3–0 win over West Brom with two goals from Agana and one from Deane. Both players were clearly keen to carry on in the way that they had finished the previous season.

Brian Talbot, West Brom's manager, was quick to criticise our playing style again after the game but, when you have been hit by as much verbal flak as I have, one tends to become immune. It was tempting to remind him of our conversation back in Magaluf but, as it happened, I didn't need to. I later discovered that Harry Redknapp, who had kept relatively quiet at the time, had actually followed our chat at the bar by placing a £50 bet with Brian that my Sheffield no-hopers would beat West Brom. Needless to say Harry was very quick to rub salt into Talbot's wounds by ringing him at home to say how he would like to be paid. Anyway, at the end of the season Brian Talbot sent me a congratulatory letter which stated: 'I think your achievement is fantastic ... I can assure you that I'll keep my big mouth shut in future.'

Our first home match saw us beat Talbot's former club, Ipswich Town, 2–0. Deane was again on target and Mark Morris, making his home debut, became an immediate hit with the crowd by scoring the second. In September I was able to strengthen the squad by acquiring both Carl Bradshaw from Manchester City and former Watford player Wilf Rostron from Sheffield Wednesday. I took them both on loan and subsequently signed them on more permanent terms. Both of these players proved vital in our push towards the First Division.

We extended our unbeaten run to ten games with four draws and four more victories, including a home thriller against Brighton which we won 5–4 after blowing a three-goal lead. It was all good stuff and it kept the fans happy. We were at the top of the Second Division and feeling pretty pleased with ourselves when our egos were rudely punctured by a 2–0 home defeat at the hands of West Ham. To be fair, the Hammers defence soaked up everything that we threw at them – even when we forced 23 corners in the second half.

Fortunately, that defeat proved to be just a temporary hiccup. Normal service was resumed in the second half of October, during which we registered four successive wins, including a 3–1 victory over Steve Harrison's Watford team at Vicarage Road – oh, how sweet that victory tasted! I enjoyed it all the more because it was one of our finest performances of the season so far, despite the appalling weather conditions. Because of high winds we changed our tactics at half-time, adopted the short-ball game and cruised home with a goal from Brian Deane and two, in the second half, from John Francis who came on as substitute for Agana. I think we must have shocked everyone by changing to a short-ball game – it had been assumed that Bassett's boys could only play one way.

Our run-up to Christmas saw us win three, draw three and lose only our second match of the season, to Newcastle United who had been on the tail of the promotion pace-setters for most of the campaign. Despite this set-back, however, we had lost only two of our first 22 matches – which was the best record in the entire Football League. Even so, we had been edged out of our top spot by Yorkshire rivals Leeds United, who we were due to face at Bramall Lane on Boxing Day.

It was a rare occasion – the two top teams in Division Two with the added bonus of the passion and rivalry of a Yorkshire derby. We went one down – then

Wilf Rostron shot through a crowded goalmouth to equalise. Five minutes before half-time Bryson and Booker combined well to lay a goal on for Agana and the Sheffield crowd went potty. The lead was short-lived, though. Five minutes after the restart Leeds equalised through Carl Shutt and, although it was gripping stuff for the next 40 minutes, both defences held out for a 2–2 draw.

The crowd of 31,600 beat our next best home attendance of the season by more than 10,000 but, pleasing though it undoubtedly was, it was still less than half Bramall Lane's record gate. Coincidentally that was also against Leeds, in February 1936 for a fifth-round FA Cup match when 68,287 fans were shoe-horned into the ground to see Second Division Sheffield United beat their First Division rivals 3–1. That was a momentous year for the Blades, who went on to reach the Cup Final only to lose to the all-conquering Arsenal side – which contained ten internationals – by the only goal of the match. The scorer? Ted Drake from a Cliff Bastin cross.

That was the last time Sheffield United reached the FA Cup Final and while the year has been proudly chronicled in the pages of Bramall Lane history, it was also a season tinged with regret because the Blades finished third in the table and missed promotion to the First Division by one place.

Three days after we met, Leeds slipped up by losing at Barnsley. We had only to win our home match against Blackburn to regain our place at the head of Division Two. Despite taking the lead with a Brian Deane goal we blew it, going down 2–1. Two days later, on New Year's Day 1990, it happened again when we turned in a remarkably inept performance in driving rain at Oxford and went down by three clear goals.

Our next Second Division match took us to Ipswich where we were leading, again with a Brian Deane goal, with only three minutes to go but we cracked and came away with a disappointing draw, knowing that our performance had merited three points rather than one. We had now gone five matches without a win and our tally had been just three points – hardly promotion form and not quite the right image to lay on for the BBC production team which had just invaded us to commence shooting *United* – a six-part documentary on life behind the scenes at a football club. It was to have a gripping climax which was much more suited to the pages of fiction than the world of fact.

I introduced some changes to the team for our next home match, against Middlesbrough, and Agana's goal settled what must have been one of the most entertaining games of the season. Leeds were still ahead of us but other results had strengthened our position, opening up an eight-point lead over Swindon Town who were in third place. It seemed as good a time as any to have our interests diverted by the FA Cup. We had already disposed of Bournemouth in the third round and, as you can imagine, I wasn't too disappointed at drawing Watford at home in the next round.

Another chance to rub their noses in it?

It should have been, certainly. We took an early lead but they equalised in the final minutes to force a replay. This game, incidentally, was goalkeeper Graham Benstead's only appearance of the season and was to be his last for Sheffield United. He had now been usurped as first-choice by Simon Tracey and, anxious for first-team football, he later signed for Brentford.

I was fairly confident about the replay at Watford. There were still plenty of people at Vicarage Road who blamed me for the club's fall from Division One and they had been pretty sick when we had won there in the League. For many of them, ending my interest in the FA Cup would at least help to redress the balance. There was little to worry about, though. The team knew exactly what was at stake and they really turned it on for me. Brian Deane scored first, then they equalised with a very dodgy penalty – honestly, it really was – and it was left to the old war-horse Paul Stancliffe to score one of his two goals of the season to give us our second win over my former employers.

The euphoria sparked by beating Watford for the second time in three months soon evaporated as we returned to League action with a miserable goalless draw against Hull City at Boothferry Park. The result was disappointing. Hull were a poor side and they had started the season by going 16 League games without a win – an achievement with which I was to become closely identified the following season.

The Hull match signalled a mini-run of six League games without defeat, during which we also took the chance to extend our Cup run. Having disposed of Watford in the fourth round, we drew near-neighbours Barnsley at home and were disappointed to be held to a 2–2 draw in a game which we should have won at the first attempt – even though we were 2–0 down at one stage. The replay, a goalless draw, must have bored the pants off anyone who had the misfortune to see it, and foul weather intervened to twice postpone the second replay.

So, leaving our Cup tussle in abeyance, we returned to League action and that successful mini-run of three wins and three draws, during which recent signings Paul Wood from Brighton and Billy Whitehurst from Hull were introduced to the side. Wood is an ideal play-anywhere utility man, while Whitehurst had plenty of experience up front and I saw him as a perfect cover for our strikers, particularly since we had been jinxed by injury from the start of the season.

I have always looked at players for their cover value – once an insurance man, always an insurance man.

They both opened their League scoring accounts in

the 2–2 draw at Brighton but it was Wood's goal against his former club which gave me more pleasure. Whitehurst suffered the ignominy of heading a corner past his own goalkeeper, but he made amends three days later when he completed his each-way double by scoring his first goal for United in our 3–0 win over Wolves. It seems that I had bought Whitehurst at precisely the right time. Before the Brighton game we had looked pretty impressive at Bradford City when we won 4–1, but Tony Agana had been injured in a vicious late tackle as he scored our fourth goal. It was to be seven League matches before he was fit enough to play a complete game again.

The match against Bradford City marked the beginning of a frenetic 11-day period, during which we played four matches, two of them in the FA Cup. Two days after Bradford City we faced the long-awaited FA Cup second replay at Barnsley. It was another sloppy game, not much better than the first replay but was finally settled by a penalty goal scored by Tony Agana, who was still nursing the injury from the previous game. Not much to shout about really but by reaching the sixth round we had enjoyed Sheffield United's best FA Cup run for 22 years.

Our reward for 330 minutes of gruelling FA Cup fifth-round football was another home draw – this time against the mighty Manchester United. Alex Ferguson was getting a bit desperate to win something. He had been at Old Trafford for more than three years without success and both the media and the public were beginning to climb all over him. His United had beaten Nottingham Forest, Hereford and Newcastle to get this far and had been drawn away each time.

We had the bit between our teeth and they had the bit between theirs. It had all the ingredients of a great FA Cup-tie and 34,344 spectators turned up at Bramall Lane on 11 March 1990 to see it. When you saw names like Leighton, Anderson, Bruce, Pallister, Ince, McClair and

Hughes in the match programme, you knew that you were in for a game and a half.

Played on a Sunday with a 12.30pm kick-off – which never feels quite right – it was a fairly disappointing game with both teams performing well below their ability It is now history that Manchester United won with a Brian McClair goal and went on to collect the Cup after beating Palace in a replay. It certainly relieved Alex Ferguson of a great deal of mounting pressure. For us it was a shame really – victory would have put us into the semi-finals for the first time since 1961 when Sheffield United, then in the Second Division, were deprived of a place at Wembley only after losing 2–0 in a second replay against Leicester. It was almost a memorable double in that season – the club finished one point behind Alf Ramsey's Ipswich and gained promotion to Division One.

By mid-March we were cruising. The comprehensive 3–0 dismantling of an in-form Wolves side had reinforced our confidence and we had gained 63 points from our 33 games played so far. If only we could average something close to two points from each of the remaining 13 matches, I reckoned that we would finish in the top two. An unusually symmetric pattern of draw, win, draw, win and so on, had seen us take 16 points from our previous eight games – and I felt confident that we were on course, even though seven of those 13 fixtures were away from home. I wasn't feeling complacent – far from it – but there was, as the man said, a strong case for mild optimism.

Then we came up against West Ham – the team which had halted our run of ten games without defeat at the start of the season. They simply tore us apart. We came second in just about every aspect of the game and I willingly concede that there was very little that we could do about it. It wasn't so much the five-goal drubbing that we received that worried me so much – it was the mental effect that the game would have on my team.

Later I was proved right. It had been something of a culture shock. The players suddenly seemed very unsure of themselves and that crushing defeat by West Ham started a disastrous period of four defeats in six games. Even our next game, against neighbouring Barnsley ended in a home defeat, which was extremely disappointing after having already beaten them in the fifth round of the FA Cup, albeit at the third attempt.

We rallied briefly with away wins at Oldham Athletic and Stoke City. The victory over Oldham was the Latics' first home defeat in 18 months. Unfortunately we then slumped at home to Sunderland and away at Portsmouth. The game at Fratton Park marked Tony Agana's return to the side, but even he couldn't weave the necessary magic. Defeat meant that Newcastle were now only three points behind us in third place – and we no longer had any games in hand.

With only six points gained from six matches, it was clear that a swift revision of the points equation was necessary and I estimated that we needed 18 points from our final seven games to be sure of one of the promotion places. That meant that we could afford to drop only three points – four at the most – and, while I was pleased that only three of the remaining matches were away from home, I was very much aware that one of them was at Leeds.

The first of those critical seven games was at home to Watford, who we had already beaten twice. Fleetingly I feared the worst when we went a goal down within four minutes, because I knew that the Watford players – not to mention the fans – having failed to halt our Cup run would enjoy nothing better than messing up my promotion hopes. I needn't have worried, however, as goals from Messrs Agana, Booker, Deane and Whitehurst gave us a decisive win. I derived considerable satisfaction from the fact that, out of four meetings with Watford that season, we had won three and drawn one.

One down, six to go – and Newcastle were still breathing down our necks, still only those three points behind.

Oxford United were our next challenge and we were forced to struggle right up to the last minute when a fortunate – for us – own-goal gave us a 2–1 victory. Five left to play and everything so far was going according to plan. Then came Easter Monday at Elland Road.

Far from being a classic 'Clash of the Titans', it was a scrappy and disappointing game, marred by persistent niggling among the players and some quite inconsistent refereeing. Leeds had paid Wimbledon £600,000 to acquire my Wealdstone 'find', Vinnie Jones, to boost their promotion challenge and I'm sure that he did the business for them – I'm only sorry that he did some of it at our expense. Despite holding Leeds United to a single goal for most of the match, our defence crumbled late in the game and we finally lost 4–0.

The journey back to South Yorkshire that Easter Monday evening was miserable to say the least. A heavy defeat was bad enough but Newcastle United had also beaten Stoke City 3–0 and had edged into second place by virtue of a much superior goal-difference. Not that it had been all that superior before the day's kick-off, when they had been only six goals ahead of us – but now, because of their win and our defeat, they had a cushion of 13 goals over us, and even had one in hand over Leeds. Other pretenders had fallen away in the previous couple of weeks and now it was just a three-horse race. With four matches each to play, Leeds United with 78 points were clear favourites, with Newcastle and ourselves both on 75 points. All very tight, give or take a goal or two.

We next faced Port Vale at home. Anything but a win would probably condemn us to the Play-offs – and we were drawing 1–1 with less than a minute to go. I had really given up all hope of victory when Brian Deane popped up to slam the ball through a crowded goalmouth for yet another of his dramatic 90th-minute winners. Those three points were particularly valuable since both Leeds and Newcastle drew away from home. Three games to go and we were now within a point of Leeds and two ahead of Newcastle.

The following Wednesday saw us resting while our rivals sought to consolidate – or even improve – their position with home games which, according to the form-books, appeared to present few problems. Newcastle United were held to a goalless draw at home by Play-off contenders Swindon Town, while Leeds United faced a relatively easy task – on paper at least – against Barnsley at Elland Road.

Barnsley, who were foundering just above the relegation zone, had been impertinent enough to snatch three home points from Leeds in their Christmas holiday clash, but I couldn't see them surviving in the cauldron of Elland Road in front of 30,000 promotion-hungry fans. I tried not to think about it – we would be all right as long as we won all our remaining games – but a little outside help would not come amiss.

I was in the car when the score was flashed through and I just couldn't believe it. Leeds 1, Barnsley 2? Impossible. It must either be a mistake, or else someone was taking the mickey Then I heard confirmation of the score, followed by a brief match report and I almost swerved off the road in my delight. Barnsley, who had severely dented our own promotion charge a month earlier, had achieved an unlikely double over Leeds. So there we were, with just three games to go, one point behind Leeds, one point ahead of Newcastle – and a game in hand over both of them. Now it wasn't merely promotion that was the all-important target – the championship had become a very real possibility. And Barnsley? Suddenly I'm their greatest fan and I love 'em dearly!

The following Saturday saw all three of us win at home. Leeds United beat Leicester City – who we would be facing on the final day of the season – while Newcastle United had a creditable 2–1 win over West Ham. Our task against Bournemouth should have been relatively easy – particularly after Ian Bryson's two early goals had dispelled any sign of nervousness. Bournemouth, like Barnsley were also among the relegation candidates but they proved to be a tough nut to crack and I was more than a little miffed when former Blade, Richard Cadette – who I'd sold the previous season – scored one and then came within an ace of equalising. Tony Agana eased the pressure before another of my erstwhile associates – one Luther Blissett, formerly of Watford – did his best to ruin my day by scoring from the penalty spot before Deane eased my blood pressure with a fourth.

No change at the top, then, with two points separating the top three teams. We were still sandwiched in the middle and, although we had improved our goal-difference, there was clearly no way we could finish ahead of either Leeds United or Newcastle United if we finished level on points. We still had two games left to their one, but both of them were away from home.

May Day – Tuesday, 1 May – marked our big chance against Blackburn Rovers at Ewood Park. It was our game in hand and a win would see us go into the last match two points ahead of Leeds and three in front of Newcastle. In the event the date seemed particularly apt since we could have done with our own Mayday distress call to help us find the goal.

The boys gave everything, completely outplaying Blackburn Rovers for long periods at a time, but unable to get the ball into the net. Wood dribbled through the Blackburn defences but his shot lacked power, Agana narrowly missed with a half-chance and Deane shot high and then headed over the bar in a situation where he would have scored in nine cases out of ten. Then it was Blackburn Rovers who looked dangerous for a spell before the Blades came back with efforts from Wood and Morris, both thwarted by great saves. In the dying moments Whitehurst stretched for a high Deane cross and his stunning header went just inches wide.

No goals and a single point which had taken us level with Leeds United and two ahead of Newcastle United. With just one away game for each of us, nothing was settled. Any one of us could lift the title, any one of us could miss automatic promotion. For Leeds and ourselves, the fixture computer had thrown up an odd quirk – reversing the situation of the previous Saturday when we had beaten Bournemouth and Leeds had won against Leicester City. Now the Elland Road side would have to overcome Bournemouth at Dean Court to win the championship title, while we knew that we must triumph at Filbert Street to be assured of promotion. Newcastle United would have to win at Middlesbrough to have any chance at all. However, if both Leeds and Sheffield lost, then Newcastle would win the title on points, and if we both drew they would still win it on goal-difference. Are you still following me?

At three o'clock that afternoon there could not have been a more electric atmosphere anywhere in Britain than there was at Dean Court, Ayresome Park or Filbert Street, where we were each doing our particular thing. Geoff Taylor and I had finished our tactical talk at lunch-time. After that it would have been impossible to achieve anything at the ground, which appeared to have been taken over – first by the press and then by the BBC camera crew who were catching the pre-match tension for their TV series *United*.

Fortunately the players seemed to be oblivious to the

intrusion as they sat in their away strip of bright yellow, black and red – preparing themselves mentally for the task that lay ahead. I wondered if they would miss the influence of club captain Paul Stancliffe, who had appeared in 40 of our League matches but could not play in this one because of an injury sustained in the Port Vale game. In an unaccustomed fit of optimism, before the season had started, he had told his wife that, in spite of media predictions, he really fancied our chances this year. In a couple of hours we would know if he had been right.

For the final few minutes before they were due to run out on to the pitch I stood in the doorway and watched my team as they whispered, comforted, cajoled, eased tension and finally shook hands and noisily wished each other good luck. A team which had been built for around £400,000 and had been written off as a bunch of no-hopers at the start of the season was now only 90 minutes away from football in the top flight of the English game. I felt proud – very proud – of all of them.

Of the 21,000 who packed into the Filbert Street stadium, at least half must have been Sheffield United fans. The roar which erupted when stand-in skipper Bob Booker led them on to the field was unbelievable. It would have needed a stronger man than me not to have a tear in his eye and a lump in his throat.

It did not take long for that overwhelming feeling of emotion and elation to turn into depression. Leicester had obviously not read the script and when they went ahead through Mills, I started to fear the worst. But not my players. They set out to prove what a faint-hearted wimp I really was as they took the game by the scruff of the neck and subjected Leicester City to intense pressure. A perfectly-flighted cross from Bryson enabled Wood to equalise and soon afterwards Deane ended an absorbing game of ping-pong in the Leicester goalmouth by slamming in a fierce drive.

At last the frown disappeared from my face and I almost began to smile. Two more goals by Agana and Rostron and I was totally relaxed – well, as relaxed as I'm ever likely to be. Even when Leicester scored a second before the interval, my inner-man told me that we were already there – a 4–2 lead at half-time, while Newcastle United were behind at Middlesbrough and Leeds were being held at Bournemouth. The future was looking quite rosy.

Tony Agana's second-half goal confirmed my suspicions – and even the news that Leeds United had gone one up at Bournemouth, and were therefore on course to snatch the championship on goal-difference, did nothing to dampen my spirits. When the final whistle blew on a scoreline of 5–2, the Sheffield supporters erupted.

They had waited 14 long years for First Division football and they were not slow in showing their appreciation for the players who had got them there, and even the manager – not considered to be among life's shrinking violets – was mildly embarrassed to be carried around shoulder-high by the euphoric United fans.

Although wins by ourselves and Leeds meant that Newcastle United were condemned to the Play-offs, I must record that they self-destructed at the final hurdle – losing the North-Eastern derby with Middlesbrough by 4–1 – but still finished up with a superior goal-difference to ourselves. Promotion apart, there was much interest in the results at Ayresome Park and Dean Court for other reasons. Middlesbrough's defeat of Newcastle guaranteed them another season in the Second Division by jumping above Bournemouth, whose defeat by Leeds condemned them to the relegation Play-offs and, ultimately the Third Division. Rarely can there have been so much at stake in two matches.

We had been kept in touch with the scores at both Bournemouth and Middlesbrough courtesy of Leicester's computerised scoreboard. Sadly, however, it also kept us abreast of Sheffield Wednesday's unsuccessful bid to escape relegation to the Second Division – which appeared to delight a small section of the fans, but saddened me. There had been no Sheffield derby in the First Division since 1967–68 – 24 years previously – and it would have been really good to have both teams in the top flight for the following season. Good for football, good for Sheffield and, perhaps more pertinently, good for both Bramall Lane and Hillsborough.

However, as has often been said – that's football. My main concern was that we had won promotion for the second year running, and that my reputation as shit-or-bust Bassett – the man who'll either take you up or pull you down – was still intact.

9

The Jaws of Doom

I DOUBT IF THE BBC COULD BELIEVE THEIR LUCK with the timing of the *United* series. When negotiations started several weeks before the start of the season, we were very aware that nothing was certain as they were also considering another Second Division club at the time. We also knew that the proposed programme might not even go ahead at all.

They simply came to sound us out in the planning stages, probably to establish what level of co-operation they could expect from us. Would we allow them into the board-room? Would a camera crew have access to the dressing-room prior to a match? We agreed to all these things, promising them our full co-operation. Nevertheless, they had no way of knowing that we would still be among the promotion contenders four months later.

The first time that cameras appeared was before our FA Cup match game against Bournemouth – and it proved to be a good omen, heralding the start of our best run in the competition for 22 years. The series was screened during the last few nail-biting weeks of the season and the production team were able to up-date the situation week by week, thus catching the full drama of those final matches – culminating in that decisive game at Leicester City when we finally gained our promotion.

I think that the producer, Paul Poirot, will admit that he didn't have a clue that we'd figure in the promotion race when he first approached us. He wanted an average football club, perhaps one which was struggling to recapture its former glory days and he also needed the blessing and complete co-operation of the manager. Total access to all areas of the club was vital to the project, as was the freedom to catch moments and moods without fear of upset.

That is almost certainly why they eventually chose Sheffield United from their shortlist of two. I imagine that my reputation had gone before me and that the BBC felt that I was the sort of manager who would co-operate by allowing their cameras into all sorts of places which would have been strictly vetoed by many others in my position. As it happened, I never found their presence in any way intrusive and, after a couple of weeks, they seemed just like any other member of the office staff.

My final verdict? I was pleased with the overall result of the series, but felt that it could have been a little more accurate in places – particularly when taking a behind-the-scenes look at the players' personal lives. They portrayed Ian Bryson's wife, for example, as a stay-at-home – an almost lonely, or distant, type of person – which she most certainly is not. They intimated that Wilf Rostron's wife didn't even like the game, which is totally wrong. She could never be said to be anti-football even though she has little interest in the game as an entertainment.

Apart from one or two rather niggling deviations from the truth, I have to say that, all in all, it was the best programme about football that has ever been on the box – even though I have to point out that I don't normally speak through a series of bleeps. They wanted realism and that is what they got. I'm not the sort who dilutes the content of an important pre-match team talk simply because there are TV cameras there – and they knew it. I do have to admit, however, that I didn't realise the full extent of my verbal enthusiasm until the programme was screened. It's not surprising that some critics in my family likened my dialogue to a certain little robot in *Star Wars*.

If I have one gripe about the series it's that the producers were less than fair to our fans – painting them as the villains of the terraces – and this is where Bassett gets on his hobby-horse.

Fans are not incited to violence by what they see on the pitch, despite the claims of certain MPs, social workers and the myriad of observers who have prepared reports and recommendations on the state of the game and the behaviour of its participants. Football is an emotional game, but the behaviour of the fans is not dictated by the actions of the players.

It is my belief that the basic behavioural patterns of any youngster – not just those who attend soccer matches – are determined by education, the attitude of parents, environment and the structure of today's society which, in many cases, has broken down. Genuine football fans are no more likely to cause trouble on the terraces than they are in a department store.

On the other hand, if a group of yobs are out to make trouble, then nothing on God's earth will stop them. The tragedy of it all is that the image of football has suffered greatly through the actions of a touring mob of agitators who will attend a game – any game – purely to start aggravation. The result is organised mayhem, and then you have thousands of self-appointed do-gooders starting their tut-tutting and pointing an accusing finger at football, publicly denouncing the game as being solely responsible for the decline in social values and the increase of hooliganism.

What's the answer? I am not a politician but I consider that I have been blessed with a certain amount of common sense and I believe that the police in the UK should be given far wider powers. Not just when dealing with hooligans who start trouble at football matches, but in dealing with all sorts of civil unrest. There seems to be much more respect for officers of the law on the continent – particularly in Germany, Italy, Holland and France – where the police go in hard to sort it out and ask questions afterwards.

Does that seem extreme? No, I don't think so. Particularly if it helps to rid the game of its unwanted troublesome element. Mind you – I think that the Italian authorities did go a bit over the top at the 1990 World Cup Final, when they impounded a bottle of Christine's favourite expensive perfume ... just in case it contained alcohol!

I'm more in favour of broadening police powers than introducing membership cards which, quite frankly, don't solve anything. What about those people who may want to attend only half a dozen matches a year? There are thousands of football aficionados who don't want to go to a match every week any more than a theatre buff wants to attend the local theatre for every performance. Apart from that, such schemes are open to abuse and could almost be seen as a challenge by the troublemakers to attempt to beat the system. I was glad that the original scheme proposed by some politicians did not materialise.

Once the extravagances of the 1990 World Cup had passed our attention, we reverted back to preparations for the forthcoming season and I was well aware that, if we were to survive in what was then Division One, I had a real need to strengthen the squad. I was quite happy with the attack – Deane, Agana and Bryson had all proved themselves in the Second Division – and we had adequate cover with Messrs Whitehurst and Bradshaw. However, I had been less than happy with our defensive record during that promotion season. We had conceded 58 goals – six more than Leeds and three more than Newcastle who had finished behind us. It was also more than West Ham and Oldham, neither of whom figured in the final run-in – and only five fewer than Stoke, who finished bottom.

One defender who had impressed me was John

Pemberton of Crystal Palace. He is quick and also has the ability to finish a long penetrating run with an accurate cross – an art that he illustrated perfectly in the FA Cup semi-final when he set up the goal which sent Palace to Wembley while Liverpool stayed at home.

'Pembo', as he is known throughout the footballing fraternity, was a junior with Manchester United, playing alongside the likes of Mark Hughes, Clayton Blackmore and David Platt. Neither he nor Platt figured in Old Trafford's future plans and they eventually came together again at Crewe – under my ex-Wimbledon boss, Dario Gradi. Later, the old pals act between Gradi and Ron Noades saw Pemberton move to Crystal Palace. When I decided that he was just the player I needed to shore up our defence, I decided to use the old boys' bush telegraph, too, and asked Dario to do a bit of homework for me. The player seemed keen on a move to Sheffield and I came to a deal with Ron Noades while his manager, Stevie Coppell, was on holiday. Wolves were also keen to sign 'Pembo', but his desire to play in the top division meant that we were always the favourite for his signature. He has since gone on to become a very good youth coach.

I paid £250,000 for Pemberton – plus another £50,000 after 50 games – and slightly more for Paul Beesley, a central-defender-cum-midfield player from Orient, who had been attracting the attentions of several top clubs. My third close season signing – which pushed up my expenditure very close to the £1 million mark – was Jamie Hoyland, a midfield player from Bury and son of a Blades' favourite of the 1950s, Tommy Hoyland.

With three new players I felt confident that we could do the business in Division One. My aim was not simply survival – it was to do so in a manner which would provide a suitable gesture to the many seers of the game who had written us off before ever a ball had been kicked in contest.

I had already planned a ten-day tour of Scandinavia as part of the pre-season warm-up, with four games in Sweden and one in Finland. Most Scandinavian teams comprise only part-time players and we were hardly stretched as we rattled in over 30 goals in a series of impressive-sounding wins. I was quite pleased with the way in which my three new signings fitted in, both on and off the pitch. Two abiding memories that I carried back home were of Billy Whitehurst's insistence that he was a reincarnation of WC Fields, and Derek French's pessimism about the airworthiness of an ageing turbo-prop on a short internal flight in Sweden. He had real tears in his eyes as he said his fond farewells to each member of the team and then administered the last rites.

We returned home from the tour with a few question marks about our prospects – the most obvious being, were we strong enough for life in the First Division?

If competitive football is a drug, then I am an addict. For me, the new season could not begin early enough. The fixture computer had given us a dream curtain-raiser, at home against champions Liverpool – and the mood of optimism at Bramall Lane was contagious as everyone prepared to hail a new and successful era for Sheffield United.

The signs were good. There was no way of predicting that life was about to kick me in the lower regions again, or that the next four months would prove to be one of the most frustrating and disappointing periods of my entire football career – bringing with it the new and unfamiliar pain of failure.

The crowd erupted as Paul Stancliffe, making his First Division debut after 14 years in the game, led the Sheffield United team out of the players' tunnel into the warm August sun. The club had been deprived of First Division football since 1976 and had even been condemned to a year in the Fourth Division before climbing back to take their rightful place among the game's élite.

As I watched them take the field I briefly compared my team – which had cost a little more than £1 million to assemble – with the expensive stars of Liverpool. Rush, Barnes and Beardsley had cost almost £5 million between them – and poor Beardsley, after his great World Cup performance with England, wasn't even named as substitute.

It would have been sheer luxury to have had him in my side and I recall wondering at the time – how many clubs could have taken such a decision? Time was to show that he was omitted from the Liverpool team on several occasions during the season for reasons which are beyond me. I can only assume that the name of Peter Beardsley must have been a contributory factor which eventually led to the sudden and ill-timed departure from Anfield of manager Kenny Dalglish. The reasons for Beardsley's omission were said to be tactical, and that he was fully aware and agreed with the decision. All I can say is that, like a lot of other managers, I was pleased to see his name missing from the opposition team sheet.

I watched my squad of hopefuls go through their warm-up exercises, hoping that my dressing-room message had got through to them and that they wouldn't be over-awed by either the opposition or the occasion. Of the 11 players who started the game, only three – Pemberton, Hill and Rostron – had any useful experience of First Division football. Of the others, goalkeeper Simon Tracey had played one game – in which he conceded five goals – and Tony Agana had made only a handful of appearances with Watford.

On paper, at that time, it didn't add up to much – particularly against the most consistently successful team in British football history – but I felt that we still had a lot going for us. The players were fit, keen, confident and, above all, anxious to bury the ghost of the last time that the two sides met in Division One – when the Blades held Liverpool to a goalless draw at home, then lost to the only goal scored at Anfield. Three hours of football and a single goal between them, yet the records show that Liverpool won the League championship that year – while Sheffield United finished at the bottom of the table and were relegated.

I knew that it would do much for my long-term prospects to improve on both of those performances – starting with a home win. It might happen, it might not – but I was quietly confident that I would at least improve on the opening sequence of results in that relegation year – when United played their first eight matches without a win and then went a further 20 games before recording only their second victory of the season in mid-February. Surely, nobody worthy of the title of manager could expect to do as badly as that?

I knew that the fates were not on our side when, after just 13 minutes, Ian Rush collided with Simon Tracey who sustained a fractured cheekbone and was carried off. Losing your goalkeeper in any match is bad enough, but against a team like Liverpool it compounds the ill-fortune because virtually everyone on their side is well able to score goals. It was a wicked slice of luck – we were holding Liverpool and playing with confidence – but I now found myself having to change the team structure.

Full-back John Pemberton had kept goal during a couple of training sessions on tour, and I had no alternative but to disrupt his debut by asking him to put on the green jersey and pray that he could keep a clean sheet against the best players in the land. He soon won over the crowd but later made a couple of basic errors which anyone who is not a trained goalkeeper would be quite entitled to make and, as Liverpool rattled in three goals, it became very obvious that Tracey's injury had cost us the match. You are entitled to say that we might well have lost it anyway, but I would have realistically fancied our chances of holding them to a draw – especially since Brian Deane had put one away to get us level at one point.

I had just signed Phil Kite from Bournemouth as cover for Tracey and he was now thrown in at the deep end, making his club debut in a 1–1 draw against Derby at the Baseball Ground, Deane scoring a vital goal in the very last minute. I now knew that Tracey would be out for up to eight weeks and I must say that, during that time, Kite acquitted himself very well. However, time was to prove that our trouble didn't lie in conceding goals – but in our inability to score them.

The match against Derby had given us our first point and we had every reason to feel optimistic about a visit to Crystal Palace. They had gained a win and a draw in their opening two games and were obviously still feeling confident after their two Wembley appearances against Manchester United. Even so, I felt that we had the ability to come away with at least a point. Not for the first time in my life I was wrong. I had reshuffled the midfield because I wasn't sure that all the players were happy. I brought in Wood and Rostron to start the game, with Bryson named as substitute. Unfortunately, none of their boots appeared to be working that day and we went down by the only goal of the game. It was a poor performance and we should have lost 4-0. With only one point from three games we were not exactly setting the First Division on fire but languishing in 19th place, level on points with Aston Villa and one place ahead of Everton who had lost all their matches.

Then it became time for our second home match, this time against a rejuvenated Manchester City side who had my former Watford player, Tony Coton, in goal and who were handily placed with six points from three games. We had already lost Tony Agana with an injury at Selhurst

Park and I was now prepared to gamble in the hope that we could stem the tide against us. I re-organised the defence, leaving out Paul Stancliffe and introducing 19-year-old Mitch Ward to the side. To say that we 'clicked' might create the impression that I had found the instant solution to all our problems – but at least we managed to salvage a 1–1 draw with a goal from Deane and I felt that we were, at last, beginning to get our act together. However, I also realised that there would have to be even more changes.

A manager can never do anything right. Whatever course of action he chooses, he is acutely aware that where he will be pleasing some people, he will be inflaming others. He knows, too, that he must put emotional and personal feelings behind him when making any decision which is in the long-term interests of the club. It is never easy, particularly when he has to break the news to a loyal and long-serving professional that he can no longer be regarded as an automatic first-team choice.

Such was the situation I faced with Paul Stancliffe, captain of Sheffield United and a Blades player for seven years. The man who had led the on-field charge from Third to First Division in successive seasons. 'Stan', as he is always known by Blades' fans, was in every way a model professional who could represent his club at any function at any level. He had been a tremendous asset to the club but I felt that, in his own interests, the time had come to part company. He was probably surprised at the suddeness of my decision, but I have always believed in being totally honest with my players and letting them know exactly where they stand.

I offered Paul a free transfer, which would enable him to negotiate a lucrative short-term contract for himself with a new club, and we promised him full support throughout his benefit year. He immediately returned to Rotherham United, his former club, on a month's loan and later signed a contract with Wolves where he jumped straight into their first team. In many ways I was sorry to see him go and, although a handful of bright juniors who I had inherited three years earlier still remained with the club, the departure of Stan from Bramall Lane marked the severing of the final link with the Blades' old guard. I wished him every success and I still do.

I was now minus one club captain and an experienced defender, and it is now part of football history that I saw the much-maligned Vinnie Jones, formerly of Wimbledon and then of Leeds United, as the answer to my problem. Vinnie was not being selected for the Leeds first team at the time. His fee, £650,000, was almost twice the record sum I had paid for Paul Beesley just a few weeks earlier, and my critics were not slow to suggest that it was a panic purchase and that I was rebuilding my Wimbledon empire with a view to further denigrating the game.

These accusations angered me and were very unfair to the player. As far as Sheffield football goes, Vinnie Jones was never intended to be the next Tony Currie. Vinnie is a footballer of much character and a great deal of skill, and he was to prove a great driving force in a team which was beginning to lose faith in itself. He has also proved to be a great source of help and strength to individuals and families outside the game.

I immediately appointed him captain. He had matured in his year at Leeds and I felt that he was now ready for the responsibility. I knew, too, that he had learned how to motivate players and that his hatred of losing might just rub off on other members of the team as they prepared for the fifth match of the campaign at Southampton. Sadly, it was a no-joy day all round. We were a goal down within five minutes, thanks to Matthew Le Tissier, and Rod Wallace made it two within half an hour. We battled well, but the Saints' defence held out and it proved to be a pretty miserable coach ride back to Yorkshire.

Despite that defeat at Southampton, I felt reasonably confident about this defence. The big question mark now was in attack, where an horrendous bout of injuries had deprived me of Agana, Wood and Whitehurst. Bradshaw's form had dropped and there was no secret about it – we had problems. I had heard on the grapevine that Arsenal might be prepared to part with Brian Marwood, who had won both a League championship medal and a place in the full England squad in his two years under George Graham. I spent a few hours on the hotline to Highbury before meeting the player to discuss terms and it was plain that he was keen to move back to Yorkshire. Brian had spent four years at Hillsborough after having turned down a move to Sheffield United when the Blades were managed by Ian Porterfield. The directors – bless 'em – came up with some more money to make it £1 million within a week, and Brian had the chance of only one training session before being pushed straight into the team for the home game against Leeds United. As it happened, he didn't live up to expectations during his spell with the Blades, although in fairness he did have a number of injury problems.

Apart from needing the points desperately, I was still smarting from that 4–0 walloping which Leeds had given us during our run-in to promotion the previous season and I was anxious to redress the balance. With Marwood in attack and Jones keen to impress against his former club, I sensed a positive – if somewhat rare – buzz of confidence about the team as they started the game. We could easily have been two up as Jones and Beesley hammered shots against the post, but we were eventually sunk by two late goals. Now we had played six and won none – many of the game's paid observers were already gleefully dispatching us back into the Second Division.

Two days later we had to struggle to beat Fourth Division Northampton Town in the first leg of the Rumbelows Cup – which didn't auger well for our visit to Chelsea and a reunion with Dave Beasant and Dennis Wise. Came the day and we were two goals down in 30 minutes, but goals from Jones just before the interval, and Deane, in the 89th minute, again earned us our third point of the season. Not much to shout about perhaps, but an away draw against a well-equipped outfit like Chelsea was a great confidence-booster and, mentally, was worth considerably more than that single point.

A week later there was another reunion – this time at home to the old firm from Wimbledon. Whatever warmth I might have felt for my former club was rapidly cooled by the 2–1 defeat they inflicted on us with goals from my old mates Fairweather and Fashanu. Behaviour like this can test even the strongest of friendships.

We had a brief respite from our run of failure when we beat Northampton again to graduate to the second round of the Rumbelows Cup – but then it was back to reality again with a 4–0 thumping at Tottenham, which I think gives a rather distorted view of the game. We held them until the final half-hour when our defence seemed to crumble after David Barnes had been sent off for what seemed to me to be nothing at all. The match marked an unhappy return to the side of Simon Tracey, who had recovered from his injury sustained in the first match of the season. In addition to conceding four goals, he was also booked for dissent. The game was otherwise memorable for the fact that Paul Walsh scored a hat-trick, and Paul Gascoigne spent most of the time making stupid gestures at me following my claims in the morning press that certain players of his ilk were over-protected by referees and seemed able to get away with murder on the pitch. He was substituted before the end.

That defeat by Tottenham cemented us firmly to the

foot of the table. We had zero wins, and only three points from a total of nine games and even Derby County had edged above us. Things didn't improve a week later when fellow-strugglers Coventry City came to Bramall Lane and repaid our hospitality by stealing three points. This was followed by another brief respite as goals from Deane and Bradshaw put Everton out of the League Cup competition. However, with due respect to Mr Rumbelow, I have to say that I would much rather have kept results like that for a League match.

Conceding three goals at Norwich didn't do much more for our confidence and I was feeling pretty low towards the end of the match when a remarkable thing happened. The few hundred fans who had braved the difficult voyage from Sheffield to Carrow Road started to sing, 'There's only one Harry Bassett.'

I could hardly believe it – here we were, heading irrevocably for our 11th result without a win and the supporters were actually showing signs of confidence in myself and the team. That moment of faith, born in the face of defeat, provided a very moving gesture and I would like to say a very simple 'thank you' to those fans who were responsible – especially as they had every right to be screaming for my head.

Our next challenge was Everton, who had just sacked Colin Harvey after an uncharacteristically poor start to the season. The match marked the return of their former manager, Howard Kendall, who had returned to England after a spell with Athletic Bilbao and joined Manchester City in the job which I had blown out in sensational kamikaze style. It was quite an odd connection because both Howard and I had been in the frame for Atletico Bilbao and Manchester City, and later he was to manage Sheffield United. From Spain, Howard had been enticed to Everton and immediately reinstated Harvey as his right-hand man. Everton's visit to Sheffield marked their first match under the 'new' management and also Brian Deane's 100th appearance for the Blades. Everton were in 17th place – three above us – and they must have felt pretty confident about coming to Bramall Lane, where we had thus far gained only one point from our five home League games. True, we had beaten them the previous week in the Rumbelows Cup, but that doesn't count for much when you've run out of confidence in the League.

It was never going to be a classic but we really did enough to win – if only someone could have found the net. The result was a goalless draw to give us our fourth point from 12 games. That record was bad enough, but you don't win games without goals and I was particularly perturbed that we had failed to score in each of our last four League matches.

The cauldron of Old Trafford, with most of the 46,000 fans baying for three points at our expense, proved too much to overcome and we went down 2–0. Now it was only four points from 13 games – and we hadn't scored in the last five. Yet, remarkably, the fans were still behind us and almost 20,000 turned up at Bramall Lane to see us take on fellow-strugglers Sunderland.

It was a vitally important bottom-of-the-table battle and I told myself that surely this one must go our way – but I was wrong again. The game turned out to be a scrappy comedy of errors and the players' heads had sunk down to navel level as they trudged off the pitch having lost the match 2–0 – failing to score for the sixth consecutive League game. Three days later we entertained Spurs in the fourth round of the Rumbelows Cup and an amazing 25,000 turned up to watch the game and to see us lose 2–0. I was beginning to think that these Sheffield United fans must be a macabre lot – wanting to be in at the death. Either that or they must be taking the mickey.

The first day of December saw us at Villa Park for our 15th League match and, although we lost 2–1, I found some consolation in the fact that we actually scored a goal – albeit from defender Vinnie Jones. I found rather more satisfaction in our overall performance which did little to suggest that we were stuck at the foot of the table, still with only four points from 15 games and well adrift from the rest of the pack. It augured well, I told them, for the following week when we would be playing Derby at home – a match we really had to win if we were to stand any chance of extricating ourselves from the mire into which we had sunk – and which most people outside Bramall Lane regarded as a joke.

We were in the right frame of mind for a win, but then sod's law intervened and the game was postponed after heavy snowfalls. Then a remarkable thing happened. Oldham Athletic, top of the Second Division, came to Bramall Lane for a Zenith Cup match and we put seven past them with defender Paul Beesley grabbing his first two goals for the club. Seven goals. That equalled our League tally for the season so far – and for the team, and the meagre 3,000 fans who turned up, it was a great morale-booster and it confirmed my view that we weren't nearly as bad as our current position suggested.

With our confidence starting to return, the last thing that we needed was an away match at Liverpool. They were top, we were bottom, and the result was not only predictable but also inevitable. Goals from Barnes and Rush saw us go down 2–0 and the media hounds were swift to point out that we had now recorded our 16th League game of the season without a win – thus equalling Hull City's miserable record of the previous season. Not many of them bothered to point out that Hull had actually managed to get out of trouble – and those who did scoffed at the idea that Sheffield United might be capable of doing exactly the same.

Christmas loomed and next on our agenda was the ubiquitous Mr Clough – the man who has figured so prominently among the more memorable results of my career. Could he be relied upon to do it again? The answer was a resounding 'yes' and in a thrilling game against Forest we recorded our first win of the season on 22 December, thanks to two goals from Bryson and one from Deane – giving our faithful and success-starved fans an early Christmas present.

It is normal practice for me to talk to the press after a match and this is usually handled in two sessions – one for the Sunday papers, which tend to concentrate on match reports, and the second for the Monday editions which are more concerned with comment and news emanating from the game, rather than the game itself. We had just chalked up our first win in 17 games and I honestly hadn't a clue as to what I would say. I'd said it all before anyway so, for the first time in my managerial career, I passed the buck. Instead of facing the press myself, I sent my captain – Vinnie Jones – to tell them that I had gone for a drink and that he would be happy to answer any questions they might like to throw at him. They thought he was joking at first, but then they took him seriously and Vinnie handled it well. Apart from anything else, it was a change which was good for the player, good for the press and good for the club.

Boxing Day saw us perform on Luton's 'drastic plastic' where another Deane goal saw us gain our second win in four days and, although two successive wins can hardly be described as a run, it made the team feel almost invincible. The fans were now singing, 'We're going to win the League.'

Then came Arsenal and a 4–1 defeat at Highbury which brought us down to earth – not so much with a bump, as with a mighty crash. Then again, that match was always going to be a tough one.

I made only one enforced change by bringing in Carl Bradshaw for the injured Marwood for the New Year's

Day tussle at home to Queen's Park Rangers. We were still bottom of the table by an uncomfortable margin, but 21,000 fans turned up to see Brian Deane – again – score the only goal of the game to give us our third win and nine valuable points from four matches. We did not really deserve to win but the points were greatly appreciated and it seemed that fortunes were at last beginning to change.

The festive holiday period had been good to us and I remember thinking just how sharply it contrasted with the Christmas of three years before when I was experiencing so much misery at Watford. Then it had marked the end, but now it had offered us a lifeline which everyone at Bramall Lane was keen to grab. With 20 games gone and 18 left to play, we still had approximately half of the season's programme ahead of us and, given a bit of luck and a following wind, I knew that we had a realistic chance of surviving against the odds.

In our mood of the moment, a home tie against Luton Town in the third round of the FA Cup should have presented us with few problems. Surprisingly, the early rounds of the Cup seem to be less popular with the fans than League matches – even when you're going through a bad run – and a crowd of less than 18,000 turned up to watch us face our first challenge on the road to Wembley. I'm sure that most of them wish that they had never bothered as we made a swift exit from the competition, losing 3–1 to a team that we had already beaten on their own ground barely a week earlier.

Crystal Palace then completed their League double over us by scoring the only goal of the match at Bramall Lane. Once again I went out into the market place, this time for someone who could provide some much-needed fire-power up front.

Not for the first time I decided to gamble on the talents of Glyn Hodges, a player I knew well, to pull us through. He had been with me at both Wimbledon and

Watford, and I had tried unsuccessfully to sign him before the start of the season when his contract with Watford had expired. He had disappointed me by opting to join Crystal Palace instead but I later learned that he had been having a few personal problems at the time and, for that reason, had felt it was better to remain in London.

It seemed, however, that he never really settled at Palace and when the chance came to sign him on loan, I put aside the prejudice created by his earlier reluctance to join the club, and happily took him on board. He made his Sheffield United debut the following week at Manchester City, but was unable to perform instant miracles in a match which we lost 2–0. Three days later we met again when City came to Sheffield in the Zenith Cup and, just to rub it in, they repeated the scoreline.

In 17 days we had been booted out of two Cup competitions and had lost two vital League matches. I feared that our mini-revival had burned itself out and I knew that the next game – the re-arranged home fixture against fellow-strugglers Derby County – was probably the most crucial match I had faced in my three years with the club.

Originally planned for early December, the game now assumed the magnitude of a Cup Final. It was a game we simply had to win if we were to prise our way out of the coffin. Peter Shilton was in brilliant form in the Derby goal but Glyn Hodges repaid my faith in the best possible way by hitting an 88th-minute winner to send most of the 18,000 fans home happy and, more pertinently, to start a remarkable sequence of nine matches in which we gained eight wins and a draw sending us up to an almost respectable 16th place.

The week after beating Derby County we faced Southampton at home without Vinnie Jones, who was taking an enforced one-match rest at the request of the FA. Former Saint, Chris Wilder, who had joined on a free transfer, captained the side and it was a perfect time for Bob Booker to score his first two goals of the season, with two more coming from Hodges and the ever-reliable Deane as we cruised to a 4–0 success, our most emphatic League win so far.

By now the team was oozing confidence and there was a positive feeling that our next match – away at Everton – would continue the run. They were right. Despite us trailing by a goal after only two minutes, Hodges scored his third in three games to put us level and Brian Marwood picked the perfect moment to score his first goal for the club with a last-gasp winner. Later, in April, after the maximum three-month loan period, £410,000 ensured that Hodges remained a permanent member of my playing staff.

Three days later we faced Manchester United at home and I was very aware that Alex Ferguson's team had put a few over on me in recent seasons. Although Wimbledon had chalked up a creditable double over the Reds in my last season at Plough Lane, the situation had been reversed the following term when I was at Watford – and I still had vivid memories of that 'stolen' 1–0 victory shortly before my departure from Vicarage Road. There had also been the narrow sixth-round FA Cup defeat during our promotion year and we had already lost at Old Trafford earlier in the season. After four successive defeats, nobody could have wanted to win this one more than me.

We held them in the first half and then, five minutes into the second, most of the 27,000 crowd went crazy when Deane put us ahead. Two minutes later they were strangely subdued as Blackmore equalised from a penalty-kick. Then, normal exuberance was restored by Carl Bradshaw's winner. Four successive wins had given us 12 golden points and we were now not only ahead of Derby, but level on points with the handful of clubs struggling above us. Suddenly, First Division survival looked very much on.

Next came Aston Villa at home and they went the same way as their immediate predecessors – courtesy of Messrs Bryson and Deane who provided our part of the 2–1 scoreline. Our sudden charge had put us above Sunderland, who now occupied one of the relegation spots, and it became clear that our forthcoming match at Roker Park was not likely to be one for the faint-hearted. We were on a run and our spirits were high, so nobody in the football world was surprised when we came away with the points – thanks to another goal from Bryson. Nevertheless, it was a very tough match and the mood of the battle can best be illustrated by the fact that, for the first time in his career, John Gannon was sent off for retaliation and, after the final whistle, Glyn Hodges was involved in an incident outside the players' tunnel which led to his suspension for the last five matches of that season – and the first of the next campaign.

What actually happened was this. We were defending a corner and Sunderland's Gordon Armstrong and our Glyn Hodges, who had always had a bit of a history between them, found themselves face to face. Armstrong ran into the box and Hodges blocked him. Armstrong got the hump and kicked Hodges in the worst possible place. Hodges went down. Vinny saw the incident and came straight in to clump Armstrong. Kevin Ball saw Vinnie go in and so he went in as well and kicked Vinnie. John Gannon saw Ball do Vinnie so he then came in and clumped Ball. It ended up with the people who had started the whole thing walking away, while Gannon and Ball were sent off. Hodges was furious so I subbed him to get him out of trouble. He sat on the bench with us but at the end of the game he ran on to the pitch and the first person he saw was Armstrong, so a new ruckus started. The police came into the dressing room after the game and were talking about prosecutions. To be honest, I picked up most of what had happened when I watched the video on the following Monday and, in my opinion, all five should have been sent off!

Now we had achieved six wins out of six and found ourselves to be the team of the moment as we prepared to greet Chelsea – who had proved to be nothing if not unpredictable throughout the season and, thus far, the only team to inflict defeat upon League leaders, Arsenal. They had also seen off Manchester United the previous week to end a bad run – and that is when a team can be most dangerous. Complacency, however, was not a disease from which we suffered at Bramall Lane. Indeed, we'd had precious little cause to suffer from it during the season so far – and yet another goal from Bryson saw us record our seventh win in a row.

The following week saw me make an emotional return to Plough Lane, Wimbledon, for the first time since I had left almost four years before. Nothing seemed to have changed much – not even the style of play – and the ball zapped from end-to-end so quickly that the match would have been better suited to the All-England tennis club just up the road.

The Wimbledon team included two of my former strikers in Alan Cork and John Fashanu, both of whom made their contribution. Cork scored first to put Wimbledon ahead and Fashanu handled in his own area to give us a penalty which Deane stroked home. Then unbelievably – in the dying minutes – Fashanu leaped high to handle again in his own area – falling to his knees unable to believe what he had done. Amazingly, the referee didn't believe it either, even though this second transgression was ten times more blatant than the first.

That draw marked the end of our winning sequence but I willingly settled for just a point at Plough Lane. Wimbledon are nobody's fool. They had been consistently in the top third of the division and even at this late stage of the season had lost only three home League matches — to Arsenal, Liverpool and Manchester United.

Normal service was resumed a week later when we met Luton Town at home and completed our first League double of the season with a 2–1 win — the goals coming from Hodges and Bryson. Sadly, that rare double also marked the end of a remarkable run which had seen us gain 25 points from a possible 27 in nine games. A wider view shows that of our last 15 games, we had won 11, drawn one and lost only three to take 34 points and pull us back from the edge. It was a rather better record than in the previous 16 games, when our total harvest was a meagre four points.

Ironically, it was Nottingham Forest — against whom we had started our charge for survival — who also brought it to an end precisely 16 games later. A 2–0 away defeat against Mr Clough and Co was followed by a home game with Arsenal who rode their luck and scored two breakaway goals to maintain their title challenge and, with only five games to go, left us still not out of the woods. One bright spot here, though — I was presented with the Barclay's Manager of the Month award for March, during which we had gained four wins and a draw.

A final effort was still needed to guarantee our safety. We were faced with three away matches and two at home. Every goal scored would be golden and every point precious. The first of these five games was away to Queen's Park Rangers and a goal apiece from Deane and Booker outweighed the one scored by Rangers. Three points and an away match completed. We all breathed a little easier — but not too easy.

Tottenham visited us a week later. They had already put six past us without reply in two games earlier in the season and we were determined not to go down again. Beesley and Deane did the business for us, although Spurs also scored two. I was happy with the draw but now we had to face two tough away games on the trot. Incidentally, this game was the last before the old Kop stand was pulled down and replaced by seats.

Coventry were ready for us. It was their last home game of the season and they wanted to have a party at our expense. We put up the shutters and came away with a 0–0 draw. That was OK, but I felt that we could have sneaked it. We had to do better on our next trip – away to Leeds who were fourth in the table. We were their last home game too – and they also wanted to party. We could not be party poopers at Elland Road. Brian Marwood scored for us, but Leeds hit two and left us with just one game left to play and a need to get maximum points.

Norwich were our visitors and they also wanted a win to lift them to a more respectable position in the table. The supporters did us proud and, with more than 21,000 cheering on the Blades, Tony Agana popped in two first-half goals and we finished as 2–1 winners.

The celebrations went on for ages and anyone watching from another planet would have thought that we had just won the championship. On *A Question of Sport*, this moment has been featured a couple of times because the players were all throwing bits of kit into the crowd as part of the celebrations. I joined in the party and, by the time I had thrown my shirt, boots and socks into the crowd, I had just my shorts and underpants left. The question is: 'What happened next?' Well, I took my shorts off and threw them into the crowd as well and was left standing in just my underpants. My wife was disgusted. We actually finished 13th out of the 20 clubs. Sunderland and Derby were relegated, and also below us were Southampton, Norwich, Coventry, Aston Villa and Luton, the Hatters having done one of their famous Houdini acts. Arsenal were champions.

From the seemingly inescapable clutches of relegation

we had fought back and finished in a half-decent position. Once again we were to rub shoulders with the cream of English football.

After the season was over, I went to Marbella on holiday with my family and Doug Ellis, the Aston Villa chairman, came to see me. He was also in Marbella with his boat and he came to lunch. We had the afternoon and the evening together and he talked to me about going to Aston Villa. He made it sound very attractive and offered me good money. It was tempting because Aston Villa is such a big and great club. But, after all I had gone through with Sheffield United and their fans, I just didn't feel that I could be so disloyal to them. I told Doug the next day over lunch and, while he was disappointed, he said he admired my loyalty.

Ironically, it was Ron Atkinson who got the Villa job and left Sheffield Wednesday just after winning them promotion. The circumstances in which he left were not very friendly and I am glad that I had not done that to the people of Bramall Lane.

10

Harry Houdini Strikes Again

WHEN YOU OVERDOSE ON OPTIMISM AS I DO, it is very easy for people to keep you on a staple diet of bullshit. You really want to believe every positive thing that you are told because it fuels your own optimism. In fact it makes you a very easy prey for a certain kind of person. It has happened to me far too often for comfort – and it happened in no more an outstanding way than at Sheffield United, where boardroom changes and broken promises were more frequent than roadworks on the M1 – and that's saying something.

I shall be going into the musical chairs of the Bramall Lane boardroom a little later, suffice it to say that I should have taken a little more seriously what I had been told in the first place – when the directors said quite openly that there would be no money for buying in good players. It was the one promise that the directors really kept. If I'd had a shoe-string budget it would have been an improvement – as it was, there was not enough in the kitty for a midget's fly-button.

Having escaped relegation and finished in a reasonably respectable position, the Blades' supporters were probably holding their breath throughout the summer, waiting for the big names to start arriving. They had a long wait. Those fans had been brilliant during the season and I knew that they were avidly reading the local newspapers and listening to the local radio every day in the hope that the stars were going to start flocking to Bramall Lane.

As the season ended the newspapers were talking about Sheffield United – but it was all about how I could have a job for life at the club if I wanted it. I'm sure that Derek Dooley told the *Daily Express* in good faith that, 'I speak for the board in saying that Dave has got a job here for life. When I pack up, Dave can have my job as well. We realise that we have got a manager who is unique.'

Dooley was managing director at that time and was a nice man who has never been treated as he deserved to be by either Sheffield United or Wednesday. There was talk that our great escape would generate at least half a million quid in ticket sales and another £200,000 in television payments – and that I could use the lot to strengthen the side.

'I'd back Bassett to do well whether he'd got money or not, but it's not realistic to ask him to carry on like that,' said Dooley.

Guess what? I bought Tom Cowan from Rangers for £300,000, Nathan Peel from Preston for £50,000 and Clive Mendonca from Rotherham for £110,000. Where did the money come from? Well, I sold Mark Morris to Bournemouth for £95,000 and, just after the season started, Vinnie Jones went to Chelsea for £575,000. I'll let you work it out.

Before the season, we went on a 12-day trip to Sweden. I like to take teams there for pre-season because the Swedes are fit and provide stiff opposition. It is a lovely country and the facilities are good – I see it as an ideal preparation trip.

On this particular trip, there was a bit of a fracas when Billy Whitehurst and Vinnie Jones tangled with some locals. The story made the *News of the World* and we were none too happy about that because it was a mountain out of a molehill story that had been sold to the paper by someone who should have known better.

The new season began with a trip to Norwich. We were leading at half-time thanks to a Brian Deane goal, but, in the end we had to travel back with only one point in the bag as the final score was 2–2. At least we hadn't lost and we could go into our first home game with an unbeaten record. We came out of it with an unbeaten record, too, because we drew 1–1 with West Ham thanks to a Paul Beesley goal.

That was as far as our unbeaten record went – we lost all of the next five games and fell from 16th to 22nd in the table. Our tumble was faster than a one-legged man in a bum-kicking contest. It wasn't difficult to see what the problem was – we weren't scoring goals and we weren't stopping them either. I wouldn't have blamed the supporters if they had immediately demanded a refund on their season tickets – but they stuck by us and I was grateful to them for that.

It was all a bit *déjâ vu* – that's French for 'we're playing crap again'. It would not have been so bad if we had been losing to the really big clubs – but we lost to Southampton, Coventry, Crystal Palace, Chelsea and Oldham. All right, Chelsea are a smart side now – but in the 1991 season they were nothing special even though they did have some top names – and, of course, Mr Vincent Jones had joined them only a few days before we met.

I thought that we had turned a bit of a corner when we beat Everton 2–1 at home, but then we lost 3–1 to newly-promoted Notts County at home a few days later. We hardly had time to scratch our heads before Arsenal stuffed us 5–2 at Highbury. By the end of October we had firmly established ourselves at the bottom of the First Division. A 4–2 win over Nottingham Forest cheered us up a bit, but that was only our second victory of the season. We had drawn three and lost the other nine games.

I didn't panic – I never have done. In fact, I was not really too displeased with the way that things were taking shape. We could, and should, have been playing better, but I kept seeing signs that showed me that we were capable of better things – and as long as I could see that I knew that anything was possible. It's when your players are playing at peak and you are still losing that you have a really serious problem.

When we lost 4–3 to Leeds at Elland Road, I saw something that I liked very much. At half-time we were 3–0 down and Leeds were giving us the run-around. I gave the lads some earache over a cup of tea and sent them out to do better. Within minutes Leeds had made it 4–0 and I was beginning to wonder if my lot had actually been listening. Then came the transformation – and three goals. By the end, Leeds were desperately hanging on to their one-goal lead and I was proud of my team as they trooped off even if they had not quite managed to salvage anything.

November started with a 2–0 defeat at Old Trafford. We didn't help our cause when Paul Beesley put through his own-goal. It was just one of those things and typical of the way our game was going at that time. Manchester United held that lead at half-time and Andrei Kanchelskis made it 2–0 before the end. We were still firmly planted at the bottom of the table.

There were some who rubbed their hands in delight whenever they saw us propping up the rest of the division, and among them were the supporters of Sheffield Wednesday, our rivals across the city. Wednesday had just been promoted back to the First Division and it shows what a difference there was between the two clubs when you realise that they were able to spend £750,000 on Paul Warhurst, £1.2 million on Chris Woods and, just after the season started, a further £800,000 on Nigel Jemson.

There was a sharp contrast between that £2.75

million and the £210,000 that I had been able to spend. The real test of financial strength came around the same time as Trevor Francis was spending on Nigel Jemson. I wanted Brian Gayle who was then with Ipswich. A fee of £700,000 was agreed – which was a record for Sheffield United – and Brian signed on the dotted line. I should have known that it had all gone too smoothly. What followed was deeply embarrassing when Ipswich later revealed that they had not actually received the money and were legally within their rights to recall the player.

The matter was finally resolved, but not before the press had had their bit of fun with it, and I had personally loaned the club £100,000 to help clinch the transfer. It was all very messy and once again it showed that all was not well behind the scenes at Bramall Lane. Sheffield United were being shown up as the poor relations of the First Division. This was even more bad news for our supporters, who were still having to take constant stick from their rivals, the Wednesday fans – even though the Owls had only just returned to the First Division, having been relegated in the season that we were promoted.

The scene was set for the first Division One meeting between the Blades and the Owls for 23 years. It was on Sunday 17 November at Bramall Lane and the Wednesday fans arrived in party mood. Apart from Ian Bryson coming in for Tony Agana, I put out the same side that had been beaten by Manchester United. The result was sheer magic. Dane Whitehouse put us one up in the first half, and Brian Deane wrapped it up in the second half. Wednesday played well, but we played better and all the potential that I had seen in flashes during previous games suddenly came together in a really good 90-minute performance. We beat our rivals and moved one place up the table. Now I knew for certain that we could climb well away from the relegation zone.

I think that win kick-started our season. We beat

Tottenham at White Hart Lane in our next game, got a point from Luton, lost to Queen's Park Rangers and then beat Aston Villa 2–0. After drawing away to West Ham we were ready for the busy Christmas schedule in 19th place and just out of the relegation zone.

Christmas was a bit too full of goodwill for my liking — and it was all one-way. We took one point out of the nine and developed a trait which I definitely did not like. Coventry gave us a 3–0 seeing-to on Boxing Day on our own ground. Two days later, Crystal Palace came visiting and we allowed them back into the game after taking a 1–0 lead. They went home with a 1–1 draw and smiles on their faces. Four days later we were at Anfield. Brian Deane shocked Liverpool by giving us the lead and we held it until the second half when Ray Houghton and Dean Saunders hit a goal apiece and sent us home with nothing to show for our honest endeavour. The trait that I didn't like was that we were turning it on, getting ahead, and then throwing it away. There's no excuse for that and I let them know it.

We were back in the relegation zone but we had learned a lesson. In the following four games I had no complaints. Now when we took the lead we held it. We dumped Luton out of the FA Cup with a 4–0 stuffing, and in the League we beat Southampton 4–2, Norwich 1–0, Nottingham Forest 5–2 and Manchester City 4–2 — as well as beating Charlton 3–1 in the FA Cup fourth round. Six wins in a row and things were looking much better. Luton gained some revenge by beating us 2–1 and Queen's Park Rangers held us to a goalless draw but by the time we were due to face Sheffield Wednesday again, we were a lot happier than we had been before our previous encounter.

When Wednesday had made the short trip to our ground in November 1991 they were fourth in the table and we were bottom. Now in March, they had moved up to third and we had improved to 18th. They were determined to avenge the 2–0 defeat we had inflicted on them at Bramall Lane – and most people seemed to think that they would do it too. I didn't – and neither did my players. We were confident and we really fancied picking up maximum points again. At the very least our supporters deserved it for the stick that they were forever having to take from the Wednesday fans. The match took place on a drizzly Wednesday evening at Hillsborough, with steam floating up from the pitch. The crowds were served up what I can only describe as a blood and guts local derby, no quarter asked and no quarter given, in the finest tradition of Rangers v Celtic, United v City, Liverpool v Everton and Arsenal v Tottenham.

I had taken the former Derby striker Bobby Davison on loan from Leeds just a few days earlier and I think he was quite keen to prove something. Dane Whitehouse opened the scoring and then Bobby went to work and put us 2–0 ahead before the interval. The dressing-room was pretty excited at half-time but we calmed things down and I told everyone that I wanted a repeat performance. Davison took me at my word and planted another one in the net. Wednesday got a consolation goal through Phil King but it was the Blades' day and we had quite a party that night. Bobby Davison became a folk hero and entered the Sheffield United Hall of Fame.

We then set about the run-in for the rest of the season. Chelsea had knocked us out of the FA Cup at the fifth-round stage, so we were pleased to beat them in the League 2–1. Even better than that, we beat Liverpool 2–0 – and then Oldham, Everton and Tottenham by the same score. We beat Notts County 3–1 and drew with both Arsenal and Aston Villa. Those were heady days and, with two games remaining, we were suddenly in seventh place in the table.

I should have known that our run could not continue right to the end – especially since our last home game was to be against Leeds who were vying with Manchester United for the title. Leeds wanted every available point and in the end they got the lot. Perhaps it was all a bit too friendly — we even scored a goal for each other. Brian Gayle scored their third goal for them and Lee Chapman scored our second for us. Eric Cantona was substitute that day otherwise the damage might have been greater. Whatever, we lost 3–2 but our supporters did not let that upset their party mood which is a tradition at the last home game of the season.

We still had one game to go and, of all places, it had to be at Wimbledon. They were 17th at the time and wanted to finish on a high note. They did, too. I think we must have slept through the first 45 minutes because we barely seemed to notice as they took a 3–0 lead by half-time. John Fashanu hit the first and Robbie Earle then scored two more. I politely explained to my players that, although they had studied the holiday brochures, the plane had not actually taken off as yet. We shut up shop in the second half and the score remained at 3–0 to the Dons.

I was not thrilled to bits by the way we had ended the season but at least we were able to look at the First Division table in the evening papers and see that we were in ninth position — meaning that, taking the season as a whole, there were only eight sides better than us in the country. It seemed that we had turned a corner. We had consolidated our position in the top division and, by the time the whistle blew to start the next campaign, we were going to be in the new Premier League.

Of course, the question remained as to whether or not we would all still be together when that new season kicked-off. There was a summer ahead of us, during which anything could happen and there was constant talk of take-overs at the club. In a sense, as we travelled home from Wimbledon, it seemed as if we had won the battle of the season but the war for the future of the club was still raging.

I could not have asked more from the players that season. Clive Mendonca had been one of our most expensive signings but it had not quite worked out for him. Injuries had not helped him at all and, to give him some confidence, I loaned him to Grimsby in January and it seemed to suit him. He played ten games for them and scored three goals. He also played ten games for us that season and scored just once. He later joined Grimsby on a permanent basis and the move looked to have done him a power of good as he banged in around 20 goals for them in 1996–97, in a struggling side. He is an excellent player. We paid £110,000 for him and sold him for £85,000. He remained a model professional, finally joining Charlton Athletic and helping them in their promotion push back to the Premiership. He has just retired through injury, and I wish him well in retirement.

I had signed Alan Cork on a free from Wimbledon. He has the distinction, therefore, of being the only player ever to play for the same manager in the Fourth, Third, Second and First Divisions, and the Premiership, for me for both Wimbledon and Sheffield United. I knew he would do a job for us and he certainly didn't let us down. The fans liked him, too, and admired the way he led the line wearing the number 9 shirt. He was a gutsy player and football fans love that whether they follow Sheffield United or Wimbledon.

Probably the surprise transfer of the season was when the club sold Tony Agana to Notts County for £750,000 in the November. It split up the very successful Deane–Agana partnership and probably the fans were expecting a high-profile replacement signing. If they were expecting it then they were to be disappointed.

Brian Deane had a few injury problems but still managed to finish the season as top scorer with 12 League goals and two each in the FA Cup and the League Cup. The previous season he had been voted Player of the Year, but this season it was left to Simon Tracey to pick up the award. Since he was our first-choice goalkeeper it shows you where the supporters considered our chief strength to be.

That March I had signed another goalkeeper. Phil Kite was understudy to Simon Tracey but I needed another experienced 'keeper on the books and so I paid £25,000 to bring Mel Rees from West Bromwich Albion. As well as being a good goalkeeper, he was a nice bloke and it was tragic that his life was to end so unexpectedly early.

When the early fixtures were announced, all eyes were focused on the Premiership. Leeds had won the last League championship and I was very pleased for Howard Wilkinson because I feel that he is not only a decent fellow but a much-maligned fellow. He had gained promotion for Leeds at the same time as Sheffield United. He had taken them to second place in his first First Division season and then won the Championship itself. Leeds have not done it since, and I don't think he has ever received the credit fully due to him. Also, when you look at the young Leeds players of today, they are there as a direct result of the youth policy introduced by Howard. I think it is convenient for people to forget his role in that.

Howard has never had the best rapport with the press. I think he has seen them as a necessary evil and, as a result, they have given him something of a hard time. As an example, when he had to step in at the last minute to take over the England team, he was slaughtered because they lost to the World Champions. Once again, he was an easy target for the press but I defy anybody to have got a better result against France under those circumstances. Also, when Keegan left and Howard had to take charge for the Finland game, he received no credit for stepping into the breach and sorting things out. I have a lot of respect for him, but I can see that he is not media-friendly and that puts him at a great disadvantage. It was politics which removed him from being in charge of the England under-21s and I think that was very short-sighted. One day, people will look back at the career of Howard Wilkinson and realise just how successful he has been as manager of Sheffield Wednesday and Leeds and in his role with the FA.

Our first game of the new season in the new Premiership was at home to Manchester United. That optimism that I was telling you about was due to be tested to the full.

11

Christmas in August

I HAD PLENTY TO THINK ABOUT IN THE SUMMER OF 1992. Sheffield United had defied the odds and finished ninth in the First Division and the new challenge of the promised land of the Premiership was looming. There was still no money to spend at Bramall Lane, however, and the boardroom shenanigans were continuing to worry everybody – except, it seemed, the board itself. I had the uneasy feeling that life was going to get even tougher in the top division and we really did not have the necessary ammunition for battle. On top of all that, there was a lot of newspaper talk about Brian Deane being chased by the likes of Leeds and Manchester United. I had a sneaking suspicion that if a £1 million carrot was dangled in front of our donkey of a board, they would follow it all the way to relegation. There was not a lot that I could do about it except to have my say, if and when that time arrived, so I decided to stop biting my nails over it.

As I kept looking at the free or nominal transfers around the country, other people were writing cheques as if money was going out of fashion. Tottenham forked out over £2.6 million in one day to capture Darren Anderton, Dean Austin and Peter Beadle. A month later they bought Jason Cundy for £800,000, and Neil Ruddock for £750,000. Then, when the season had started, they paid £2.2 million for Teddy Sheringham. They did some good business, too, because they sold Paul Stewart to Liverpool for £2.3 million, and Paul Walsh to Portsmouth for

£400,000. At the end of the day they had spent something like £4 million. Kenny Dalglish spent £3.3 million on Alan Shearer at Blackburn, and a further £1.3 million on Stuart Ripley, and everyone else, too, seemed to be getting in on the transfer act.

We weren't totally out of it. We sold Clive Mendonca to Grimsby where he had done well on loan. Grimsby paid us £85,000. Leicester bought Colin Hill from us for £200,000 and I signed Alan Kelly for £150,000 as deputy for Simon Tracey. He now plays for Blackburn Rovers and is a valuable member of the Republic of Ireland World Cup squad. Chris Wilder went later, as the season started, for £40,000 – so our books balanced at a profit of £175,000. To put it into perspective, Bristol Rovers invested more than we did and yet we were a Premier League side preparing to open our season against Manchester United, and they were a Division One side preparing to face Oxford. I have always said that I would use whatever was available even if it was nothing – but don't run away with the idea that I actually liked having nothing in the kitty. I don't.

There was no point in moping and enviously looking at what other people had, so instead I tried to think of ways in which we could improve with what we already had. I have always been a firm believer in the value of team spirit, which is why I always do my best to ensure that, from the minute the team reports back training, something interesting is going on that will pull them together as a unit as closely as possible.

The Sheffield United players knew that they would be going on a club tour to Sweden, and they also knew that they would be going to an army training camp to be put through some special paces. The army training camp idea is something I began when I was manager of Wimbledon. The players spent several days undergoing commando-style training. They don't have it easy. The whole point is to toughen them up as quickly as possible after their summer relaxations. Since it is pretty gruelling you always get one or two moans – but you also get a lot of laughs. Either way, it acts to bring everyone together, either out of fun or in sympathy. Before the 1992–93 season the army training was done in Devon and it was pretty tough too – or so they told me. You see, while they were being put through their paces by a fierce sergeant-major, I went on holiday. Well, I couldn't stand to see my lads suffering – at least that's my story.

I did join them on the club tour of Sweden, though, and I had another little surprise lined up for them there. We were away for ten days and since they had all worked so hard I thought that a nice little river trip would help to relax them. We split up into groups of eight to go into the special boats that were provided and I couldn't help but smile as they cheerfully joked among themselves as we set off. The river was beautiful and we glided along with not a care in the world. They hardly noticed that the flow of the water was getting faster by the second.

The serenity of the water actually had one or two of them nodding off – but they didn't doze for long when the realisation of my little surprise finally dawned on them. That river trip was a natural white-knuckle ride as it included the boats shooting the rapids. It was one of the most exhilarating, frightening experiences that I have ever known – and I know that all the players thought the same. Just to round things off nicely we all ended up in the river – and that water was so cold that I swear I saw three brass monkeys go past with high-pitched voices. My boat with Frenchie, kit man John Greaves and myself became a target for warfare by the other players, but we survived to tell the tale.

The army training camp and our successful tour of Sweden proved to be really useful for the morale of the team – but I wasn't finished yet. I had another surprise up my sleeve for when we started the season proper.

I had noticed that we had become a second-half team – not so much in the individual matches we played, but taking the season as a whole. It was almost as if we were out Christmas shopping for the first half of the season and then, after the festive season, we rolled up our sleeves and got down to business. So, I thought, why not bring Christmas forward? Then perhaps the whole season would be like the second half.

The players thought that I had totally lost it when I told them we were going to have a Christmas party a few days before the start of the season. I ordered them all to turn up in Christmas gear and, to be fair to them, they all went along with it. We had the Bramall Lane suite decorated, a turkey, a visit from Father Christmas, the lot. The press turned up to make sure that it wasn't just a rumour that Bassett was off to the funny farm and, as they say, a good time was had by all.

Did the idea work? Just ask Manchester United. They were our visitors on that lovely opening day of the new season and the new Premier League. It was quite exciting – even I felt more of a buzz than usual. Alex Ferguson was still a bit bruised about losing the championship race to Leeds the previous season. He had his jaw set and I remember thinking at the time that he had the look of someone who was not going to settle for second best this time around.

The Manchester players seemed to be in good humour when they arrived but they knew they had a job to do. When you see a team bus coughing out players like Peter Schmeichel, Ryan Giggs, Mark Hughes, Gary Pallister, Paul Ince, Dennis Irwin and the others that made up that day's United team, it can make you gulp a little bit. I think that's why Bill Shankly used to watch the opposition arrive and then rush down to his own team's dressing-room to tell them how unhappy the other side looked – how so-and-so is limping and all that sort of stuff. I don't know who he was reassuring the most – himself, or his players.

The game kicked-off with 28,070 people inside Bramall Lane – about 6,000 more than the previous season's average, and that meant that we had the chance to prove that, against the odds, we could compete with the cream of the land. Within five minutes Brian Deane had landed himself a place in the football history books. He scored a great goal and became the first man to find the net in the new Premier League. United threw everything at us but we stood firm and at half-time I told them to keep calm and keep playing the same way and they would be sure of the verdict.

Fergie must have had a bit of a rant and rave because United came at us as if their lives depended on it. Perhaps they were over-anxious because they didn't really turn their play into any serious threat and it came as no surprise to me when we scored the next goal. Deane struck again, albeit from the penalty spot after we had caught them on the hop. Funnily enough, it was after five minutes again – this time in the second half. Mark Hughes popped up 11 minutes later and pulled one back for his side, but I never saw us losing and when the whistle went to end the game we all went home happy. That was some Boxing Day on 15 August 1992!

The hangover was inevitable, but it could have been much worse. Just a few days after beating the prospective champions we were away to one of their chief rivals, Liverpool. Their season had begun with a 1–0 defeat at Nottingham Forest so they were just about ready for us when we arrived at Anfield.

The scoreline will show you that we lost 2–1. We held them 1–1 at half-time with Brian Deane scoring our goal. Mark Walters had hit theirs and Paul Stewart made a name for himself by scoring their winner on his home debut. I can put my hand on my heart and say that we deserved a point. I thought that we played well and it was encouraging that we had faced two of the best teams in the land, beaten one and narrowly lost to the other.

It was a bit disappointing, then, when the fire on the Christmas pudding fizzled out into a soggy mess. We went to Queen's Park Rangers and chased the game throughout. They beat us 3–2, which might not sound too bad but, again, I knew that we should have got at least one point from the game. Wimbledon were our visitors for the next match, our second home game of the season. I looked forward to doing something I had never done before – managing a side that beat them. It had never happened since I left Plough Lane and I was beginning to think that Sam Hammam had put some sort of Lebanese curse on me. I was believing it a bit more after the game. We drew 2–2, but the Dons fully deserved the point they had come for.

Four days later we were at home again, this time to Aston Villa. Garry Parker had brought his shooting boots and they beat us 2–0. No excuses – we were not performing and it was time to make changes. I gave Adrian Littlejohn his first start of the season and brought in Paul Rogers to give us some extra life in midfield. Paul was another of my non-league finds, this time from Sutton United, and proved to be a great servant for Sheffield United. As is the way with these things, there was a fly in the ointment. His name was Teddy Sheringham. A Spurs fan all his life, he had just signed for them in a £2.2 million deal from Forest. He had played in Tottenham's 1–1 draw at Ipswich a few days earlier, but against us he was going to make his home debut.

You have probably already guessed what happened. Sheringham scored about a minute before half-time and that had us reeling. We gritted our teeth for the second half, determined that 'they shall not pass'. Within a minute Gordon Durie had netted and we were two down. Somehow we managed to contain them for the rest of the match with one little problem near the end – when our goalkeeper was sent off for a second bookable offence.

The sending off was just part of a night to forget – and yet a night to remember as well. The referee, Ian Mitchell, booked Simon Tracey after 90 seconds for handling outside the area. Mitchell was a replacement referee because the appointed ref, Howard King, had been taken ill in the dressing-room before the game. The irony continued when Mitchell was also taken ill during the game and had to be replaced with 15 minutes left. Then Simon Tracey executed a rugby tackle on Spurs' Andy Gray that would have been applauded at Twickenham, and off he went. You can chuckle when you look back at these things, but they are not so funny at the time. In fact, at the time, I described Simon as having the brains of a rocking horse.

We had played six, won one, drawn one and lost four and had a trip to Middlesbrough coming up on Saturday. I won't bore you with the details of a match best forgotten – but the upshot was that we lost 2–0 again and, after our grand opening day performance against Manchester United we had slumped to 21st place in the table.

Sensing my frustration the press began their 'will Bassett stay?' routine, suggesting that, with all the poor delivery from the players and the rubbish going on in the boardroom, I might go for a hike. The supporters began pleading with me to stay and I have to say that I was touched, both by their astuteness and their loyalty. Usually if things are not going right, the manager is an easy target for everyone from the directors, to the players, to the press and to the fans – but this didn't happen. In fact, I had no intention of going anywhere. There is a lot of gossip in football and it is not difficult to find out which clubs might soon be looking for a new manager – but I wasn't interested. I had a job at Bramall Lane and I wanted to see it through, no matter what. I might be many things but I have never been a quitter.

On Saturday, 12 September 1992, we were to play our eighth match of the season and, by some quirk of the computer, we were at home to Liverpool. It is unusual to be playing the same side in two League fixtures so early in the season but that is how it had turned out. During that week we hadn't had a game because England were playing an international in Spain. Following our poor showing in the European Championship in Sweden in the summer of 1992, Graham Taylor took his troops to Spain for a friendly which we lost 1–0, leaving our hosts to celebrate their first home win over England for 32 years. It didn't help the mood.

The players were in no doubt as to what was expected of them. They delivered. Adrian Littlejohn got the ball past David James after just four minutes and I knew that we were on the way to victory. It proved to be the only goal of the game and I was more than pleased with our performance – and said so to anyone that would listen after the game. At last – a breakthrough.

When Simon Tracey was sent off against Tottenham he did more damage to his career than he could have realised at the time. Alan Kelly proved to be a more than adequate replacement and it was Simon who, thereafter, ended up on the subs' bench for most of the rest of the season. I always think that it is very difficult for goalkeepers, much more so than for other players. A club has got to have the best possible goalkeeper sub on the bench and – unlike defenders, midfielders or forwards – you can hardly try them in another position.

That win over Liverpool gave us a lift in every sense and our next home game was a creditable 1–1 draw with Arsenal. This was followed by a goalless draw at Ipswich and then a 2–0 home win over Southampton. Four games without defeat and we had risen to 16th in the table. Things were definitely looking up again.

Our next Premiership match was away to Leeds a fortnight after the Southampton game. There was a gap because of another international but we did play the second leg of our Coca-Cola Cup second-round tie against Bristol City. They had beaten us 2–1 at Ashton Gate and we had to do much better than that if we were not going to have red faces. Andy Cole was playing for them that day and he scored, of course – but we hit four of our own, courtesy of Dane Whitehouse, Carl Bradshaw and two from Brian Deane. That was good enough to please our supporters and to get us into the third-round draw in which we were rewarded with Liverpool as our opponents.

Leeds proved to be too hot for us and beat us 3–1. Gary Speed had a great game for them and when you look back at their line-up, which featured such players as David Batty, Gordon Strachan, Gary McAllister, Lee Chapman and Eric Cantona, it makes you realise just how strong the reigning champions continued to be. We were disappointed to be beaten, but we were not shamed.

A 0–0 draw with Nottingham Forest followed and then came our third-round Coca-Cola Cup match which also ended 0–0. Just what we wanted – yet another game against Liverpool. When we went to Chelsea for our next Premier League match, I felt quite confident. Chelsea were playing better away from home so I thought we had a chance. The game locked into a stalemate until five minutes from half-time when Adrian Littlejohn put us ahead. Within a minute Chelsea were back on terms through Andy Townsend and it seemed that the afternoon's excitement was all over in that two-minute spell. However, we were about due for a goal from Brian Deane who hadn't scored for ten League games. Sure enough he delivered just six minutes into the second half.

We were ready to go into battle with our city rivals, Sheffield Wednesday. It was the first derby of the season and it was at Bramall Lane. Wednesday were two places above us in the table at that time, so there was a lot to play for. The game never really lived up to expectations, though, and the 1–1 draw was probably the fairest result – even though it was not the scoreline that we wanted.

We played our return Coca-Cola Cup game with Liverpool and they beat us 3–0 – so that was goodbye to one piece of silverware for another season – and once again there was a break in fixtures for internationals. We had a difficult game with Norwich on the horizon – and the Canaries were top of the table at that time. As it was they beat us 2–1 and stayed top, which was quite amazing since they had the worst defensive record in the Premiership. I was peeved that we had not exploited their obvious weaknesses in that department. We could have done better and I had no hesitation in saying just that.

There were two new faces in the team that faced Norwich and I was encouraged by their presence. Chris Kamara had come from Luton on loan and I had also put John Pemberton into the side for the first time that season. I was pleased with their contributions but I knew that we still needed something extra if we were going to survive. We were seriously in need of some extra bite in front of goal. We were just not scoring enough. Alan Cork had scored our goal against Norwich. We played Coventry next and drew 1–1, thanks to an own-goal by their Andy Pearce. Crystal Palace then beat us 2–0 and I was really getting fed up with our lack of goals. In four games we had managed only two ourselves – and that was definitely not good enough.

Adrian Littlejohn did his stuff at home to Everton and we beat them 1–0, but then we lost 1–0 at Blackburn and 2–0 at Manchester City on Boxing Day. The year was ending and we were back down in 20th position. I did not take any heart from what might happen after Christmas because we had already had ours. All I knew was that we had scored only one goal in the last 450 minutes.

12

A Sheffield Derby — at Wembley

THERE IS NOTHING LIKE THE FA CUP to get the adrenalin going. With so many cups and other competitions these days, it might be easy to think of the FA Cup as devalued in some way, but believe me, nobody who sets out on the road to Wembley ever sees it as anything but the ultimate knockout competition. As far as I'm concerned all those other competitions are just Mickey Mouse affairs by comparison and little more than a good excuse for a day out at Wembley.

Our first match of 1993 was in the third round of the FA Cup and we were drawn to play Burnley on our icy home pitch. The 23,041 crowd was our best at Bramall Lane since the opening day of the season and the visiting fans must have been well-pleased at half-time to have their team 2–0 ahead. Adrian Heath had scored both goals and I could not believe what I was watching as my so-called Premiership players allowed themselves to be given the runaround by a team that was 13th in the Second Division – two divisions below them. Even our dressing-room walls were cringing as I gave them earache during the break. I was annoyed because I felt they were letting the fans down, they were letting me down and they were letting themselves down.

My tirade must have struck home because they pulled up their socks during the second half and at the final whistle it was a 2–2 draw with Glyn Hodges and Paul

Beesley hitting our goals. It had been a near thing, however – our first goal did not come until the 81st minute and the second hit the back of their net only a minute from time. We had escaped embarrassment by the skin of our teeth.

Before the replay we had a bit of Premiership business in London with a match at Highbury. That last ten minutes against Burnley must have given the United players something to think about because they gave a good account of themselves against Arsenal. When we got back on the team coach we had earned a point that nobody had expected us to get. Adrian Littlejohn equalised for us five minutes from the end, and we held on.

A few days later we were off on the coach again, this time to Turf Moor for our Cup replay. Adrian Heath tried to ruin everything by giving Burnley the lead after 16 minutes, but Brian Deane found his form and equalised three minutes later – and then hit two more for a first-half hat-trick. Adrian Littlejohn made it 4–1 and even though Burnley pulled one back, we kept control of the situation, returning home with the knowledge that we had done enough to get through to the next round – in which we knew that we would be at home to Hartlepool.

Brian Deane was showing us what a fine attacking forward he was. He virtually beat Ipswich on his own by scoring all three goals and recording his second hat-trick in only a few days. It was good news from a results point of view but it increased the speculation that he would soon be on his way, as several other Premiership sides were looking at him – among them Leeds, his home-town side and the club that he had supported as a kid.

I wasn't exactly thrilled with our performance in the fourth round of the FA Cup. We beat Hartlepool 1–0 and, to be fair, there is nothing easy about a Cup match no matter who you are playing, but it was left to Alan

Cork to score our goal a couple of minutes into the second half. It was the only goal of the game and we were through into the fifth round – but we should have buried them more convincingly.

I think it was about at this time that some reporter decided to have a pop about our tactics. It seemed to be that if Peter Schmeichel collected a ball and chucked it to the halfway line to one of his team-mates, that was great football – but if we did it, then it was crap. There were all the usual jokes about planes being diverted away from Bramall Lane when there was a match on because of Bassett's long-ball tactics.

When questioned, I said my piece. 'There's a lot of crap talked about good football. I want Sheffield United to be the dirtiest, ugliest, luckiest and most boring team in the League – so long as we're winning 1–0 every week.'

That quote did the rounds and confirmed a lot of people's opinions of me – mostly people who did not know and had never worked with me. When you need points you will accept them however they come but, like everyone else, I have always admired and enjoyed classical football and much prefer to win games with pure football. It was another example of something being said tongue-in-cheek and taken too seriously.

One other pleasing thing about our last League victory over Ipswich was Franz Carr. I had bought him from Newcastle for £120,000 and gave him his debut in the Ipswich game. As expected he was lively and he had their defenders back-pedalling every time he got the ball. I cannot understand why he hasn't had a better career. He has always had electrifying speed and tremendous ball control, but he has never really settled anywhere other than when he was with Forest where frequent hamstring injuries seemed to drain his self-belief. I had Franz on a loan deal first of all, but then bought him. I was impressed but unfortunately he sustained a calf injury towards the end of the season and that was the last we saw of him until the following year.

Our next Premiership game was away to Aston Villa who were second in the table and gunning for the championship. We knew that it was going to be tough but we managed to hold them in the first half. We had a lapse of concentration in the second half and first Paul McGrath, and then Dean Saunders, scored a goal apiece in four minutes. Our own 'Deano' – Brian Deane – pulled one back for us a quarter of an hour later and, for a while, I thought we just might sneak in another. However, Villa regrouped and gave us a hard time in the last ten minutes which led to Kevin Richardson getting a third for them just before the final whistle. We were 20th in the table and life was getting uncomfortable again.

We had a good chance to redeem ourselves the following Saturday when we were at home to Queen's Park Rangers. Gerry Francis was manager at that time and he'd done a good job in getting them to about seventh in the table – not bad for a club that was certainly no bigger than us. Les Ferdinand was with them then and we knew that we would have to keep him quiet. Of course, knowing these things and actually doing something about them are two different matters. One of the frustrations of being a manager is that you can give your players all the information, all the tactics and all the encouragement to do the job properly – but from the moment the whistle blows it is all in their hands alone. You are just a helpless bystander as they play the game.

My head was in my hands when Bradley Allen popped into a space after 19 minutes and put Rangers ahead. I was banging it against the wall in the 75th minute when Ian Holloway added another. I could barely raise a smile when Jamie Hoyland scored for us two minutes from the end. As far as I was concerned, we had the opportunity to pick up three points on our own ground and we blew it. The supporters were disappointed too, but not as much as I was. Once again I found myself questioning the commitment of the players.

We had been drawn to play Manchester United at home in the next round of the FA Cup and we had already beaten them at home on the first day of the season in the Premiership. We felt that we had a chance therefore – but first of all we had to have a rehearsal at Old Trafford in the return Premiership fixture. Since our previous meeting Eric Cantona had joined them and it was no coincidence that they were running neck-and-neck with Villa for the title.

It cannot be easy having a place like Old Trafford for your home ground because every visiting player wants to do well there. My lot were no exception and the home fans were stunned when Franz Carr put us ahead after only seven minutes. One of the qualities of Manchester United has always been their patience. They grind you down until you crack. It took them until halfway into the second half but eventually they drew level through Brian McClair and then, ten minutes from the end, Cantona struck – and any grip we had on precious points was gone. We returned home knowing that we were now bottom of the Premier League.

I have never been one to panic and did not on this occasion. I had seen all this before and I got the feeling that many other people thought that it was a deliberate ploy to put our heads on the chopping-block and then move out of the way at the last minute. I think that they actually believed that I enjoyed playing the role of Harry Houdini. Forget it! My job is to get results. If I don't, then I'm on the dole – it's as simple as that. We come back to that same argument about what is 'good football'. Our supporters want winning football — first and foremost.

William Hill already had us as evens for the drop – and on paper I couldn't argue with that – but we had to play most of the clubs who were involved in the battle of the plug-hole, and I knew that there were points to collect if we had the right attitude. The first of those games was against Middlesbrough, just three days after our defeat at Old Trafford. It was an evening game and we took full advantage of being at home. Franz Carr scored after 38 minutes and Brian Deane wrapped it up on the hour. They were working well together. 'Boro had long faces when they went home, but we were celebrating a valuable three points and were looking forward to our FA Cup-tie against Manchester United.

United had the title race on their minds as well as the FA Cup, but they must have been feeling confident when they arrived at Bramall Lane. The crowd was almost the biggest since their last visit and we adopted a nothing-to-lose attitude. Cantona was not playing that day.

Giggs played out of his skin and on the half-hour he put them ahead. It was a good goal but one that I felt we had gifted them by allowing too much space. I yelled as much from the dugout. Whether it was my yelling or the sudden realisation of what they had done I never knew, but suddenly we started to play. Within four minutes, Jamie Hoyland had put us back on terms. Another seven minutes and Glyn Hodges landed the ball in the net and we were 2–1 to the good. Fergie must have had a fit, especially when Steve Bruce planted his penalty at the foot of the post near the end. The referee Mike Reid played eight minutes' extra time but, despite all that, they managed to throw at us we kept our heads and, when the final whistle sounded, we were into the sixth round of the FA Cup and Manchester United saw another trophy disappear from view.

If we could only show that sort of spirit for the rest of the season in our Premier League matches I knew that we would be certain of survival. I was also well aware that players are a Jekyll and Hyde lot and anything could happen at any time. We listened to the Cup draw and there were cheers as we drew Blackburn away. I don't really know why there were cheers. Kenny Dalglish had bought himself a pretty tough, strong side and, even without the injured Alan Shearer, they were still among the front-runners in the title race. I can only put our cheers down to too much mushy peas with our fish and chips.

We needed to cash in on our victories over Middlesbrough and Manchester United to get ourselves out of our predicament in the League table. Our next trip, though, was away to Wimbledon and I had almost come to hate playing against my old club because I never seemed able to put one over on them. This trip was not much different. Again we came away with a big fat nothing. John Fashanu scored after two minutes and when Dobbs came in with a second just before half-time we were sunk.

Only two days later, on the Monday night, we had the chance to put the record straight as we were at home to Oldham who were bottom of the table, just one place below us. We simply had to win this one and it was a pretty tense affair for both sides. Everybody was scared stiff of making a mistake and, as the first half drew to a close, I was already thinking of what I could say to try to relax my players during the interval. I need not have worried. John Gannon popped one in on the stroke of half-time and you could almost see the tension evaporating from Bramall Lane. Adrian Littlejohn added another halfway through the second half and we sent Joe Royle's men home empty-handed. It was tight, though.

Southampton were in a mid-table position when we paid them a Premiership visit and I had high hopes that we would bring something away. My hopes were dashed when we were two goals down in the first five minutes through Kevin Moore and Jeff Kenna. Both were so-called defence players but there was nothing defensive about the way they landed a couple of knockout punches so early in the game. Brian Gayle pulled one back but then Ian Dowie made it 3–1 before half-time. I sent Ian Bryson on with half-an-hour left and he managed to pull another one back, but we were still trailing at the end of the game and another precious point or three had gone down the drain.

March was upon us and that means that time was beginning to run out. It also means transfer deadline time. I spoke hopefully to the directors about what sort of cash might be available — and got the usual response. I could not strengthen the squad in any way. I still had Franz Carr on loan at this stage and I was eventually able to actually buy him, but apart from selling Michael Lake to Wrexham for £60,000. I was very limited with what I could do on the transfer market.

If we were going to turn things round and get out of the relegation hole, we had to start some serious action during March. I conveyed that to the players and waited for their response. I didn't have long to wait. On 2 March we were at home to Tottenham and what a night it turned out to be. The match had been rearranged to accommodate Tottenham as they were playing Manchester City on the following Sunday, also in the FA Cup Sixth Round.We were four goals ahead inside the first half-hour with Ian Bryson getting two in two minutes after Franz Carr had opened the scoring and Tottenham's Andy Gray had put through into his own net to help matters along. Deane and Rogers added a couple more in the second half and we finished the game shock winners at 6–0 — easily our best result of the season. It was Spurs' worst result for 15 years and ended a run of six wins on the trot. We had a few drinks that night! Venables didn't, he had objected to the rearranged date.

The result also set us up for our visit to Blackburn Rovers for the FA Cup sixth round and we took quite a few supporters with us. My plan was to contain Blackburn and hit them on the break. We didn't do the latter, but we certainly contained them and at the final whistle he scoresheet was still blank – a result that seemed to puzzle them a lot more than it puzzled us. The following Monday night, our rivals Wednesday were playing their Cup--tie at Derby By contrast there were plenty of goals in that one – six in fact – but the end product was the same, it ended in a draw with Wednesday getting a late equaliser.

Before we replayed with Blackburn we were at home to Norwich in the Premiership. The Canaries were third in the table at that time and they were playing some fast and exciting football. A Ruel Fox goal ten minutes into be second half settled the issue and once again we had thrown away points :hat we desperately needed and had failed to score. After the six we'd hit against Tottenham I really thought that we'd rediscovered the basic idea of he game – but I was wrong and it was back to the drawing board.

We were as well prepared as we were likely to be for the visit of Blackburn and I was confident that we were going to give the crowd something to talk about on their way home. It was another cagey first half but hen the goals started to flow By the end of 90 minutes it was 2–2 with Livingstone and Newell scoring for Blackburn and Mitch Ward getting our two. We battled it out for another half an hour of extra time without a clear result and so it was all down to penalties – and a chance for Alan Kelly to win us the game.

The way of determining victors of Cup matches has long been a subject of debate. There used to be the debacle of tossing coins, or any number of replays. Sudden death extra-time has now come into play but the question of penalties remains for the present time at least.

It also put us into a good mood for our FA Cup semi-final which we now knew was going to be at Wembley It seemed very strange to be dragging two teams from Sheffield all the way to London for their Cup semi-final, but in hindsight I can see that the FA had a bit of a problem in that if the all-North London semi-final was going to take place there, then they simply had to have the other Cup-tie there too. Probably it would have been better to have had the semi-finals elsewhere but it seemed that the whole of Sheffield wanted to see history being made. And certainly the combined fans of Arsenal and Spurs could have filled the place twice over.

The FA were bombarded with phone-calls, faxes and letters from Sheffield fans who wanted to see their local derby played beneath the twin towers. Personally I was in favour of Wembley given the circumstances but in hindsight I think it probably gave Wednesday the edge especially since they knew that they would be returning there for the League Cup Final a couple of weeks later. They also had more players with Wembley experience than us, so Elland Road would probably have been better for us.

We travelled down on the Thursday and stayed at Sopwell House, near St Albans. It was like preparing for the Cup Final itself for us and, when the day dawned and we drove down Wembley Way in our coach, it was just like the real thing. There were 78,000 fans there and the place was a sea of red and white and blue and white. It was a marvellous experience and felt like the whole of Sheffield had taken a family day out at the first-ever Steel City semi-final.

The game was one of those so-near-and-yet-so-far jobs. I thought we matched Wednesday player for player and we didn't give up after Chris Waddle had put the Owls ahead from a scorching free-kick in the first minute. Alan Cork put us level just before half-time and we were in for an exciting second half. It was quite a game and one that I shall always remember, partly because of the occasion and the way we played, but also for the fact that the referee missed a blatant handball by Viv Anderson in the area that should have been a spot-kick for us. Only two people in that packed Wembley stadium missed seeing Anderson's hands go in the air and contact the ball – the referee and his nearest linesman. I still shake my head in disbelief every time I think about it.

In extra-time Mark Bright scored Wednesday's winner. We didn't recover from that, although, to their credit, the players did not stop trying. As one man they all slumped to the ground when the final whistle went – but I told them to lift their heads and go to greet their supporters. They had nothing to be ashamed of and they owed a big thank you to all those Blades fans who had travelled to Wembley to cheer them on. Wednesday's boss, Trevor Francis, rushed to greet his family in the excitement of the moment little knowing that there was disappointment ahead for him as he pitted his side against George Graham's Arsenal in both the League Cup and the FA Cup Finals during the weeks ahead.

We did not wait around to watch the next semi-final between Arsenal and Spurs the following day. I wanted to get us back to Sheffield because we had a big night looming up on the following Tuesday. Leeds United were coming to call and we needed another three points. Our last Premiership game had been the 3–1 win at Coventry and I did not want us to forget that.

We performed well and sent Leeds packing empty-handed. Our goals came from Paul Rogers and Brian Deane. It was a wonderful three points from heaven and I felt that we were going to be safe provided we continued to play that way for the rest of our campaign – which comprised three home games and four away, some of them quite difficult fixtures too.

We drew 1–1 at home to Manchester City and then chalked up the same scoreline at Oldham. Blackburn took revenge for their Cup exit by beating us 3–1 and then we completed our April programme with a 1–1 draw at Sheffield Wednesday – which was once again a game of passion. They were a bit miffed because they had lost to Arsenal in the League Cup Final and I believe that they would have liked to take it out on us a little bit. There was nothing doing, though. Deano put us ahead just before the interval and once again it was left to their defender-turned-attacker, Paul Warhurst, to get them out of trouble. I was fairly happy with a point, although Glyn Hodges was sent off following an incident with John Harkes, on the word of an unsighted linesman, that was annoying.

We now faced three games in eight days to complete our fixtures. The first two were away and the last one at home. We were one place away from relegation and had a three-point advantage over Oldham, who were our chief threat. We could not afford any slip-ups but there was a particularly emotional involvement in the first of our remaining games. It was Nottingham Forest's last home game of the season and they were faced with relegation. More than that, it was Brian Clough's last home game in charge and marked the end of a tremendous reign. There was tremendous media attention and they created an atmosphere whereby they made it obvious that they wanted Cloughie to finish with a win.

We had to ignore Forest's feelings, though. I assured my players that there was no room for sentiment that afternoon as we were not out of the woods ourselves as yet. I don't think that they really needed telling but I had to be sure. The game was half an hour old when Glyn Hodges struck the first blow for us. Brian Gayle added a second about midway through the second half and the game ended with a 2–0 scoreline in our favour. I shook Cloughie's hand and looked into the eyes of a man who seemed to be somewhere else.

With Oldham and Middlesbrough both winning, our situation remained the same and we went to Goodison Park knowing that we had to do our level best to bring home at least one point – although, really we could not afford to drop any. It was a tough task – especially since it was also Everton's last home game and they didn't want to finish with a defeat. Bradshaw and Hodges gave us a 2–0 half-time lead and we held it throughout the second half.

Crystal Palace had slumped and were now in a dangerous position, so the battle raged on to the last weekend of the Premiership season. We looked to be safe but had to be sure of getting something out of our very last game, at home to Chelsea (an omen for next year if ever there was one!). Nearly 25,000 turned up to see the match and we raced into a 3–0 lead by half-time. Andy Scott scored his first-ever League goal, his former Sutton team-mate Paul Rogers got another and Dane Whitehouse also got his name on the scoresheet. Dane repeated his performance in the second half and, despite two late Chelsea goals, when the final whistle went, the party began – we had won 4–2. It was Dave Webb's last game as Chelsea boss although he had achieved his task of keeping them up.

Our season had ended on a high note. We had climbed to 14th in the table and we were guaranteed another term in the Premiership. Not only that but we had given our supporters something that precious few teams had provided during that 1992–93 season – a day out at Wembley.

[illegible] about [illegible] the [illegible] [illegible] that [illegible] and [illegible] the [illegible]

[illegible] position [illegible] because of [illegible] [illegible] he was [illegible] [illegible] the [illegible]

[illegible] the [illegible] and [illegible] [illegible]

13

Boardroom Battles

THE DUST HAD NOT SETTLED ON THE 1992–93 SEASON before speculation began about the future of the Sheffield United club and my own future too. Perhaps this would be a good time to reveal the impossible situation in the boardroom at Bramall Lane. If you have ever been a passenger on a Jumbo jet and heard the chief pilot and his co-pilot arguing about how to fly the plane, then you will have some idea of what it was like to be manager of Sheffield United. You never knew from one day to the next if you were going to get a comfortable flight and a safe landing or if you were going to put your head round the door of the cockpit to find that both pilots had bailed out.

That same situation continued until just before my departure from the club in December 1995 – when it was obviously time for a fresh start for all concerned. When I agreed to become manager of Sheffield United I had, as already mentioned, had initial talks with Reg Brealey. I knew that there was not going to be a Jack Walker type of budget available, but I was totally unprepared for the years of financial strangulation and misinformation that were lying ahead.

Brealey had been chairman of the club since 1981. Described as an entrepreneur, it is widely accepted that he brought fresh hope to a Sheffield United that had been through the mill financially and were a poor Division Three side which at the end of the 1980–81 season were relegated to the bottom division. He had built something of a reputation among the business fraternity for his shrewd dealings and when he first arrived at Bramall Lane it looked as if his drive and ambition were going to work.

He made a few quid available and new manager Ian Porterfield spent wisely to create a squad that won the old Fourth Division championship at the first attempt. The Blades won it in style, too, with only four defeats – all away – in 46 League matches. Attendance increased and happy days were here again as far as the Blades were concerned. The club continued to progress until 1988, just before I joined. Billy McEwan had been manager before me and things seemed to be going along all right – but then it all suddenly went horribly wrong.

The question that most people ask is, 'Why?' It's a good question and one that cannot be easily answered. Perhaps Brealey's other interests diverted his attention too much. He had been hailed as an all-conquering hero in India when he took over Titaghur Jute – a struggling company situated on the Ganges delta. It employed 18,000 people and when he arrived there he was given the sort of welcome reserved for national heroes.

The euphoria was not to last long, however. It all began to go wrong with the result that Reg and his brother were investigated by the police both here and in India for several alleged irregularities – including deducting money from the Indian workers' pay-packets which should have gone into the Provident Fund, but didn't.

Few knew to what extent Brealey was wheelin' and dealin' and we were therefore inclined to take what he said at face value. Probably one of the worst incidents of myself being suckered was in 1990 when the regular topic of Sheffield United's dire finances were being aired for the umpteenth time by the media.

Brealey gave pressure of business in Florida, Brunei and India as the reason he wanted to unload his interest in the club and, on 5 March 1990, he called a board meeting and then a press conference to introduce Sam Hashimi – the man who was going to provide the cash that would transform Sheffield United into one of the wealthiest and most successful clubs in the country.

Sam Hashimi appeared from nowhere but was introduced as the 'new owner of Sheffield United'. He was a young, well-dressed man who had been born in Baghdad. It all turned out to be a 'bad gag'. Ali Baba had nothing on this pantomime. It was said that Hashimi had offered £6.25 million for control of the club using Middle East funds transmitted through Barnacle Holdings, a Jersey-based company. Barnacle Holdings? Shellfish Sureties might have been a better title – get someone to swallow it and the world's your oyster.

Hashimi played his part very well and said that finding a million pounds for new players was not a problem. In 1990 a million quid would have bought you Colin Hendry with probably enough change to invest in someone like Lee Chapman. Even Paul Ince only cost Manchester United £800,000 in late 1989. Hashimi said that the investment was financed from his 'own resources and capital from the Middle East'.

The story got even better when Hashimi announced that he had walked away from a deal to buy Manchester United so that he could take over Sheffield United.

'I had talks with Mr Martin Edwards, but he said that he was not prepared to name a price because there were 13 other interested parties, and he wanted me to name the figure,' said Hashimi – who also added that he had the backing of four sheikhs and a prince and would arrange for Egypt to send their national team to Bramall Lane for a friendly before the 1990 World Cup.

Remember what I said about the folly of being an optimist? I swallowed it all and even posed for press pictures, draping a Blades scarf around the shoulders of Hashimi.

'If he puts up the money for players I'll willingly spend it,' I said – but to save other managers rushing to put up their price tags I added the rider – 'I'm not in any hurry. If I were let loose with more than £100,000 I'd be dangerous.'

The photographs that appeared in the national press the next day have been a constant source of embarrassment ever since. Why? Because I should have known better. Money doesn't grow on trees, or suddenly turn up in Sheffield on the back of a camel.

I had my suspicions, but I didn't want to believe them. Blades board member Michael Wragg, a pal of mine and son of the former Football Association vice-president Dick Wragg, was more inclined to listen to the alarm bells that were ringing inside him. Convinced that he was a bit too old to be believing in Fairy Godsheikhs, Michael had a chat with Paul Woolhouse who had recently become a director of the club, and together they launched an investigation into the sale of Brealey's shares to Hashimi.

The board was united in its opposition to the deal and rounded on Brealey. Three weeks after the deal was announced, Brealey went public and announced that it was off. There was a token gesture of protest from Hashimi who claimed that he had a watertight agreement but it was further announced that he was now banned from the ground – and nobody ever heard of him again. He went into oblivion just as quickly as he had emerged from it, and this so-called millionaire football fanatic disappeared into the far-off horizon, until he briefly popped up in Dubai a few years later. I do believe I read a year or so ago that he had undergone an operation, and is now a woman!

What had it all been about? Was it simply a diversion to gain some breathing space for troubled Brealey? Was it a genuine bid that just disintegrated? Only a few people know the truth of it but it seemed a very strange episode to me, and I felt a complete mug after it. I felt that I had been used to give credence to something which had more to do with 1001 Arabian Nights than 1001 Arabian banks.

The problems did not go away of course. The battle of the boardroom went on longer than the Christmas edition of *Coronation Street*. Paul Woolhouse got the bit between his teeth and wanted to take over from Brealey as club chairman. Woolhouse was involved in the metals business and appeared to have a few quid to his name – but it took six months before the matter was resolved and it was finally announced, in December 1990, that Brealey had agreed to sell his shares to Woolhouse who would now become the new club chairman with immediate effect.

You can imagine what it was like to be manager while all this was going on. Not only do you not know what is happening from one day to the next, but also there is nothing that you can tell your players who are equally concerned about their futures – and even about their next pay packets. You have to try to keep them happy and concentrated on their next game while all about them is speculation. You have to keep their trust as well and be honest as to what you do or do not know. Lose your players' trust and you have lost their commitment – without that you might just as well pack up and go home.

It didn't help that there was a television investigation into Brealey's business affairs which also set the nerves jangling. We had just won promotion to the First Division and I didn't need all this aggravation. There were lulls in the storm now and then, but they were few and they never lasted long. It didn't help in trying to sign new players either. Would you climb aboard a boat that looked as if it were ready to sink?

It was in August 1991 when things reached boiling point again. I sold Vinnie Jones to Chelsea and wanted to spend the money. Nobody said anything to the contrary and so I arranged the purchase of Brian Gayle from

Ipswich. I have already mentioned what happened, but just to make the point clear – we gained £575,000 from selling Vinnie and Brian Gayle was going to cost us £700,000. I was led to believe that there was no problem with that so I went ahead with the deal – only to suffer the embarrassment of the bank refusing to honour the club's cheque. They wanted the money from Vinnie's sale to go towards a bank debt.

The official line was that the transfer deal was delayed because of a couple of 'irregularities', but the truth was that Sheffield United's bank was getting nervous. As I previously said, I put in £100,000 of my own money and eventually got my man.

Life continued like that with a hand-to-mouth situation for the next season or so. The supporters must have been frustrated when they saw reasonable crowds turning up at Bramall Lane, and what appeared to be a thriving commercial department, and yet there was still nothing substantial being spent on the players that were necessary in our annual battle against relegation. Believe me, nobody was more frustrated then Dave Bassett.

We staggered on like that for another couple of years. Stephen Hinchliffe joined the board and ultimately became vice-chairman and sided with Michael Wragg, so there were permanent battle-lines still in the boardroom.

Hinchliffe was another character. He was 6ft 4in, blond hair and larger than life. He liked the good life and was quite a flamboyant character. He was assertive but if you stood up to him you would earn his respect. He had been a successful businessman in Sheffield in his early days. Later business dealings did not work out quite so well and he ended up with a prison sentence. He had wanted to make it big in the City of London but it did not work out for him. To his credit he was a true Blade, wanted the best for the club and as far as I am aware he never did any harm to Sheffield United or me.

Paul Woolhouse was a quietly spoken man, actually a ladies' man, always smart and well dressed. He was a Blade through and through. When he came into the club I think he over-stretched himself because his other business interests were on a downturn at the time. The last time I saw him he looked a tragic figure. It was after the semi-finals at Wembley and I saw him going to his car. He talked confidently but he had many business problems which are still going on today.

While talking of the people involved in the running of the club, I must mention Derek Dooley and place on record that I have nothing but the highest regard for him. I met him when I first joined the club and had a wonderful eight years with him. He was a football man and every club should have a Derek Dooley on the board. He understands the game and acts as a great link between the playing side and directors. The board think they know everything about the game because they read the papers and watch the television but, in fact, most of them know very little.

Derek was brilliant as a mediator between board and manager. He would explain to them in terms they could understand what the manager was doing and saying and he would put them in their place if they tried to talk down to the manager. He is a very honourable man, honest as the day is long and lives for the game, a loyal servant to football and his clubs. I think the world of him. He is a true Mr Sheffield and was recently given the Freedom of the City. He is a very honourable man, respected by both Sheffield clubs and is a real gentleman.

Things came to a head again in March 1993 when it was discovered that Paul Woolhouse had not honoured the hire-purchase arrangement that had landed him his majority shareholding. Chaos reigned once again — and once again yours truly was one of the last to find out what was going on. Derek Dooley did his best to keep me informed, but even he was puzzled at times. I liked Paul Woolhouse because he had taken on the club for the right reasons. However, he just didn't have the necessary financial clout.

It all got very involved since Alan Laver became acting chairman but Woolhouse's majority shareholding was being returned to a company called Else (1982), which was owned by Reg Brierley and his brother, Len. Laver tried to prevent the Brealeys from returning by threatening to call in a loan of £750,000 which he had made to the club if they pursued in the resignation of Woolhouse. The Brealeys had also demanded the resignation of Stephen Hinchliffe and Michael Wragg and everything pointed towards a stormy extraordinary meeting of the board.

The Brealeys knew where they stood in company law and forced the issue. Hinchliffe and Wragg resigned in advance of the meeting to avoid the embarrassment of being voted out of office. I think that they wanted to do the Brealeys out of the satisfaction of forcing them out. Within days the Brealeys were back in control. They appointed Derek Dooley as chief executive, which was the one good bit of news since he was at least a trustworthy man and one who I felt that I could talk to. The rest of the news was all bad. I felt that we had taken a backward step and, if it had not been for the number of supporters who urged me to stay, I might have called it a day there and then.

The shareholders finally got to have their say at the extraordinary meeting, but really it counted for very little. I said at the time that I had taken the club as far as I felt I could without further investment and that just surviving had to stop and be replaced by the will to compete. It was all very well buying shares but it was what you were prepared to do after the buying that really counted. I said that we had to decide if we were satisfied with just hanging on by our fingernails as a Premiership side, or if we wanted to actually improve and reach Cup Finals and European competitions.

The meeting was packed and there were a lot of voices raised, but Reg Brealey was nobody's fool. His brother Len joined the board along with Bernard Proctor, a Sheffield motor dealer, and Kevin McCabe, a builder from Scarborough. Alan Laver retained his place on the board and Derek Dooley was confirmed as chairman and unpaid chief executive.

Reg Brealey delivered two master-strokes. First of all he said that he wanted his shares to go to wealthy Blades fans who had the club at heart, and that he had already sold ten per cent of his holding to Bernard Proctor. He also said that he wanted to be a director for just one month to make sure that there was a thorough audit of the club's books by his own accountants. The shareholders rejected the 1992 accounts when it was announced that the directors had charged full overdraft rates for the various loans that they had made to the club – and also that the club had incurred £340,000 extra costs as penalties for late payments of bills. Brealey met the challenge from the floor head-on and said that the club would be open to a hefty fine if the accounts were not accepted there and then. Len Brealey also said that there would be £1 million for new players. It was not true.

The outcome was that the Brealeys were running the show again, but assured everyone that they were optimistic of selling out very soon as a consortium was being put together by Kevin McCabe. A month later and we heard that the consortium's bid fell short because a backer, who had promised nearly £5 million towards the club's purchase, had suddenly vanished.

Len Brealey said, 'I can't name the party. I can say that it cost £5,000 to draw up a contract which I signed – and that the man involved disappeared.' He added that

Kevin McCabe, who was organising the consortium, had been badly let down and could no longer reach the asking price of £2.75 million. Perhaps the mystery buyer got lost in the desert trying to find Sam Hashimi.

All that was going on at the end of the 1992–93 season and into the summer.

Another new director joined the board that summer – John Plant. We now had two camps, the Brealeys and Plant versus Proctor, Laver and Dooley. Reg had the casting vote. I was very unhappy about the whole situation. In public I was trying to say all the right things in order to keep some sort of stability within the club. We did not need any more boat-rocking at that time. Privately I was more than a little fed up. I had grown to love Sheffield, my family had settled well there and I loved, and still do love, the people. If it had been anywhere else I would have gone but I felt that the fans, at least, deserved some loyalty – and so I decided to bite the bullet and hang on in the hope that perhaps there would be a buyer come in for the club who would realise the potential that I already knew was there.

There were more fireworks to come before the start of the season. I usually try to take a holiday just before the season starts. The end-of-season work has been done, the transfer work has been done, and the players have been welcomed back. I was out of the country then when the Sheffield United fans received yet another bombshell. On 14 July 1993 it was announced that Brian Deane was joining Leeds for £2.9 million. A year before I had turned down a £2.5 million bid from Crystal Palace and it was obvious that I did not want to lose Brian Deane which is why the deal was done in my absence.

It seemed that the board were split on the decision but Reg Brealey used his casting vote to push the deal through. The directors who voted against threatened to resign and when I heard about it I hit the roof. I told Reg

Brealey that he had taken a decision which would get the club relegated. I meant it too. At a meeting just a couple of months earlier, I had pointed out that we needed to improve to compete and the minute my back was turned he had sold our top scorer.

I was pacified by an assurance that the bulk of the revenue would be available for buying new players. I was therefore able to go and get Willie Falconer from Middlesbrough for £300,000 and Rob Scott from Sutton for £20,000. In the meantime we had also sold Ian Bryson to Barnsley for £20,000 – so there was a balance of £2.5 million which was supposed to have been mostly available for transfers. Had it been, I would have used it.

It was increasingly difficult to talk with Brealey – mostly because I didn't want to. The boardroom infighting and broken promises were something in which I didn't want to be embroiled. I found Derek Dooley a big help at this time. He understood my problems and did his best to keep me informed of what was going on. The boardroom battles did not ease there. I had to live with the knowledge that I was being stupid to stay, and only the hope that there really would be a buyer to put the club back on the map kept me going. It carried on like that for another two years – and it was a nightmare. Probably many people will think that I was a fool for staying – or indeed a fool for going when it changed at last – but that is another of the problems of being an optimism addict, you always believe that tomorrow will be better and you can get through an awful lot of tomorrows before you come to your senses.

We went to Norway for a pre-season tour, returning home in time to play a friendly against Sheffield Wednesday for Derek Dooley's testimonial. He had served both clubs well and we were all glad to play a part in his special match. The trip to Norway had given us the chance to get away from it all and regroup before the Premier flight started again.

The money saga didn't stop, through. On 10 August 1993, I was delighted to sign Jostein Flo, a Norwegian international striker from Songdal. The fee agreed was £375,000 plus extras which went up to £475,000. After work permit delays, he proved to be popular with the fans.

It had been a dreadful summer at the club because of the boardroom upheaval and all the ifs and buts and maybes that were the fall-out from that particular explosion. However, all of that paled into insignificance when compared with another tragic tale of 1993.

In August 1992, one of our goalkeepers, Mel Rees, had undergone an operation for bowel cancer. He knew that it was going to be a long road back but he worked hard and was back in the first-team squad much quicker than anybody ever expected. He had a relapse in March 1993 and had to go back into hospital for another operation. Even then he fought back and when we played our FA Cup semi-final at Wembley, he was there to walk a lap of honour. At the end of May he died. He was 26 years old, understudy to Neville Southall in the Welsh international squad and, for my money, was a young goalkeeper who could have held his own in any Premiership squad. He had been my first signing when I was at Watford and I had then taken him to Bramall Lane. His funeral was a typical football affair with hundreds of fans, players, managers as well as his family and friends. There were smiles and tears.

In his short time in the game Mel Rees had earned something that all the money in the boardroom could not buy – love and respect.

14

We Were Robbed!

I WARNED THAT THE SALE OF BRIAN DEANE WOULD SPELL DISASTER for Sheffield United and, as the season unfolded, there was not a lot to change my mind – although I did feel that at the end of it we were robbed of our Premiership status.

As the new season opened, I rallied the troops for the first match. We were at home to newly-promoted Swindon. They had also had their problems during the summer. Glenn Hoddle had left them to take over Chelsea and in his departure they not only lost their manager, but also a key player. We added to their woes in that first game of the season and gave ourselves a boost with a 3–1 win. David Tuttle was playing his first game for us after moving from Spurs and added some strength to our defence. Willie Falconer was also making his debut for us, and it was Willie who opened the scoring after about 20 minutes. John Moncur equalised for Swindon just after half-time but then we took control. Carl Bradshaw and Paul Rogers added two more for us, the whistle went, we all shook hands and I counted out the points as I put them in the bag.

Four days later we were away to Manchester United. Roy Keane was making his home debut after his £3.75 million move from Nottingham Forest, and United had already won their first game 2–0 away to Norwich. The stage was set for either Keane to make a name for himself among the Old Trafford fans or for Sheffield United to pull off a shock result. Keano won the day by scoring twice in the first half. Mark Hughes added a third after the break and we went home with nothing to show for our efforts. Something happened during that game which really annoyed me – and I did not try to hide the fact. Tom Cowan, our defender, did something that I find inexcusable – he took a dive in an attempt to get Roy Keane sent off. I was surprised at Tom who I considered to be a good pro, and still do. I gave him a verbal lashing and he took it. I don't mind tough play and I don't mind someone going down to let the referee see that they have been fouled – but I draw the line at getting a fellow professional dismissed.

We crossed the Pennines again for our next match. This time we were at Everton and we gave them a shock when Dane Whitehouse scored after only a minute. Everton had won their two opening games and were a little taken aback when the ragged mob from Sheffield went for their throats right at the start. They composed themselves, though, and Tony Cottee got to work. He hit an equaliser and then John Ebbrell made it 2–1 just before half-time. Cottee hit two more in the second half, his last one coming in the final minute – just after Alan Cork had pulled one back for us. Once again we returned empty-handed and had slipped to 13th in the table with three games gone. Interestingly, among those below us were Chelsea, Newcastle and Sheffield Wednesday, so things could have been much worse.

My old mates from Wimbledon were our next opponents and they came to Bramall Lane with an unbeaten record against me. A goal either side of half-time from Jostein Flo and Willie Falconer did the trick. Andy Clarke pulled one back for the Dons but it was not enough and I waved them goodbye knowing that we had another three points – and my first victory over my old club since I left Plough Lane. It would have been nice to have had another three points from our next game, at home to Ipswich. Jostein Flo put us ahead and, just as everyone was beginning to button up their coats to go home, Steve Whitton caught us looking at the *Radio Times* to see what was on telly and popped in the equaliser. Needless to say, I had something to say about that. There was no excuse for it. It was a complete lack of concentration and should not have happened. Just 60 seconds more effort and we would have had three points instead of one – and that would have made all the difference at the end of the season.

We didn't do ourselves any favours against Queen's Park Rangers either. They beat us 2–1 after we had taken an early lead – again. Their second goal was from a penalty – 'Nuff said! After a week off because of another set of internationals, in which all the home countries remained unbeaten, it was back to business with a home match against Tottenham. We trailed twice and fought back each time, thanks to Adrian Littlejohn. At the end it was 2–2 and so far we had had a win, a draw and a defeat at the hands of London clubs.

I thought that we might pull off a result away to Leeds, but once again we returned empty-handed. I was beginning to worry. The scoreline was 2–1, but our goal had been scored by them and, despite having netted eight in 12 Premiership games, I knew that we were missing Brian Deane.

When the summer boardroom crisis had reached its peak I had the opportunity to go elsewhere. My name had been linked with Crystal Palace and I won't deny that there was a possibility that I could have returned to London to take over at Selhurst Park – but I had pledged my loyalty to Sheffield United before I went on holiday to Sardinia. They had promised me that they would be looking at improving the commercial side of the club to help raise extra cash for players and ground improvements which were badly needed. They told me that they were looking to push the club forward, so I did what I have always done in that situation – I believed them. If I had felt that the right decision was to resign then I would have taken it.

As I looked at the Premiership table, I couldn't help

but reflect on that a little. Our defeat on 18 September 1993 had landed us in 17th place.

My yearning continued a few days later when we went to Blackpool for the first leg of our Coca-Cola Cup campaign. The seaside club were in the division below us and, at the end of the season they had only just missed relegation by one point, but on that night they were in form and we were not. They scored three goals and we came away with a duck again. There was an inevitable conclusion to our Wembley hopes in that competition a couple of weeks later. We beat them 2–0 at home but lost on aggregate, so that was another bad outcome on the park and the loss of some potential earnings off it.

Back on the Premiership trail, our next match after the Leeds fiasco was a home game against Manchester City. They were having a bit of a yo-yo season as well so I was confident that we could get a result from their visit. I was wrong. They wanted it more than we did and Mike Sheron scored the only goal of the match. It was there for the taking but we didn't take it. Afterwards I told the players how disappointed I was in their attitude. The truth is that I could forgive conceding a goal, but our failure to score in front of our own fans was something else.

Our next Premier League trip was to Southampton and the players had my words about the lack of goals ringing in their ears. I put near enough the same side out, except that I put Adrian Littlejohn on from the start instead of keeping him on the bench. I couldn't fault the effort this time. We were a goal down at half-time so I had a few things to say in the dressing-room, but then an amazing second half followed. Southampton hit two more but we stormed back and got three of our own. It was a hard-earned 3–3 draw but at least we had come away with a point – and more than that, we had proved that we were capable of finding the back of the net.

We did not have another game for 16 days because of

the home countries being involved in World Cup qualifiers. While I do appreciate the plight of the national team managers, such a gap between domestic fixtures can play havoc with your club form. It is all very well if you have a lot of injuries and could do with a breather but, if you were in the same position as us and had just proved a point to yourselves, you need to get back into another competitive match as quickly as possible.

Our next game after the 3–3 draw at Southampton was a visit to Blackburn – and it was the beginning of one of the worst runs that I have ever experienced as a manager. In our next 13 games to the end of December we scored precisely three goals.We won one game – against Chelsea – in which the only score of the game was an own-goal gifted to us by an opposition player. So we actually only scored two – and one of those was a penalty. We even went six consecutive games without scoring a goal.

By the time the year ended we were in 21st position and Norwich, Aston Villa, Newcastle, Liverpool, Manchester United and Wimbledon had all helped themselves to maximum points at our expense.

People sometimes have the cheek to tell me that my hair is beginning to thin a little. It's a wonder that there's any left at all. I couldn't wait to usher in 1994, I'd had my fill of 1993. The thrill of being at Wembley in April, and our great escape from relegation, were now just distant memories. We were up to our necks in muck and bullets and we didn't have the firepower to fight back. The New Year's Eve drink was no consolation.

Perhaps my real mistake was in not having a Christmas party at the start of the season as I had done the previous year. I woke up on New Year's Day with a slight headache, but also with a smile on my face. It was 1994, the second half of the season and there was everything to play for. We were at home to Oldham that afternoon and while I wanted to wish Joe Royle a Happy New Year, I didn't want to do it at the expense of three points. As it was we gave him a rotten start to the New Year by beating Oldham 2–1 which was also the score at half-time. Admittedly, our first goal was a Dane Whitehouse penalty, but Mitch Ward added a second before the break.

We were good value for the three points and I still had that smile on my face at the end of the game. Oldham had been above us in the table 90 minutes earlier, now they were below us and we had moved up three places. It set us up for a trip to London two days later when we were due to meet West Ham. It wasn't the prettiest of games but we came away with a goalless draw and suddenly we had gone two games without defeat.

Mark Hughes put paid to our FA Cup hopes. We were at home to Manchester United in the third round, which was played six days after our West Ham game. There were no goals by half-time and I was beginning to get more and more confident that we were at least going to earn a few bob from a replay but you can never take your eyes off Mark Hughes, even for a second. Unfortunately, we did just for a moment. He scored and that was another chance for some extra cash down the drain as well as the dream of another trip to Wembley.

We had to concentrate on Premiership survival now We had 17 games left, nine at home and eight away. There was no reason why we could not repeat our performances of previous seasons and keep out of trouble. Yes, of course, I was letting my optimism get the better of me yet again. We still hadn't found anybody who could replace Brian Deane and put the ball into the back of the net on a regular basis.

The next few games were little less than a disaster. Blackburn beat us 2-1 at Bramall Lane, Colin Hendry of Rovers kindly scoring our goal for us. We then suffered the indignity of being beaten 3-2 at Hillsborough by the one team that we really did not want to lose to, Sheffield Wednesday. Our goal was another Dane Whitehouse penalty.

After that defeat by Wednesday we had a short break before our next game so we flew off to Saudi Arabia to play against their national side. It was a hastily arranged trip and I am never keen adding matches to an already busy schedule, but I felt that the break might do us all a bit of good. All that sand and sun was very nice but we were not really there long enough to take full advantage of it, and you couldn't help but keep looking over your shoulder in case Sadaam Hussein had decided to invade the pitch. Incidentally, there was still no sign of the mysterious Mr Hashimi.

It was a bit of a change of scene from Hillsborough and the scene changed all too quickly when we arrived back at Bramall Lane for our next game, which was at home to Coventry who were in the middle of the table at the time. We drew 0–0 and slipped back to 21st position in the Premiership.

I had warned the directors that selling Brian Deane was virtually signing our own Premiership death warrant and, when I looked back on our last few months, I was amazed that nobody actually came forward and said, 'You were right.' In 19 League and Cup games – 1,710 minutes of football – we had scored only seven goals. Two of those were own-goals courtesy of the opposition and another three were penalties. So in all that time we had managed to score only two goals from general play. I badly needed a proven striker and the board knew that they could not put it off any longer. I found the answer in Wales – and I only wish that I'd found him a few matches earlier.

Nathan Blake had scored 14 goals in 20 games for Cardiff City. He was a new-age, laid-back striker who was prepared to get in where it hurts. Make no mistake, he had skill too, and you could equally put him on the wing or in midfield and you would get your money's worth. He had already been capped for Wales at Under-21 level and I knew that he was worth the £300,000 that he would cost. I was given the go-ahead and we had him on the bench for our away match at Ipswich.

I put him on for a few minutes in the Ipswich game, which we lost 3–2. I wasn't happy with our first-half performance but the players responded to my half-time talk and if they had played like they did in the second half earlier in the game, we would have brought home at least one point.

Blake was on the bench again for our next game away to Tottenham and I put him on a bit earlier. The supporters who had travelled to London saw why I had bought him as he scored his first goal for us – a goal that earned us a 2–2 draw and a valuable point. More than that, it was quite a confidence booster and our tails were up when Leeds came to visit a week later. We drew 2–2 with them and a few days later we drew 1–1 at home to Queen's Park Rangers. Three drawn games in a row and five goals scored, all from the run of play. Prepare for another dose of the Houdini medicine.

We did not score a goal during our next two games but neither did the opposition – and that meant a point apiece from our away game at Manchester City and our home match with Southampton. It did seem as though the tide was turning, although we still had a big fight on our hands because we were not moving up the table. The encouraging thing was that we had now gone five games without defeat. If only we could start to win.

West Ham were our next opponents and I wanted to end the month of March on a high note. I was not thrilled to bits when first Ian Bishop and then Matt Holmes put the Hammers into a 2–0 lead. Dane Whitehouse pulled one back about five minutes before half-time, but I was not happy and said so. The response was instant. Brian Gayle equalised after three minutes and then, about half an hour later, Paul Rogers put us ahead. The rest of the game was a bit nail-biting even though we did have the lion's share of it and put the pressure on them. When the whistle went we almost did a lap of honour to celebrate our first win since New Year's Day.

Nobody gave us a dog's chance of getting anything out

of our next game – away to Liverpool. When Ian Rush got on the scoresheet after only four minutes, the home fans sat back and waited for an avalanche. It didn't come. At half-time we were still a goal down and I knew that Liverpool were there for the taking. Jostein Flo shocked them with a goal straight after the restart and then headed another one halfway through the second half. We took maximum points and I was really proud of my players' performance. They had manfully tackled a man-sized job and set us up for another great escape.

Two days after our Anfield success it was Easter Monday and we were at home to Arsenal. They were fourth in the table and wanted to make sure at of least European football the next season, although they were still heavily involved in the European Cup-winners' Cup, which they were to go on and win later that season. Arsenal had the tightest defence in Britain and I knew that we were going to have a real job getting anything past Dave Seaman. At half-time it was 0–0 and I was beginning to think that was how it was going to stay. We were ten minutes into the second half when Roger Nilsen tried one of his long throws and found Paul Rogers in the Arsenal area. He had slipped his marker and the next thing we knew the ball was in the back of the net. I was on my feet celebrating along with everyone else. Perhaps those cheers were a bit premature because Arsenal drew level when Kevin Campbell headed home from a corner. The game ended 1–1 and we had fought well for a point against a team that gave very little away.

There was yet another break in our programme because of Cup matches so, when Aston Villa came to Bramall Lane, nearly a fortnight had passed since the Arsenal game. It is one of those unfortunate problems with our domestic season that you can find yourself kicking your heels for a couple of weeks and then have to play three games in seven or eight days. Villa were in no mood for niceties because they had gained only two points from their previous seven games. They beat us 2–1 and once again we were only one place from the bottom of the table with only one home game and three away games to go.

We were now looking for maximum points from every game. Nothing less would do. We travelled to Norwich knowing that one false move would mean the end of our Premiership life. We were not only dependent upon our own results but also on others slipping up around us. Swindon were already dead and buried at the bottom of the table, but the other two relegation places were available to a bunch of others including Oldham, Everton, Ipswich, Southampton, Tottenham, Manchester City and ourselves.

Nathan Blake put us ahead at Carrow Road and we held on to the end. Three points in the bag and the knowledge that Oldham, Ipswich, Southampton and Manchester City had all lost. Our rivals, Wednesday, had done us a particular favour by beating Ipswich 5–0.We moved up one place in the table – still in the frame for relegation but at least closer to escaping from it.

Our last home game of the season was against Newcastle. They had just hammered five goals past Aston Villa and they were keen to guarantee a place in Europe. The Magpies were third in the table and could not win the championship but their fans were in party mood when they came to visit us. They were still in party mood at half-time, but all that changed in the second half when Nathan Blake got to work. He scored about 20 minutes into the second half and then broke the Geordies' hearts in the last minute when he made it 2–0. Our supporters were ecstatic and so was I. Our rivals had not done anything sensational and we moved up another place in the table. At last we were out of the bottom three.

The real hard work was still to come. Two away matches in four days are gruelling enough, but when one of them is away to one of your relegation rivals, Oldham, and the other is at Chelsea, you know that you have a difficult job to do. Alan Cork delivered for us at Oldham – although Joe Royle's men also scored and we had to settle for only one point. It still meant that we were out of the relegation frame, though, as we went into the final game of the season.

The pressure was still on because the table had Swindon bottom, Oldham just above them on 39 points, Everton above them on 41 points, Ipswich next with 42 points and then ourselves with Southampton just above us. Both the Saints and ourselves were also on 42 points. We had to win to be safe, there was no question about that. Chelsea were in the FA Cup Final and they didn't want to finish their Premiership season on a low note. Our secret weapon was Nathan Blake, who had been rejected by Chelsea when he was a teenager and wanted to show them what they had missed.

Everton were at home to Wimbledon and I was hoping that my old club would do us a favour. If Everton went down it would mean their first relegation in 43 years. I heard that Sam Hammam was pretty keen to see that happen. He felt that he had been snubbed once by Everton and he wanted to see their demise. He even offered his players a holiday in Las Vegas if they beat Everton at Goodison on that last day of the season but it seems that there may have been other offers on the table.

The football bribe case involving Fashanu, Grobbelaar and Segers proved to be very interesting, especially since there were claims that Segers, the Wimbledon goalkeeper, received money for various 'deeds'. Among the games allegedly involved was the Everton versus Wimbledon match on the last day of that season.

If I say what I think I would probably be dragged through more courts than Tim Henman, but just for the record Wimbledon were 2–0 up after 21 minutes and, if it had stayed that way, our season would have had a very different ending. As it was, Everton miraculously fought back. *Match* magazine described the Everton goals like this: 'Stuart (24) penalty after Limpar was fouled; Horne (67) 30-yard drive; Stuart (81) mis-hit volley from 18 yards which deceived Segers.' There were similar write-ups elsewhere.

While Everton and Wimbledon were battling away we were at Chelsea. Jostein Flo started the ball rolling with a header from a corner after half an hour, and we went in at half-time with that lead. Chelsea equalised after ten minutes of the second half, but a few minutes later Glyn Hodges put us back in front. There was a quarter of an hour left when Mark Stein equalised for Chelsea. The way the other games were going even that would have been good enough, but disaster struck just 30 seconds before the referee ended the game. Mark Stein put Chelsea into the lead. There was not enough time for us to hit back – in fact there was only just enough time to restart the game. We knew as soon as we heard the other results that we had not done enough. We were relegated.

If we could have held on for another 30 seconds and gained a draw, Ipswich would have gone down. If the Everton result had been different even if they had drawn – they would have gone down and we would have stayed in the Premiership. I have long suffered from '90th-minutitis', but this was the cruellest time.

Everyone was totally gutted. Wally Downes punched the wall and split his hand open and all the others were justly totally devastated. I had to go and talk to the press and it is very difficult to answer questions at a time like that. You know the fans, your family and friends are there looking forward to the end of the season, a party or two and a holiday and you just know that the whole thing is like a wake. You have to try and keep a stiff upper lip but that is a very hard thing to do.

How did I feel? The same way that I feel now – cheated.

15

Promises, Promises

RELEGATION. It's one of those words that has you waking up in a cold sweat in the middle of the night. The prophecy that I had raved at the directors when they sold Brian Deane had come true, and nobody regretted it more than me. Or had it come true? We were drained when we left Chelsea, knowing that we were down and I had let the players know exactly what I thought of their season's performance. We were due to go to Australia for a pre–arranged tour but it was no celebration holiday.

We were given a bit of a lift when a possible lifeline was thrown with the news that Tottenham were in trouble for alleged administrative irregularities – the last time that that had happened there was an automatic relegation of the club involved, Swindon. Now there was the chance that Spurs might suffer the same fate and that Sheffield United could then be reinstated as a Premiership side.

The investigation into allegations of illegal payments at Tottenham had been going on for some time and I was not surprised that there was some talk of them being relegated – although I really expected that a fine would probably be the final outcome. I couldn't help feeling that the prospect of losing Sheffield United rather than Tottenham was of greater interest to the powers-that-be.

We kicked-off our tour of Australia with a 2–1 victory over the Western Australian state team in Perth. Glyn Hodges and Nathan Blake scored our goals. We were now keen to put our last-minute blow behind us and enjoy ourselves before we split up to go on holiday, to prepare ourselves for reporting back in July and attempt to get straight back into the top flight.

I kept hearing that we might not yet lose our Premiership status and the players were trying to keep up with the latest news from Britain. We probably did more for BT shareholders on that trip than all the TV adverts put together. I refused to get excited, or speculate, but when all that is going on in the papers back home, you can't help having your mind activated just a little bit. In the end I was right not to get excited. Tottenham were deducted 12 points from the following season so Sheffield United were definitely no longer a Premiership outfit.

The task now was to regroup and rebuild. The tour of Australia was a good start, but there was hard work ahead if we were going to get back at the first attempt – which is the earnest desire and motivation of any manager whose side has just dropped a division. As we flew back from Australia I couldn't help reflecting on the previous 12 months. At the end of the 1992–93 season we were still in the Premiership, we had been to Wembley and I had been voted by my colleagues at the League Managers Association to receive the inaugural Manager of the Year Award. A year later and my prophecy of doom after the sale of Brian Deane had unfortunately come all too true.

I've never been a cry-over-spilt-milk type and my thoughts soon moved on to the future. Some of the players who were on that plane with me were not going to be around for much of the fight-back of Sheffield United, and there were some tough decisions to be made in the coming weeks.

As it was, there was not too much transfer activity during the summer break – I signed Aussies Doug Hodgson for £30,000 and Carl Veart for £150,000. Tom Cowan went to Huddersfield for £200,000, and Carl Bradshaw went to Norwich for £500,000, but apart from that the attitude was 'wait and see'. There was plenty going on in other departments. While most soccer fans were glued to their televisions, pinning their hopes on Jack Charlton's almost Irish team in the World Cup, quite a few Blades fans were making pilgrimages to Bramall Lane to watch the John Street Stand being demolished.

It probably sounds a bit strange that fans would turn up just to watch an old stand being demolished. However, it was a link with the Bramall Lane past which had once seen Test cricket as well as football played on its hallowed – or hollowed – turf. There were a few tears as the bricks tumbled and crumbled – and souvenir-grabbing as well. I shared the supporters' mourning at the passing of an old friend, but I was equally gratified that, at last, the board were doing something constructive – that's if you can call demolition-work constructive.

The John Street Stand did not meet with the new safety regulations and therefore it had to go. It was to be replaced by a stunning new stand which would hold 6,000 people in comfortable seats and would also accommodate 32 executive boxes and a restaurant. We might have moved down in terms of division but we were certainly moving up in the world in terms of our stadium. Like everyone else, I could hardly wait to see the new gleaming part of Bramall Lane.

At the same time, new undersoil heating and drainage was being installed for the pitch – and it certainly did need the improvement.

So as I sat in my office, in the middle of what had now become a building site, and it reminded me of the fact that I was really just a works foreman, watching over the job and the blokes doing the work.

We prepared for the season as usual with some army training and friendlies, but it was soon time for the big kick-off and our first game, against Watford at home – or what was left of home after the demolition derby had taken its effect on John Street. On three sides the ground looked fairly normal, but opposite the players' tunnel there was a huge expanse of nothing – a wasteland which I later nicknamed 'Fred West's Garden' because there had been plenty of destruction but not a trace of construction. It didn't make for a great atmosphere, but we were optimistic of better times ahead.

The team was not so different from the last one of the previous season. As they sat in the dressing-room I reminded them of what we were about, and what their task was for the season. We wanted to bounce back after our last-gasp relegation and we owed it to our fans to show them that we were not happy at being in the First Division. I reminded them that the visit of Watford gave us a great chance to get off to a winning start.

They didn't let me down. Mitch Ward had an excellent game but I was pleased with our overall performance, too, and we were convincing winners after Jostein Flo put us ahead with only eight minutes gone. Ward scored before and after half-time and a lot of Blades fans went home happy. I was one of them.

Amzingly we didn't have another proper game for a fortnight. We were not involved in the first round of the League Cup and our scheduled second First Division match was postponed. We did have a game, though, as we were in the Anglo–Italian Cup and our first match was at home to Udinese. Perhaps if we had won it I might have had a different viewpoint but, as it was, I still think that we have enough on our plate without getting involved in more irrelevant competitions like that one. Even the supporters couldn't get excited and only about 7,000 turned up to watch – and I think that half of those were Italian waiters from the local restaurants.

The newspapers described the game as 'explosive'. That's one word for it. The Italians seemed confused about what it was they were supposed to be kicking and I think that the referee must have been appointed by

Frank Warren who had neglected to tell him to bring his guide-dog. I couldn't believe what I was seeing on the pitch in front of me and, when I told the ref that I thought it was time he visited an optician, and asked if he were related to Al Capone, he sent me off. If I hadn't been so angry at the time I would have found it laughable. Not only did I get the red card waved in the air but so did Nathan Blake, Charlie Hartfield and Glyn Hodges. One of the Italians – who I think was actually Polish – also got his marching orders and the place was in uproar. So much for a nice little competition to cement relations between our two countries. It wouldn't have caused more trouble if Mussolini had been named as the new England team manager.

After that fiasco we had to get back to some sort of normality in time for our second domestic fixture of the season – at home to Notts County. We had still played only one First Division game and, somehow, I had to get our feet back on the ground to continue where we had left off against Watford. We were definitely not the same team. By half-time we were two goals adrift and, worse than that, we had Jostein Flo sent off. We rallied in the second half but not enough and at the end of the game we had lost 3-1. Worst of all, with the season only two weeks old we had had four players and the manager all shown the red card in the matter of a few days.

We picked up a hard-won point away to Charlton and might have got all three but for a penalty. Then we were away to Tranmere. It was the first visit by a Sheffield United side for 12 years and I wish that we'd never bothered.

We lost 2–1 and I could only put it down to bad finishing because we had plenty of opportunities – especially towards the end when Tranmere lost a couple of key players due to injury.

With the knowledge that we had picked up one point

out of the last nine, we jumped aboard a plane for another waste-of-time Anglo–Italian Cup match. Actually Wally Downes took charge as I was banned. He did a good job. We were away to Piacenza, and this time only 4,000 turned up. Someone should have got the Pope to referee, it might have pulled a bigger crowd. We drew this meaningless match 2–2.

We returned from Italy unscathed and prepared for our next game, a First Division match at home to Bolton. I had been fairly pleased with our performances, especially our Australian newcomer Carl Veart, who had joined us from Adelaide just before the start of the season. It's not easy for any player to settle in at a new club and when that player has travelled half-way round the world to do it, life can be even more difficult at first.

I was even more pleased with Carl Veart when the referee ended our game with Bolton. We had won 3–1 and he had scored twice – his first goals for the club. Bobby Davison got our third a minute from the end and everything was looking much better than it had a week or so earlier. Just three days later we were at home again, this time to Sunderland. It was a tight game and there were no goals, but the worrying fact was that our captain, Brian Gayle, was sent off for what is known as a 'professional foul'. Can someone please show me an amateur foul? We had now collected nearly as many red cards as goals.

Reading hadn't conceded a goal at home that season so far and we didn't change matters when we went there. We were probably worth a point but Jimmy Quinn decided that it would be a good time to get his first goal of the season and we came away on the wrong end of a 1–0 scoreline. Things were getting serious. We were 20th in the table. This was not at all what I had been expecting, and there were other problems, too, as some players became restless. Alan Kelly was being linked with other clubs and had turned down a new contract until the situation became a little clearer. The enthusiasm and determination of the opening day was evaporating very fast.

There was not much going on with regard to transfers. Franz Carr went on loan to Leicester early in September, and a month later the move became permanent with City paying us £100,000.

After that defeat at Reading we needed to bounce back with something as a morale-booster — and we got it when we travelled to Stockport for the first leg of our Coca-Cola Cup second-round tie. Dane Whitehouse hit a hat-trick and Jostein Flo scored twice, so we came away with a 5–1 win. A few days later we were away to Port Vale in a League match. It's amazing what a difference a week can make. It's even more amazing what a difference two weeks can make. In midweek we were at home to Stockport in the return leg of the Coca-Cola Cup. I told my players that I didn't want any stupid risks of injury, red cards, or an embarrassing defeat and they played it by the book. We won 1-0 and there were no side-effects. That weekend we made it four wins on the trot with a 2–0 decision over Oldham at home and the important thing was that we had shot back into the top half of the table as October began.

Our next Anglo-Italian Cup game was a 3–3 draw at home to Ancna. Even the Italian waiters couldn't be bothered for this one, and only 1,250 turned up to watch. I've seen more people standing outside a television shop window when the lottery is being drawn. There were a few more the following Saturday when we travelled to Grimsby and they had their best crowd of the season with nearly 9,000. We came away with a 0–0 draw and I was not unhappy about that, although we might probably have sneaked the points near the end.

I took Billy Mercer from Rotherham as extra goalkeeper cover and the fee of £75,000 was set by tribunal. It was, of course, more than I had anticipated paying, but there is nothing worse than having to scratch around for a loan 'keeper at the last minute when you find your regulars are out of action. Balanced against Franz Carr going to Leicester, we were in profit to the tune of £25,000. I decided against making a bid for Alan Shearer.

We had a goalless home draw with Barnsley and followed that with a 1–0 defeat at West Brom which didn't please me very much. Suddenly we had played three League games without scoring. I was having second thoughts about investing that £25,000 in Alan Shearer. We had our chances but we blew them. West Brom had gone four defeats in a row and their manager, Keith Burkinshaw had just been given the elbow. It's amazing how players react when something like that happens. It is rare that a team whose manager has just been sacked loses their next game. It's almost as if the players are saying, 'It's not our fault.' Interesting.

I was sure that we would do better when Luton visited us the following weekend – but I was wrong. We scored first – and then we equalised. Yes, Nathan Blake put us ahead but a quarter of an hour later, Brian Gayle put through his own net. Luton then took advantage of a bad spell in the second half and smacked in two goals in seven minutes. Then they put on their hats and coats and went home with the points. I looked at the table and we were down to 17th place.

Our Coca-Cola Cup third-round game followed the same sort of pattern. We were at home to Bolton and the flying Finn, Mixu Paataleinen, put them ahead after eight minutes. I had a few words to say at half-time and Nathan Blake put us back on terms two minutes after the restart. I sat back and waited for more goals. We left it late – very late. It was the 89th minute when the winning goal came at last. Our defender Rob Scott scored it and we were out. Yes, it was another own-goal. Bolton couldn't believe their luck, especially since they then went all the way to Wembley, undefeated until Liverpool beat them in the Final.

October ended with a 2–1 defeat at Millwall. It was the home side's first win in 11 games and we gifted it to them. A lack of concentration allowed them to hit the winner in injury time. We had slumped back down the table to 19th place and I was fed up. What, I wondered, would November bring? What a month November turned out to be!

I was encouraged by a 1–1 draw at Stoke. We had suffered four defeats in a row and I was happy to stop that run at least – and I was quite pleased with our performance. We were not finishing well but we were creating chances and our defence was holding its own under pressure. I believe we deserved three points from Stoke, but I settled for the draw. Mitch Ward came to see me to discuss his future. He was unhappy with the way things were going and wanted to move. We agreed to put him on the list and put his value at £250,000, and he continued to give it his best shot – which was sensible because nobody is going to buy a player who is not playing well.

I felt like throwing a firework party on the night of 5 November because we had at last ended a run of seven games without a win. Bristol City were the victims. We sent them back to the West Country with a 3–0 hiding which did not help their cause at all since they were below us in the table. I put my feet up that weekend and relished the fact that our next game was going to be at home again a week later – against Derby.

My expectations of a trouble-free week were sent crashing on the day before the Derby game when it was announced that Mike McDonald had made an offer to buy out Reg Brealey. Now there had been rumours and counter-rumours for some time, but you could never get a straight answer from anyone. Things were really boiling though, because the fans had staged a protest during the Bristol City game turning towards the directors' box and holding up red cards. Then there had been a documentary on television during the week, alleging dodgy business dealings by Reg Brealey.

Mike McDonald and his consortium had tried to take over Manchester City earlier in the year but their bid had been unsuccessful. Now he wanted Sheffield United. His business interests were in engineering and DIY – in particular the Texas group. There was obviously some financial clout there. He told the press that there was a bid on the table and promised that, if he got control of the club, success would be just around the corner. There could be no denying that he had proved his point in business thus far and so we all waited to see what Reg Brealey's response would be.

'I have had dozens of offers for the club,' said Brealey. 'None of them stand up. As soon as we talk figures, they melt away.'

The players wanted to know what was going on and I even had people stopping me in the street to ask if I could tell them what was happening. Quite simply, they knew just as much as I did. I could not blame the fans for their treatment of the board. It created a very strange atmosphere at our previous home game because you could almost feel that our own supporters wanted us to lose just to strengthen their case against the board. It did not help us in our attempt to get our playing-act together. However, when I looked across the ground to the site that had been the John Street Stand – where nothing had happened since its demolition – and I looked at the money that was available for new players, I knew that the fans had a strong argument for change. They were not against me or the players, but the board were really getting some stick.

We played our match against Derby and beat them

2–1, but the action was almost a side attraction to the main event of board-baiting. Nathan Blake's 50th career goal was almost overlooked, as was Billy Mercer's debut in goal. At half-time the biggest cheer echoed around the ground when Reg Brealey had a message put up on the electronic scoreboard to announce that he was intending to sell the club.

After the game, Brealey issued a further statement which basically said that he had decided that the time was right to make available the majority shareholding of the club. He added that he would only sell to someone who had the cash to not only buy the shares, but to also inject a fair bit into the club. He said, quite candidly, that he would not sell to anyone who only had the money for the shares. He also said that the rebuilding of the John Street Stand would continue as planned in the meantime and that the club was in a stronger financial position than at any other time in its history.

While all this was going on, we had the extra thrill of completing our Anglo–Italian Cup fixtures with a 4–1 away win to Cesena.

Then it was back to the domestic bliss of First Division football and we had a Sunday game at Burnley I had never lost there before but all that was to be forgotten as they beat us 4–2. We had been putting a half–decent run together before that game so it was disappointing to say the least. However, we made up for it the following weekend with a 2–0 home win over Southend that put us back on course. We were now tenth in the table as November ended. What a month.

December got off to a flying start. Luton had already beaten us at Bramall Lane earlier in the season and so I sent the players out looking for revenge. We were also chasing our first away League win since the end of September. We gave them an own-goal through Brian Gayle and we also gave them a penalty, but I couldn't complain. Although they scored three against us again, we hit an amazing six goals with Gage and Veart getting two each and Hodges and Scott adding the others. It was a great performance and I was proud of the fact that the players had applied themselves to the job in hand, despite all those behind-the-scenes indecisions that were still bubbling and fermenting.

We took our run to six wins in seven games when we beat West Brom 2–0 at home. The only flaw was that Nathan Blake had got himself sent off again, this time for dissent. We all do it – argue with the referee that is – but it's a stupid thing to do really because you just cannot win. The following weekend we were involved in a 0–0 draw at Watford and after that we were at home to Middlesbrough where the result was 1–1. Paul Beesley was sent off for a second bookable offence and our red card collection was beginning to grow to an uncomfortable level. Still, we had now gone nine games with only one defeat and, as the rest of December unfolded, we beat Swindon 3–1 away and then Portsmouth 3–1 at home.

It was New Year's Eve again and we were fifth in the table. The boardroom situation was still the same, but that could be forgotten for a few minutes as we saw in the New Year – with all the prospects of it being a happy one.

16

At the Sharp End

JANUARY 1995 BROUGHT ALL THE HOPE OF A NEW YEAR. I wondered if this time the following year we might be back in the Premiership. I might as well have been wondering if I would receive a knighthood in the New Year's Honours List. In all fairness though, we did give it a good shot.

Our first game of 1995 was away to Wolves and it turned out to be a game which, once again, had me banging my head against a wall. We played well and went 2–0 up through Nathan Blake, who had not taken part until I sent him off the bench in the second half. Another three points in the bag, I thought and started to look at my watch. With a minute left, Wolves pulled one back and then, straight from the restart, they scored again and equalised. I couldn't believe it. I guess I did a good impression of Victor Meldrew as I expressed my disbelief – although my language was a good deal stronger in the dressing-room. Fancy letting in two goals in the last two minutes – and this was only the start of 1995.

Our next opponents were Manchester United. They had done the double for the first time the previous season and were keen to repeat their performance. Of all the sides that we could have drawn in the third round of the FA Cup, they had to be the toughest – even allowing for the fact that we had been drawn at home. What was easily our biggest crowd of the season turned up at Bramall Lane for the Monday night match – arranged then to provide for the demands of television. I had bought Phil Starbuck from Huddersfield a few days earlier for £158,000. He had been with us for a lengthy loan period and I decided that he was worth the investment, so I was able to field a fairly strong side against United who we had met before in the FA Cup on a regular basis in recent seasons. To the winner went the spoils – a fourth-round tie against Aston Villa.

Call me a dreamer if you like, but I actually fancied our chances against United. We had lost only once in our previous 12 games and we were at home. There was confidence in our camp and the desire to win. Put those ingredients together and you have to come up with a reasonable prospect.

Of course, confident dreams are one thing – refereeing decisions and a bit of magic from players in the right place at the right time are something else. The game was only 14 minutes old when Charlie Hartfield did something very silly and tried to get physical with Eric Cantona. He said that he was provoked, and he probably was, but no matter who did what to who it's better to stay out of things like that. The result was that he got the red card from referee Robbie Hart, who was a bit prone to whipping out red cards like they were discount vouchers from the local supermarket.

I was not happy with Hartfield getting sent off and told him so. He was handed out a fine by the club and the FA punished him as well. I also believe that it cost us the game. It is hard enough playing against Manchester United, but when you have to play 75 minutes with only ten men it is almost impossible.

We held out, though, until the last ten minutes and I still think that we were denied a penalty when Steve Bruce brought down Nathan Blake. The players worked so deperately hard but Mark Hughes scored with ten minutes to go and our shoulders sagged. Cantona, who had run the show in his own magical way, added a second two minutes later – and that was the end of our FA Cup 'run' for another season.

I don't think that game did us a lot of good psychologically because we should have taken it out on Millwall, who we played at home the following weekend. As it was we drew 1–1 even though they were reduced to ten. True, we had gone another First Division game without defeat, but our performance was jaded and I didn't like the look of it.

While all this was going on, the speculation of whether or not Reg Brealey had a buyer continued to mount. I tried to shield the players and myself from it because there seemed to be so many wild goose chases and, to be perfectly honest, the whole thing was becoming something of a farce. I needed to keep our attention focused on promotion so I treated everything that I heard with the air of someone reading about yet another Elvis sighting.

We were off to Bristol City the following Saturday and we didn't know for sure that we would be playing until two hours before the kick-off. In hindsight I wish that we hadn't. The West Country had been drenched by torrential rain and there was a constant threat that it would turn to snow – which it did before the afternoon was over. Our troubles started just before the game when Alan Kelly turned his ankle in the warm-up and I had to replace him with Billy Mercer. The pitch conditions did not get any better and decent football was out of the question. It was goalless at half-time and it did not look as if anyone would get the ball in the net. Our skipper, Brian Gayle, proved me wrong again. First he got himself into a tangle about ten minutes into the second half and put one into our net – but then, to make up for it, he scored another at the other end 12 minutes later to put us back on terms. Just before our equaliser the referee, Paul Allcock, decided that he should muscle in on the act and get his name in the papers for more than just allowing a game that should have been called off. Kevin Gage tangled – and I do mean tangled – with City's Rob Edwards and Allcock sent him off. Even Edwards was amazed because they had really just tangled. There were no fisticuffs and no foul, although the referee saw it as a foul. I watched the video over and over and the more I watched it, the more ridiculous it seemed. I even wrote to the referee and the FA and asked them to reconsider, sending the video as evidence of a mistake. It didn't make any difference of course. Funnily enough, the referee was the same Paul Allcock who gained some further fame later, for sending off Paolo Di Canio amid a scene that looked like something out of WWF.

We made up for that disappointment with a useful 3–2 win at Derby. It was a particularly satisfying win since Sheffield United had not won at the Baseball Ground for nearly 50 years – and we did so without half of the first team. Injuries and suspensions had taken their toll and I thought that we were in for a hot afternoon as Derby had been doing well up until then. One of the aspects of the win that really pleased me was the number of Blades fans who had made the trip. There were so many that the kick-off was delayed to get them all into the ground. A good performance, good support and a three-point result. I was beginning to think that we really had turned a corner.

We were undefeated throughout February. The Derby win was followed by a 1–1 draw at home to Stoke, and then a 3–1 win at Southend. That game was a bit of a nightmare in that once again we had half the team out for one reason or another. We also beat Burnley 2–0 at home but it was a dreadful performance. Nathan Blake scored both goals but I was very disappointed that we did not play much better against a struggling side like Burnley. To be blunt we were awful and it was only the fact that Burnley were no better that saved the day for us.

The game at Oldham was not for the faint-hearted. It was not a dirty game – hard, but not dirty. The thrills were from the all-out attack and the six goals that we shared. We were a goal down after four minutes, level three minutes later, ahead a quarter of an hour after that and level again by half-time. Oldham took the lead again half-way through the second half and then Jostein Flo scored our equaliser eight minutes from time and we all went home exhausted.

That point against Oldham had taken us to fourth in the table. We were in with a realistic chance of at least a Play-off place, and it was not out of the question that we could do even better than that. However, I was very aware that we had a very fragile squad. A couple of times I had been forced to dig deep into our reserves when half the first-team regulars were not available and I realised that, while we had some very good young reserve players, we still needed a bit more experience. I sounded out several clubs but there was not a lot doing at the sort of money that I had available and deadline day was fast approaching. I took Kingsley Black from Nottingham Forest on a loan deal and that was about all I could manage. Everyone else was either out of financial reach or just didn't fancy a move to our part of Sheffield.

I was pleased that Jostein Flo was returning to form. I had made a mistake with him. He had been in the 1994 World Cup with Norway and, like a lot of players, he had needed a rest which he hadn't got. His form had suffered as a result of that and the fans were beginning to get at him a bit. He was an honest player, though, and worthy of support. As we began the wind-up to the climax of the season he was beginning to hit form again and I thought that he might benefit from the service of Kingsley Black.

I took the players to Cyprus for a week before we began our March campaign. It was a sunny week of sea, sand and air which, I hoped, would set us up for the run-in. We returned to a home match with Port Vale and they turned out to be a tough nut to crack. We drew 1–1 and with better finishing we could have taken all three points.

The chances were there but it just didn't happen and we had to be content with only one point while our potential Play-off rivals took three. We were still fifth, though, which meant that, with only one team being automatically promoted as champions, we were still in the Play-off frame – but with a battle to keep ahead of Wolves who were a point behind and had played three less games than us.

Tranmere were top of the table and they were next on our fixture list. We had to beat them to keep our hopes alive – but they also had to beat us if they were to keep their place in pole position. Two days earlier they had won at Sunderland in a Sunday game, so John Aldridge and his men were pretty confident when they arrived at Bramall Lane. Kingsley Black made himself an instant hero when he put us ahead after only three minutes and an exciting game followed. It remained in the balance until a great flick from Jostein Flo put Nathan Blake in a perfect position and he wrapped it up for us with our second goal. We had now had only one League defeat in 17 games and that Play-off place was looking comfortable.

It was a blow when Notts County beat us in our next game. They had not been going very well and we should have had at least a point. As it was, we lost more than the game with that 2–1 defeat. We also lost Mitch Ward who had been in good form in recent weeks. He suffered a punctured lung in a collision and that was the end of his season. We lost another player in our next game, at home to Charlton. John Reed sustained the dreaded cruciate ligament injury and that was his season finished. We won the game 2–1, but it was far from convincing.

Nathan Blake had attracted a bit of interest from various clubs and I had put a £1.5 million price-tag on him. I knew that other managers were into six figures every time that you asked about a player, so I thought that I might as well join them. I didn't want to lose him anyway so I had stuck to my guns as the transfer deadline approached, and I was glad that I had because he had been playing so well. He was like a man inspired when we played away to Bolton, who were one of our chief rivals. Probably he tried too hard and would have scored more goals if he had been more relaxed. As it was he hit one and that was enough to bring us a valuable point.

The club had organised a 'Family Day' for our next home match, against Reading, and 19,241 turned up for it. I did wonder where some of them had been while we were battling away for promotion, but I decided to keep my mouth shut for a change. It was a happy day for David Tuttle who was making his first appearance of the season after recovering from a cruciate ligament injury. He had a great game and must have inspired John Reed who was just embarking on his lay-off with the same problem. Nathan Blake scored again but Reading went home with a 1–1 draw in their pockets and I was left looking at the First Division table which clearly showed that we had just slipped out of the Play-off frame.

We went to Sunderland for April Fool's Day. Peter Reid had just been appointed manager and the Roker boys had a fight on their hands if they were going to get away from relegation. John Wood, one of the Sunderland directors, lived in Sheffield and he approached me to have a chat about things and then asked me if I would be interested in filling the vacancy at Sunderland. This was before Peter Reid was appointed, of course. I thought about it and I did travel to York to meet Bob Murray, and then later met the whole board at Sunderland. The upshot was that I was offered the job, and I must say that I do not have many regrets but I do regret not accepting that offer. Again, I felt loyalty towards Sheffield United and the fans. They could have given me a lot of stick when we were relegated, but they didn't. I could have had my contract reduced but it wasn't so I felt that I still owed the club something. I thought long and hard about it and decided to stay at Bramall Lane. It was a mistake.

Bob Murray and the Board had been superb and I should have joined them at Sunderland. I would go so far as to say that they are the best Board I have ever met and been interviewed by. I spent an anguished evening and night mulling it over. In the end, I turned it down and Bob Murray accepted my decision in a very professional manner. Since then, of course, Peter Reid took the job and has done a fantastic job for the club. I am not envious of him because I had the chance and walked away from it. I regret not taking it, as I regret not having taken the Blackburn job when it was offered in the Autumn of 1999. I should have listened to my wife who told me to go for it on both occasions. It doesn't surprise me that Sunderland has made so much progress, because the club had such a professional Board at the top, and a fine Chairman at the helm.

Anyway, when we played Sunderland, it was a windy sort of day and that meant that it was not going to be a football spectacular. Sunderland turned the screw on us and there were a few frayed tempers in what proved to be a very physical game. In the end we lost David Tuttle who was shown the red card for a so-called professional foul. Then, with a minute to go, Alan Kelly – who had been our best player – found a shot from Russell too hot to handle and it went into the net. No blame to Kelly but most of the others were a let-down and I told them so.

A Play-off place had been in the palm of our hand and now it was trickling through our fingers. A few days later we were on the road again, this time to Portsmouth who were in the relegation battle and not optimistic of survival. We were without a few key players but, even so, there was no reason why we should not revive our own hopes. In the first half we completely dominated the game and it was amazing that we were not three or four goals ahead at half-time. That gave Terry Fenwick's men

Blades boys together. From left to right: the legendary Vinnie Jones, myself, Derek French and Bob Booker.

South of the Watford gap once more! The picture above shows me starting at Crystal Palace and the picture below was taken the morning after I turned down the Manchester City job and decided to stay at Palace.

Above: The Manager and new General Manager of Nottingham Forest in March 1997.

Below: A training session with Nottingham Forest. Here, I am listening to Liam O'Kane, the coach.

Above: Holding aloft the First Division Championship trophy at a civic reception, on Nottingham Forest winning Nationwide Division One.

Below left: Christine and me at the celebration party.

Below right: The trophy, a bottle of bubbly and me!

Time to celebrate. Me with my Manager of the Month award.

Off to Oakwell with Barnsley.

Dennis Wise and I find time for a photo opportunity at Leicester.

Above: Sir Alex Ferguson presents me with a trophy to mark my 1000th game as League manger, in April 2002

Below: The 'old codger' and the 'young sexy one' on the day we were appointed at Leicester.

renewed heart and they went for our throats in the second half. Gerry Creaney scored the only goal of the match on the hour. I watched helplessly as he collected the ball on the halfway line and sprinted untroubled towards our goal before planting his shot perfectly. Our whole season flashed before my eyes in that moment and I knew that we had blown it.

Swindon were just about doomed to relegation but they had not given up fighting and, at the very least, were playing for pride. We did not show the same resolve as Steve McMahon's men when they visited us and the game ended disappointingly in a 2–2 draw which had the supporters shaking their heads and me banging mine against a wall yet again. I said so at the time and I'll repeat it now we were appalling in the first half and not much better in the second. You would never have thought that we were a side who needed every possible point to fulfil a slim chance of a Play-off place.

I began to wonder what would motivate the players. My answer came in the very next game which was away to champions-elect, Middlesbrough. There was a full house and a great occasion to which my players rose almost by their own spirit. They were transformed and looked more like the side heading for the Premiership. The game had its rough moments as well. Fuchs was sent off and quite rightly so, and I felt that the referee could have paid closer attention to Fjortoft who seemed over-keen to win free-kicks and get everyone else into trouble. The game ended in a 1–1 draw with both Bryan Robson and myself giving it some verbal — although for different reasons. He thought that the referee was wrong in sending off Fuchs and I thought he was wrong for not taking firmer action with one or two more of the 'Boro players.

With only three games left, it would have been easy to have started looking at the holiday brochures again — but there were more fun and games still to come. Our next game was at home to Wolves on the following Saturday but, on the eve of that game, the newspapers were once again engaged in take-over talk.

Stephen Hinchliffe was the latest knight in shining armour to be paraded through the streets around Bramall Lane. A local millionaire, it was said that he was ready, willing and able to take over from Reg Brealey, and a figure of £3.5 million was being thrown around. The supporters were trying to get excited again at the prospect of a new lease of life for their club but Reg Brealey played it down.

I looked at my own position. I had a year left on my contract and I was the third longest-serving manager in the entire Football League. I had served for seven and a half years under three different boards and, under the circumstances, I thought that I had done fairly well. The fans seemed to think so, too, because our relationship was excellent and still is to this day. Yes, I had had a few whispers in my ear from other clubs, but I had never seriously looked beyond the horizon of Sheffield. Now I didn't know what to think. A new owner might not want me to stay and, on the other hand, I might not want to stay if the situation was going to remain just the same. I knew that if there was no extra income we would just be going through the same motions for season after season. I looked at the dump which used to be the John Street Stand. Still nothing had happened there, and I felt that it was symbolic of the state of the club.

We still had three games to go. Technically we were not out of the promotion race but, in all sincerity, even the most optimistic person could see that it would take a miracle for the Blades to be in at the Play-off kill. When Wolves came to Bramall Lane, Graham Taylor was their manager. It was a fairly hammer-and-tongs sort of game which could have gone either way, rather like our previous encounter at Molineux when they scored twice in the last two minutes to grab a point. This time it was us who did the grabbing. Wolves were winning 3-2 until Jostein Flo hit the equaliser just on the final whistle.

I don't think that Graham Taylor was very happy, but he was to get a lot less happy just a few minutes later when someone spat on him as he was about to go up the players' tunnel. He dived into the crowd to confront the so-called fan and managed to grab him for a moment but then lost him in the general melee. We were able to identify him, though, because he was known to a few of our youth players and, as far as we were concerned, he was banned from that moment. Nobody deserves that sort of foul treatment. It was a cowardly and disgusting thing to do and I had no hesitation in apologising to Graham on behalf of the club. To his credit he decided not to make a fuss and left it to us to sort out.

Our final away game of the season was at Barnsley, a typical SouthYorkshire derby with pride at stake – and for the home side still a chance of a Play-off place. It was a niggly sort of a game. Barnsley went ahead but we equalised just before half-time. I thought that we were probably going to get at least a point but, somehow we just dried up in the second half after Barnsley took the lead again within a few minutes of the restart. Five minutes from the end, Glyn Hodges received his third red card of the season for using 'foul, abusive language', which still puzzles me. I didn't see how the referee could single out Glyn when there were 10,844 people watching the game, most of whom were using the same sort of vocabulary.

And so, in eighth place, we came to our last game of the season. We were at home to Grimsby Town and, despite the disappointment, Bramall Lane was in party mood. We had missed out on promotion, but we had had more successes than failures and the fans were delighted when Reg Brealey played a master card by announcing, on the last day, that work would definitely be starting on the new John Street Stand.

The game was played in a festive spirit. There were no bookings, we won and at the end there was a lot of singing and dancing on the terraces. I even got carried away at the sight of so many fans in fancy dress and threw them some of the clothes that I was wearing. I didn't go as far as I had done on one or two past occasions, but most people, other than my wife, seemed to think it was a bit of fun to see the manager running around Bramall Lane in his underwear. We had failed in our bid for promotion, but that didn't seem to matter at that moment.

We went on a six-day club tour to Sicily just to wrap up the season but, before we went, it seemed that Reg Brealey had been busy. He had clinched a sponsorship deal with Ward's the Sheffield brewers, which was reported to be the biggest deal outside the Premiership. It meant that the ten-year association with the Arnold Laver company was at an end but that was the price of progress. Brealey had also revealed plans for a new £3.5 million training complex, reiterated that work would soon start on the John Street Stand and that there would be money available for new players. That was the sort of music that my ears had been wanting to hear for some time.

'If Dave Bassett is recommending changes, we will do our best to support him – and there will be a certain amount of money available,' said Brealey. He added, 'He will have to revise his squad but there will be no need for wholesale changes.

'Off the field we have finished the season on a high, and hopefully this will inspire the team. People must realise, however, that we don't have Jack Walker or Jack Hayward's millions. There will be a lot of belt-tightening across football this year and I will not put the club in a vulnerable position. Relegation cost us around £1.5 million and we have needed good management to put things back in place. I am now optimistic that we will get the roll-of-the-board next season.'

It was quite a speech. I had said all along that all I wanted to hear was that the club had ambition. I was not clamouring for millions of pounds — just a million-dollar attitude towards progress. Brealey had said nothing about other parties taking the club over, and really he said little that had not been said before, but — with the increase in sponsorship — there was the chance that this time it really might work out.

Since we are now on the countdown to BE Day (Bassett's Exit), perhaps it would be good to take a fleeting stock of the situation. Stephen Hinchcliffe and Bernard Proctor were on the boardroom scene and I was able to talk to them openly about how I felt. When the Blades were relegated I felt that I should have left and the club be given a fresh start with someone else. I had had such overwhelming encouragement, from football fans all over Britain and overseas to stay on and take the Blades back to the top, that I would have felt as if I were deserting a ship full of goodwill if I had. I also had a number of encouraging letters and faxes from other managers. During the time that followed, whenever I got uptight about the situation, I was able to discuss it with Hinchliffe, Proctor or Derek Dooley and they all encouraged me to hang on.

Reg Brealey had promised money for players and I had a good look around to see who was available. I ended up with Mark Beard who cost us £117,500 from Millwall at the start of the 1995–96 season, and Paul Holland who I had signed in June from Mansfield for £200,000. Paul Beesley went to Leeds for £250,000, and so, by the time that the new season was under way, I had spent the princely sum of £67,500. The big money for players would 'be available soon' — as I was frequently told.

I had heard a whisper that Crystal Palace would be interested in me joining them and the newspapers soon got hold of that. It was also said that Manchester City were interested but I can honestly say that nothing was ever said to me about it. I thought about the Palace possibility but no other club was involved at all. Someone even suggested that I might replace Trevor Francis at Sheffield Wednesday – but that was never mentioned to me either. Managers get linked with all sorts of clubs but it is nearly always just newspaper conjecture, instantly forgotten when a new manager has been appointed – or perhaps boasted about if, by some fluke, the writer's prediction happens to come true.

There was still a year to run on my contract and an extended version was being negotiated. Hinchcliffe and Proctor were the prime movers in getting me to stay. They were the only ones who actually seemed keen for me to remain. Brealey wasn't like that. If he even discussed it, he went about it with the same attitude as someone buying a bag of crisps – it wasn't a matter of life and death and he never actually said that he wanted it.

In the end I agreed to a contract which would go to 1997 with a one-year roll-on. I had never actually wanted to leave Sheffield United, but I did want assurances that the club wanted to go forward. We seemed to have gone backward for a couple of seasons and I needed to know that this was not to be a long-term proposition. I was told that until new funds were in place I could only spend what I generated in sales of players – but that was nothing new. I could handle any situation just as long as I knew we were all striving for the same goal.

The loyalty of the fans meant a lot to me, too, and I wanted to at least try and give them back their Premiership status.

I went to France to sign Paul Holland. He was playing for England Under-21s in the Toulon tournament and I was keen to get him before anyone else stepped in. At the back of my mind was the fact that I also had players back at Bramall Lane who had not yet signed new contracts and I didn't want to lose any of them. Kevin Gage, John Gannon, Simon Tracey and Adrian Littlejohn were all players that I felt would be necessary for our campaign.

The Blades Independent Fans Association amused me when they formed a band called 'Hanging on to Harry' and started doing gigs around the Sheffield pubs. It was a great gesture and provided some light moments at a tense time.

I did not manage to keep Adrian Littlejohn. He went to Plymouth for an initial £100,000 leading to £200,000 – so, in the end, my summer dealings brought a small profit to the club. However, the biggest bombshell came when Reg Brealey made another of his startling announcements.

Brealey had signed a contract with Mowlem Construction to build the new John Street Stand and they were waiting for the go-ahead to start work. The bombshell was that the club's bankers would not sanction the £3.5 million investment without some very concrete guarantees. The job was supposed to have been started in June and a month later Mowlem were still kicking their heels waiting to get on with it. Brealey said that he knew that, if he asked me to raise the money by selling star players, I would do it – but that it would never come to that. I wish he had asked me.

The red and white side of Sheffield was in uproar. The phone never stopped, the letters flooded in and the shareholders demanded an extraordinary meeting. Brealey had once again placed himself in the middle of the dartboard. At the same time, I personally received a number of messages from supporters saying that, if it were not for me, they would give up – their way of making sure that I was not about to walk out.

July continued in pandemonium. Mike McDonald confirmed that he had been having buy-out talks with Brealey. Stephen Hinchcliffe remained in a position to take over the reins and nobody knew what was really happening. Brealey had admitted to signing a contract which the club could not afford when he did the deal for the new stand. The consequences being that the club was committed to the deal and that meant spending money one way or another – building the stand or in legal fees. I got on well with Stephen Hinchliffe and he told me that he felt that he was getting closer to a deal but that, at the same time, Mike McDonald was also getting closer. Bernard Proctor, who didn't have confidence in Brealey, kept assuring me that it would turn out all right in the end but, while all this was going on, I must admit that I was getting the hump because I could not get on with the team rebuilding job that I wanted to do.

We reached the end of July and I took the team on a pre-season tour of Norway. While we were away, Mike McDonald's bid seemed to hit a stumbling block over the rebuilding of the John Street Stand because he wanted his own company to take on the project and also wanted a different design. Personally I was past caring who would build the stand or what it would look like. I was beginning to think that perhaps we could make a few bob by renting out allotments.

Just before the season started I offered Trevor Francis the chance to join us. He had just left Sheffield Wednesday as manager and everybody thought it was another 'Barmy Bassettism', but I was serious. I didn't expect him to play a 90-minute game for us, but I thought he would be handy on the bench, or even to start a game, and I knew that the players would benefit from having him around. Trev thought about it but didn't want to take himself out of the management market so we shook hands and forgot about it.

It all went very quiet on the takeover front as the season started. We began away to Watford and they beat us. It was the first time that they had put one over on me since I had left there. It was not the start that I wanted but it was still early days. Our first home match followed and Tranmere were the visitors. John Aldridge proved that he is ageless by scoring twice and I had to give my players a roasting for losing 2–0 in front of their own fans. At Oldham in the next game the trend continued, and it didn't help when Brian Gayle was sent off after 26 minutes. We lost 2–1. I was unhappy with Brian Gayle after that and I fined him after watching a video of the incident in which he stamped on Sean McCarthy. It was clear that McCarthy had been provoking him, but there was no excuse for losing his cool like that and it probably cost us the match. The £1,500 fine gave him something to think about.

So far we had scored twice, both goals from Nathan Blake, and we had conceded six goals. I could live with defeat but I could not tolerate poor performance and I gave the players a going over in public. I said that I was ready to ditch the experienced players and bring in the kids if they did not improve. I meant it too. If you are losing you might as well gamble on enthusiasm and at the very least bring on the young players together – rather as Alex Ferguson has done at Manchester United.

To end August we entertained Crystal Palace. My demand for an improvement by the players appeared not to have fallen on deaf ears as we went into a 2–1 lead. What was strange was that I was without several players who would have been automatic first choices. The first half was a bit lacklustre but we came to life in the second half. With five minutes left we were heading for our first points of the season – but we were then hit by an attack of generosity and in the next few minutes Palace scored twice to win.

The players were booed off the pitch and that said it all. There was no point in giving them another roasting. The trouble was, I knew that they were capable of winning us promotion. If they could only take their abilities and ambitions on to the pitch with them we would be all right. For me personally it was one of those weeks. The morning after the Palace match I was fined for speeding and the following day I got a parking ticket. I didn't bother buying a lottery ticket that week!

After a fifth defeat on the trot – going down 1–3 at West Bromwich – we were bottom of the table and had dropped 15 points.

So when Norwich came the following Saturday we knew that we just had to get something out of the match – but we didn't quite expect it to happen as it did. Norwich have always been a good side and I thought that we were going to be in trouble again when they took the lead. However, just before half-time Nathan Blake headed us back on terms. Bryan Gunn, the Norwich goalie, went loopy at the referee and carried it on as they went down the tunnel at half-time. He didn't come out for the second half because the ref showed him the red card for his language. The second half was just over 20 minutes old when another Canary was sent back to the nest. Robert Fleck got the red card for dissent. You would have thought that he would have learned from what had happened to Gunn. Four minutes after Fleck went, Carl Veart put us ahead and it stayed that way. It was a strange game but a brilliant scoreline for us. A few days later we beat Charlton 2–0 at home and then our next game resulted in a 2–2 draw at Barnsley. It was a great improvement and there was light at the end of the tunnel – I didn't realise that it was the light of an onrushing train.

We got another shock after the Charlton game when it was discovered that the month's salaries had not been paid. These were usually paid direct into everyone's accounts on the 14th of the month but it hadn't happened. It was humiliating for the club but it did, at last, prompt some further action since Brealey was forced out into the open once again. Bernard Proctor went on the warpath a bit and told Brealey that something had to be done to overcome the takeover stalemate. We all received payment cheques but the worry was whether or not we would have to go through the same problem the following month. To their credit the players shrugged it off, as could be seen by their commitment when we played at Barnsley that weekend.

At last the takeover was announced. Mike McDonald had won the day and Brealey was out. I had meetings with Mike McDonald and, to be honest, I got the impression that he really didn't want me there. Some press contacts had told me that he had leaked the news that I was going to be removed. He went through the motions of talking things out but his body language was more that of someone who, although he is interviewing you, has already placed the job elsewhere. Also I had taken David White on loan from Leeds and knew he was acting as a mole for his dad, who was then a director of the club. My suspicions were further aroused when I was told that Adrian Heath was making a study of our players when we played at Port Vale some weeks later. Heath was closely linked with Howard Kendall.

McDonald brought in a new wave of enthusiasm. The supporters were told that the new stand would be started immediately – and he was as good as his word. As far as I was concerned, McDonald publicly said that he was happy with me and that he had no problem with my being there. I believed him. I'm that kind of a person. I wasn't sure that it was a good idea for me to still be there, however. And we all know the old joke about a vote of confidence from the directors being the same thing as a kiss of death!

Towards the end of September we played Huddersfield and beat them 2–1. Our results continued to be a bit topsy-turvy and I made several pleas for some real money to strengthen the squad. It wasn't until the middle of October that we discovered that Mike McDonald was bailing the club out financially, even though his deal with Brealey was not yet fully completed. There was a legal wrangle over some of the shares which were still in the hands of Paul Woolhouse. It was all a bit messy and McDonald threatened to jack it in at one stage – although I don't know if he really meant it.

The matter was resolved, of course, and I was waiting for some cash for transfers. At that stage I was still in profit from sales and, at the very least, I wanted that to be released to me – but it was not forthcoming. I made a move for Kevin Muscat, an Australian defender who would cost us £200,000 from South Melbourne, but the deal was blocked by my own directors and I was told that I would have to wait until the transfer of control was finally completed. I had no choice but to accept the situation as it stood, but I was far from happy about it.

It was the middle of November when we played at Port Vale and Adrian Heath was seen looking at our players. We won 3–2 at Vale Park and we should have been smiling, but there was so much happening behind the scenes that the games were almost an interruption. The salary situation was still up in the air and the PFA even loaned the club £50,000 to help pay the players. I had David White on loan from Leeds, as our transfer ban remained. It was very frustrating, no, much more than that – I was very annoyed.

I finally blew my stack at a board meeting at the end of November. The takeover had still not been resolved and I still could not buy anybody. I was fed up to the back teeth. It was the worst situation that I had ever faced as a manager, and all because people were not telling the truth or living up to their promises. I felt that most of the board just didn't care what was happening. It was all some sort of game. I told the board that I was fed up with hearing lies about everything. I don't think that I won many friends, but I was sick to death of this supposed takeover and all its implications and the fact that it was taking longer than the Magna Carta to work out.

At last, however, the takeover was completed. I demanded money for transfers again and I was fobbed off for a short while. It was ridiculous. Mike McDonald knew what he wanted and said all the right things. Unlike Brealey, I think that he mostly meant them too. He had annoyed me earlier when he publicly had a go at the players even before the deal had been done. I have never agreed with that. I don't blame directors for airing their views to the manager, but I don't like them having a go to the press about the players. It undermines morale and you don't need that when things are already difficult.

Should I stay and fight on, or should I go? That was the question. I didn't feel that McDonald wanted me there, and all the signs pointed to the fact that it was only a matter of time before something else happened that would force a conclusion. On 9 December 1995 we were at home to Huddersfield and lost 2–0. It was my last game in charge. Funnily enough, I won a lottery prize of a £2,000 holiday during half-time. We lost, but we opened a bottle of champagne after the game in the physio's room and everyone knew that it was the end. I told Stephen Hinchliffe and Bernard Proctor during the weekend, and then told Mike McDonald formally on the Monday.

It was the end of the Bassett era at Bramall Lane.

17

What Happened Next

I WAS NOT BITING MY NAILS WHEN I LEFT SHEFFIELD UNITED. I actually felt that a weight had been lifted from my shoulders. I was saddened at leaving behind the supporters and the staff, all of whom had become good colleagues during my years at Bramall Lane, and it helped that I was not leaving Sheffield itself because I knew that I would be bumping into those people fairly often. When I first joined the Blades a lot of people thought that this 'Chirpy Cockney' would never settle in Sheffield – yet the truth is my family and myself took to the place instantly and, even when I left the club, we did not start packing our bags or begin house-hunting back in London. We had no intention of leaving. In fact, we still live there and, when I was at Palace, we had a flat in Wimbledon but returned home to Sheffield as often as the job would allow.

There was no rush for me to find a job but it did not take long for the telephone to start ringing. It was mostly media work, match comments for television and radio and the after-dinner appearances that I had done so often before. There was a full-time job going that interested me and I made a number of enquiries. Jack Charlton had ended his wonderful reign as manager of the Republic of Ireland side and a replacement was being sought. There were a number of favourites for the job but I fancied it myself and I wondered if I might be considered. Most of the names being suggested were of Irish origin – but Jack Charlton wasn't of course – and I wondered if they might give another Englishman the chance. I had all the qualifications – I didn't have an Irish accent but I did enjoy a glass of Guinness.

I didn't really think that I had a chance but Bobby Gould encouraged me to have a go. He had been successful in his application for the Wales job and urged me to chance my arm. I phoned Johnny Giles and asked him if he thought I would be wasting my time. John made a few enquiries among his many contacts in Ireland and called me back to say that the Football Association of Ireland would not be averse to hearing from me. I telephoned the FAI and I was invited for an interview which would be held at the Marriott Hotel at Heathrow Airport.

By this time there were just three names in the frame. Mick McCarthy seemed to be the favourite but Joe Kinnear was also in there and, of course, yours truly. I was the odd one out because the other two knew the name of the river that flows through Dublin. I seemed to have acquitted myself quite well, though, because I was later invited to a second interview – this time at Gatwick. The following day Mick McCarthy was named as the new manager, but I think I came very close to becoming an international manager. That would have given the critics plenty of mileage, wouldn't it?

As I went through the motions of the Ireland job there was another post open to me. Ron Noades and I had been talking. Actually we had been talking for some time. We were old acquaintances, of course, and we were bound to talk to each other – but there were suggestions that the seat at Crystal Palace was available if I wanted it. I had to smile a little later on when Ron complained about Nottingham Forest making 'illegal approaches' to me, because it was a bit naughty of him to say that. His several suggestions about the Palace job had fallen into the same category because not all our conversations along those lines took place after I had left Sheffield United. It is common practice in football for managers to be approached by hints and suggestions, on a direct basis or through a third party – often a journalist, or someone in a similar position.

I was talking to Ron about the Palace job while I was also applying for the Ireland post, and I had made no secret of the fact that the international job would be my first choice. He respected that and I kept him in touch with developments. When it fell through we agreed that I would become the new manager of Crystal Palace.

Of course it was not the first time that I had been named manager of Palace and there were some who were quick to point out that I had left in record time when I was last appointed. You learn to take those sort of remarks in your stride. I was more interested in getting my new club on their way up the table. Ray Lewington had been joint manager with Peter Nicholas before me and he became first-team coach when I arrived. Ray knows his stuff but somehow things had not gelled and when I became boss, on 8 February 1996, Palace were 16th in the table after a goalless draw at Charlton.

Ron Noades had earned a bit of a reputation that he interfered with team selection and so I made it quite clear from the start that I was nobody's puppet. As manager, all team responsibilities were mine, and mine alone. Ron knew me well enough to realise that I meant it and he had no problem with that. My head was on the block if it all went horribly wrong, so I reserved the right to make my own mistakes and not to be helped in making them.

Steve Coppell was still at the club as technical director and he concentrated chiefly on the development of youth-team players. Steve and I got on very well and I have always had the utmost respect for him. I had a two-and-a-half year contract, which took me to the end of the 1997–98 season, and I had a job to do. I welcomed the input of Steve, Ray and Peter Nicholas – who was the joint first-team coach. When I talked to Ron about joining Palace I was keen that there should be no casualties just because of my arrival. I didn't want people out of work because of me. I learned that there had been some differences of opinion over tactics between Ron Noades and Ray Lewington, which is why I made it clear, both to Ron and through the press, that I would not stand for any interference from the chairman on other team matters.

The scriptwriters could not have dreamed up a better scenario for my first game after joining Palace. We had a home match – against Sheffield United. I wanted a win, of course – but no more than I would have done against any other team. I didn't even select the team because I wanted the chance to watch everyone. Ray Lewington and Peter Nicholas chose the side and we went into action with me as an almost innocent bystander. Howard Kendall had changed a number of the faces at Bramall Lane so there was only a handful of my old players on duty for the Blades that day – but we all shook hands and got on with the game.

One of the reasons why Palace were well down the First Division table was not because of their lack of victories. Now I know that seems a pretty stupid thing to say, but in fact it was very true because they had not really suffered that many defeats. They had failed to turn home advantage into three points on too many occasions – and it was no different when we played Sheffield United. The game ended in a 0–0 draw and the club had now experienced 12 drawn games out of 27 – more than anyone else in the First Division. They had lost only seven games so we had to work on turning those stalemates into victories.

My first real challenge was at home the following Saturday when we were due to play another of my old clubs, Watford. We made just a few changes but the performance was completely different and two goals each from Doug Freedman and Bruce Dyer gave us the best win of the season at 4–0. It was just what the doctor ordered.

We travelled to Tranmere a few days later, full of confidence. At half-time we were shaking our heads because they were two goals to the good. We hadn't played badly but I knew that we could do better and I said so. We scored three goals in the last half an hour and brought home the points. We came a cropper at the weekend, though, when we caved in to a first-half onslaught from Huddersfield and were three goals behind when we went in. There was no way back this time but we did not concede any more goals.

Bruce Dyer returned from a two-match suspension in time for our home game against Birmingham — and he celebrated with a hat-trick. Birmingham put up a fight but we finished as 3–2 winners and Barry Fry was gracious in defeat when he said that his men had been beaten by a team he expected to see in the Premiership the following season. That was quite a statement considering that we were only in the middle of the table — but it nearly turned out to be true.

A goalless draw at Luton was followed by the biggest Palace win of the season, 5–0 at home to Grimsby. It was sensational stuff as we scored all five goals in the first 24 minutes with Dougie Freedman helping himself to a hat-trick in 11 minutes. Grimsby shut up shop completely otherwise we would probably have gone for a cricket score. The supporters had the time of their lives and did so again the following weekend when we beat West Bromwich 1–0 at home.

During that week I had been in touch with my old club and did a deal to bring David Tuttle and Carl Veart to Selhurst Park in exchange for Gareth Taylor and £400,000. I thought that they could give us just the options we needed if we were seriously in for a chance of the Play-offs. By the time that the results came in from the other games played while we were beating West Brom, we found that we were now fifth in the table and were indeed in the frame for the Play-offs. Now we had to make sure that we stayed there.

We did the double over Tranmere when they visited us. It looked as if we were heading for a 1–1 draw, but a late goal from David Hopkin proved to be the winner. Then we completed the double over Grimsby by beating them 2–0 at their place, and we were all set for the run-in when Bruce Dyer got both goals as we beat Luton 2–0 at home. We were now third in the table and there was a chance that we might do even better than the Play-offs – although Derby and Sunderland were in commanding positions above us. Portsmouth were our next visitors and they had clearly come for a point. They strangled us with their offside trap and we didn't show the initiative to beat it. As a result we drew 0–0. Our cause was not helped by the referee who disallowed a 'goal' because the ball crossed the line as he blew the final whistle. It was a ridiculous and costly decision.

Confidence is all-important in football. Sometimes you can build it up so much that the players think that they can walk on water. At other times you have to be very careful that one slight hiccup does not undermine the whole job. I was aware that the Portsmouth result was a disappointment and that we had to bounce back very quickly. An away match against South London rivals Millwall was next on the agenda and would give us the perfect opportunity to restore our positive attitude.

It worked. Millwall put up quite a fight but we remained cool in a highly-charged atmosphere. George Ndah kept up his impressive scoring record with two of the goals as we beat them 4–1.

We were within range of second-placed Derby in the First Division, and a win over Port Vale in our next game would have helped – but they were on a run of six successive wins and had ambitions of their own. The 2–2 result was probably a fair one but not the one we wanted – especially since Derby lost on the same day and Sunderland drew. If we had taken maximum points it might have made a difference. In fact, if we had taken maximum points from both this and the Portsmouth home game, then we would almost certainly have been second in the table and in a place for automatic promotion.

There was worse to come because we then lost 1–0 at home to our rivals Leicester City. We threw everything at them but their defence held firm and moved them to within one place of the Play-off frame, while we remained third.

I received the Manager of the Month award which was very nice but sometimes brings with it the kiss of death. The number of times that managers have been handed their award before a game, which they then go on to lose, is quite frightening. As it was, we returned to winning ways with a 2–0 success at Reading. David Tuttle was sent off for getting two yellow cards but that was the only set-back. I suddenly realised that if only we could beat Southend at home in our next game we were assured of a place in the Play-offs. Dougie Freedman duly obliged with both goals in a 2–0 win and we started to get into party mood.

We were only two points behind Derby, who were in second place, so when we went to Wolves we were determined to bring home all three points. Derby drew that day and we delivered a great performance to win 2–0. It was now neck and neck with two games to go.

Our penultimate game of the season was the big one – a crunch match at Derby County's Baseball Ground. If Derby won it, then they would get automatic promotion and we would face the slog of the Play-offs. Any other result and it would go to the last game, where Derby had to visit West Brom and we were at home to Norwich. It was as simple as that. The rest of the First Division played on the Saturday and a goalless draw was enough to confirm Sunderland as champions of the division.

To say the least the atmosphere at the Baseball Ground was electric. The players were wound up, not only with the will to win but also with the fear that one mistake could mean all the difference between finishing second or third. Derby's lightning-fast striker Dean Sturridge had the place in uproar when he scored after only three minutes – and the noise had not died down when Bruce Dyer put over the cross that Kenny Brown, on loan from West Ham, sent flying into the net for our equaliser. We were all on our feet and the game kept us that way right up to half-time. I called for a last big effort and I could not fault the work that was put in. It was one of Derby's two Dutchmen, Robin Van Der Laan, who sealed the game. We left him unmarked at a corner and he headed home. Derby knew that they had the initiative and marshalled their defence for the rest of the game to keep us out. Our shoulders sagged at the end of the game and we trooped off while Derby went on a lap of honour, knowing that they had clinched promotion.

We had to play Charlton of all people in our Play-off semi-final and both legs were well worth the entrance money. The first game was at The Valley and they scared the pants off us when Shaun Newton scored after 55 seconds. We tried everything to get back into the game but nothing was working until Kenny Brown latched on to a rebound about halfway through the second half and put us back on level terms. Carl Veart, who I had signed from Sheffield United and who was in a rich vein of form, put us ahead about seven minutes later and that was the advantage that we took to the return leg a few days later.

It was our turn to set the game alight early on and Ray Houghton did just that with a cracking goal after only four minutes. It proved to be the only goal of the game and the aggregate 3–1 scoreline meant that I was taking a team to Wembley again. Leicester City's 1–0 aggregate win over Stoke put them in the opposite corner.

We played the 1996 First Division Play-off Final on the Bank Holiday Monday at the end of May with just over 73,000 people at Wembley. Memories of my previous visit with Sheffield United came flooding back to me and I didn't want to go home empty-handed for a second time. When Andy Roberts scored with a 20-yard beauty after 13 minutes, I began to see places like Old Trafford and Anfield flashing before my eyes. The score remained the same until 14 minutes before the end when the referee judged that Muzzy Izzet had been tripped in the box by Edworthy. Garry Parker took the penalty, Nigel Martyn did his best but the ball went into the net. Leicester had put us under a lot of pressure and there were those who said that the equaliser was deserved – but you don't always get what you deserve in football and I was annoyed that we were back on level terms.

Extra-time followed and, if anything, I would say that we probably deserved a goal but, like I said, you don't always get what you deserve. Just as the referee was looking at his watch at the end of 120 minutes, Steve Claridge decided to have one last shot. He completely mis-hit the ball from 18 yards out – but that only served to fool everyone and somehow the ball bounced over the line. It was a total fluke and we all stared in disbelief; but it was enough to put Leicester in the Premiership and leave Crystal Palace as also-rans – another bout of 90th-minutitis.

My mother had been unable to attend the play-off final due to being unwell and confined to her bed. I went to see her in the evening after the match, and then again a few days later in hospital, but little was I to know that this would be the last time I would see her. On 6 June, the next day, she died peacefully. She was a strong character and a little intimidating – perhaps that's where I get some of my stubbornness from.

Not a lot happened that summer. Nigel Martyn went to Leeds for £2.2 million, and Chris Day came from Tottenham for an initial £250,000 going up after a number of games. I was not too happy about the Day signing. It was not that I had any doubts about his ability, but I wanted to sign Simon Tracey from Sheffield United because I felt that we needed to replace Nigel Martyn with another experienced goalkeeper. Ron Noades did not agree and, at the end of the day, he was the one who had to sign the cheque. I feel that my views have been vindicated, however, because many of the defensive errors which let Palace down early last season must be attributed to the need for a more experienced pair of hands between the posts. I cannot stress enough that this is in no way intended as an insult to Chris Day. I just felt that he needed another season or two under his belt before regular first-team action for Palace.

Apart from that difference of opinion with Ron, everything else went fairly smoothly during the summer of 1996. We were all interested in watching the European Championships and had plenty to say about it. Once it was over we took our knotted handkerchiefs off our heads and got back to work. We were placed among the favourites for promotion and expectation was running high. We had to try and live up to it.

Our first game was the day after everybody else had started. We were to travel to Birmingham City for a Sunday game in front of the Sky TV cameras and, once again, I found myself sitting in the opposite dug-out to Trevor Francis, my old adversary from Sheffield. He seemed to be enjoying his new job as Birmingham's manager and I was pleased for him. It was an incredibly hot August afternoon – so hot in fact that two of the

Birmingham players were taken ill. The result went against us when Paul Devlin took advantage of a defensive error and sent a shot in off the post. It was the only goal of the game and we had started just as I had not wanted – in defeat. It was little compensation that we had played them off the park.

When we played our first home game the following weekend, we were determined to make amends. Oldham were our visitors and we had the game wrapped up in the first half. We led 3–0 at half-time. Oldham pulled one back but they didn't trouble us beyond that and I was quite happy with our performance. We drew our next two games, 0–0 at home to West Bromwich and 1–1 away to Huddersfield – but there were other things going on in a different part of the country that were also to involve yours truly.

Manchester City had been relegated at the end of the previous season and they had also got off to a bad start in Division One. Alan Ball had endured a lot of stick for more than a year and, with the new season just a few weeks old, he finally resigned. Francis Lee was on the search for a replacement but I had no idea that he had me in mind. He made an approach to Palace and was given permission to talk to me – or perhaps that should read that he was given permission to talk at me.

There is no doubt that Francis Lee was a great player and, as chairmen go, I have met a lot worse – but, like so many in his position, I think he would really like to be manager and immersed in team affairs, training and travelling with the lads, picking the team and all that sort of stuff. When we met he told me all about himself, his thoughts, his experience, his ambitions – in fact he almost told me his shoe size. I began to wonder who was interviewing who. He never stopped talking about himself, so much so that we had to arrange another meeting so that I could get a word in.

I wanted to ensure that I would be left to run the team and that I could have some cash for players and all the usual requirements that a manager needs to make sure he can do the job properly. I got all the right answers and yet I still felt a little uncomfortable. In fairness, I gave an indication that I would probably accept the job but I said I would go away and give it some more thought before making a final commitment.

That night, in my flat in London, I couldn't sleep. I was concerned that Francis Lee and I would not be compatible. I tossed and turned it over in my mind. I had already discussed it with Chris, my wife, and she was delighted that I would be going to Manchester since it meant that I could live at home in Sheffield. I phoned her again and we talked until midnight. A few hours later I phoned her back again and said that I was still not happy about it. She simply said that she would rather have me home once a week feeling happy than living there all the time being miserable. She was right. Inside I knew that I was going to be unhappy and that it was just not right for me. I phoned Malcolm Webber, my accountant and friend, and told him that I was not going. I don't know why I did that but, when you are having a sleepless night, you like to share it, don't you?

It was seven o'clock in the morning when I phoned Franny Lee. I thought it was a bit presumptuous of him when he told me that he had organised a press conference for later that day to make the official announcement. He didn't believe it when I told him I was staying at Palace. He had a bit of a moan at me – well, a lot of a moan really – and was worried about his image and relationship with the fans. I understood his position but my mind was made up. The more that I had thought about the City job and recalled the things that Franny Lee had told me, the more I realised that the job was not for me.

While all this was going on, the Palace directors were

very understanding. Bernie Coleman and Doug Miller both talked to me and said that they realised what a dilemma I had, but stressed that they wanted me to stay. Ron Noades said virtually nothing. I had no idea whether he wanted me to stay or whether he would have been glad to see the back of me.

At the end of the day I was still manager of Crystal Palace with a job to do, and I got on with it. City finally solved their problem with Frank Clark, but not before Steve Coppell had given it a go and given up after just a few weeks. I think that the same thing might have happened if I had gone to Maine Road.

Don't get me wrong. I would have loved to have gone to Manchester City, a great club with terrific fans, but it was not the right time as the next couple of managers proved. It was not until Francis Lee left and there was a Boardroom reshuffle that the club started to make progress again.

One of my biggest surprises was when Steve became manager of Manchester City. We used to jog together and at no time did he ever ask me anything about the job, Franny Lee, the interview, why I had turned it down or anything related to it. I would have willingly given him whatever information he had wanted without any sort of bias and, since we got on well, I was surprised that he had not taken advantage of my knowledge and recent experience. As it turned out, he had a disastrous time at Maine Road. He knew within days that he had made a mistake and I know he hated every minute of it.

When I saw him a little later, he looked unwell and I could see that he was suffering greatly from stress. If only he had talked to me, he might have had a bit more information on which to base his final decision.

We ended the month of September 1996 by running riot at Reading with a 6–1 away win. It was the first game since I had decided to stay and we were all in celebration mood. At half-time we were two goals ahead and we turned it on in the second half to give Reading their worst home defeat for nearly 30 years. We both had a player sent off too. Ours was Andy Roberts, for a second bookable offence. We were now fifth in the table and seemed to have found the rhythm of the previous season's exploits.

We sailed through the Coca-Cola Cup second round with a 7–1 aggregate win over Bury and then went goal crazy again a few days later with another 6–1 win, this time at home to Southend. I honestly believe that we could have gone into double figures if we had not got a bit blasé towards the end. We had become the second highest scorers in the entire Premiership and Football League and things were looking good.

We foolishly dropped a couple of points away to Portsmouth when we let them in for an equaliser five minutes from the end. We had done all the hard work and looked good for our 2–1 lead, but that slip kept us fifth in the table when we could have gone up to third. Our next game was at Barnsley and we were grateful to pick up another point there. Barnsley were an under-rated side and, but for a terrific penalty save by Chris Day, they would have beaten us. As it was, I was happy with the 0–0 draw which meant that we had still not been beaten since the opening weekend of the season.

At Port Vale we scored twice in the first quarter of an hour and then consolidated to keep the home side at bay They threw the kitchen sink at us and chipped the woodwork a couple of times but, at the end, we held our 2–0 lead and took all three points. Then we had to face Swindon at home in what turned out to be more of a punch-up in the park than super soccer at Selhurst. We lost 2–1 after scoring the first goal and the game was chiefly remembered for the vendettas breaking out all over the pitch, climaxing in a 16-man brawl in the centre circle. Swindon had Mark Walters sent off but my lot all stayed on. Some of them probably wished they had got an early bath after I had said a few words in the dressing-room when the game was over.

I broke a personal record when we signed Neil Shipperley from Southampton. He cost us £1 million, the most I had ever spent on a player. I considered that we needed him to strengthen our attacking department. He turned out to be a good investment. He was not available when we travelled to Ipswich for the next round of the Coca-Cola Cup but I don't suppose he minded that too much. We scored after four minutes and then mentally went home. Ipswich smashed four goals past us and that was the end of the competition. Things had not gone better with Coke for us.

Our old friends from Grimsby cheered us up a bit the following weekend. They came visiting, Neil Shipperley made his debut and we won 3–0 without too much trouble. If only they were all like that. We ended October in third place and when November started we seemed to have got the bit between our teeth as we won 3–1 at Tranmere. We then beat Queen's Park Rangers 3–0 at our place and drew 2–2 with Bolton, the runaway leaders, at their ground. Bolton had gone two ahead in the first 20 minutes but we were level by half-time and I was pleased with the way we had fought. On reflection we deserved that second place in the table.

More than 20,000 fans turned up at Selhurst Park to see our home match with Wolves and they were treated to one of the most exciting games of the season. Wolves were winning 2–0 at half-time but in the second half we stormed back and made it 2–2. They then got a third and we launched an all-out attack that had them pinned back with every player in their own half for most of the rest of the game. We hit the woodwork and just about everything else but could not get the ball into the net again and, at the end, we had lost 3–2. Somehow that became a turning point.

We were still in second place when we went to Grimsby for our next game. They were struggling near the bottom but on the day they fought for their 2–1 victory. Neil Shipperley had put us ahead after four minutes and the Grimsby fans must have thought they were in for another hiding but, to their credit, the home side fought back and we went home empty-handed.

When we only managed to draw 2–2 at home to Oxford, we slipped to fourth place and, even allowing for injuries, there was obviously something wrong. At Norwich things took a turn for the worse. We drew 1–1 but we had played well enough and three minutes from time there was another mass punch-up in which we had both Ray Houghton and Kevin Muscat sent off.

I was relieved that we beat Charlton 1–0 at home in our next game because we had gone six games without a win and the old nerves were jangling a bit. I was not so happy when we lost again at Ipswich where they followed their League Cup win with a 3–1 First Division victory. It was Boxing Day and I was sat at home with 'flu and it didn't make me feel better to see my team slide down to fifth place having failed to consolidate a position at the top of the table. To make matters worse, the FA charged and fined both Norwich and ourselves with misconduct over the Carrow Road punch-up.

The FA Cup programme was hit by the weather so we did not play our third-round match until after our first Division One game of 1997. We were away to Manchester City where Frank Clark had just been appointed manager. I wished him well, of course, and it was even honours as the game ended 1–1.

When our FA Cup third-round tie was finally staged it still did not reach a conclusion. We drew 2–2 at home to Leeds and we had Nigel Martyn to thank for denying us a victory as he saved a penalty two minutes from the end. It was a bit mean of him, especially as Leeds' second goal was one that we had scored for them! We were the better side on the night and deserved the result. Instead we had to go to Elland Road for the replay – but not before we had lost at home to Portsmouth. We had now gone ten games with only one win – and had even tumbled out of the Play-off zone.

I signed Andy Linighan from Arsenal to bolster our defence and would have liked to have had him in the side for our trip to Leeds for the FA Cup replay. Again we played well, but a brilliant goal from Rod Wallace beat us and now promotion was our sole target.

We continued to be a Jekyll and Hyde side with some really good results, like a 3–0 thrashing of Wolves at Molineux, but some lousy performances, too, and as a result we were up and down the top of the table like a piston. Ron Noades muttered a few times in the background and the atmosphere was beginning to get a little uncomfortable – not among the coaching and playing staff particularly, but just in general.

On 22 February 1997 we were at home to Tranmere Rovers and it was to be a significant match. They had never won at Selhurst Park and it seemed as if they had come with the idea of not losing this time. They put up a wall of defence and relied upon occasional breaks to threaten us. With about 20 minutes left they scored from one of those breakaways and, try though we did, we just couldn't get the equaliser. Tranmere had broken their duck and we had slipped to sixth place.

For me, although I didn't know it at the time, the real significance was that it was to be my last game as manager of Crystal Palace Football Club.

18

Deep in the Forest

NOBODY WAS MORE SURPRISED THAN ME when I got a call asking me about joining Nottingham Forest. I'm not going to say that I wasn't pleased because, quite frankly, I was getting less and less happy at Palace. We were getting results that pointed to us finishing at least in the Play-off zone, but I didn't feel comfortable at Selhurst Park. I wasn't entirely confident that I would not be getting some boardroom interference, and there was a lack of consistency about some players. I wasn't all that pleased about sharing with Wimbledon either. The idea of ground-sharing is all very well but it does mess up your pitch when you have twice as much football being played on it. Contrary to all the jokes, I do like to have a pitch in good condition, partly because of the quality of passing, and partly because it is safer for the players.

I was not looking for a way out of Palace, though, and had Forest not come in for me when they did, I probably would have continued at least until the end of the season. I don't know if I would have stayed any longer than that. Ron Noades was also stalling on extending my contract which gave me an uneasy feeling about the future at Palace. When your family is in Yorkshire and you are having to spend most of your time in a one-bedroomed flat in London, it takes away any pleasure that there might be in managing a decent club like Palace. I not only love my family, I like them as well — and I like to have as much meaningful time as possible with them.

Nottingham Forest presented me with a new challenge. When that was coupled with the prospect of living at home in Sheffield, it was a 'no-contest' decision really. I had no qualms about leaving Palace because I had ensured that there was a clause in my contract which gave me freedom of movement if Palace received sufficient compensation. I know that Ron Noades was reported to be shocked that I left but, with all due respect, he knew the situation and he and I have always understood that our friendship and our business relationship are two entirely separate areas. If he had not been happy with my input at Palace he would have shown me the door without hesitation. That's how it works! Football is a volatile business in which major changes can happen in a shorter time than it takes to play a match. I think Ron had lost interest because, in my opinion, he seemed to have other business commitments which were taking up his time. I am certain he did very well out of the deal when he sold to Mark Goldberg who claimed to have been a life-long Palace fan, although I had never heard of him before. I am sure that Goldberg would have bombed me to get Terry Venables in so I was happy that I had left before it all went totally pear-shaped at the club.

One reporter did question my loyalty. It annoyed me a bit because I had spent 13 years at Wimbledon and eight years at Sheffield United. All the way down the line I had put my clubs first – and had even put my hand into my own pocket to help when it became necessary. The decision to join Nottingham Forest was one of the few in which I put Dave Bassett first.

I talked to Stuart Pearce before agreeing to join the club. Stuart had taken over the running of the team at a difficult time. Frank Clark had left a little earlier. The club was in disarray because of the impending take-over. I came in at the invitation of the new consortium – headed by Nigel Wray – but I would not have agreed if I had sensed any resentment from Stuart.

It was a little ironic that Stuart and I should end up at the same club. When I was in charge at Wimbledon I had tried to sign Stuart. I had been very impressed with him in trials and I could see a lot of myself in him. He was with Wealdstone at the time and I offered them £10,000 for him. They were ready to sell but Stuart didn't like the personal terms and, after listening to a Bassett speech about how I saw him fitting in with the Dons and what a great future lay ahead, he just shook his head and said, 'Nah! I think I can do better!'

He was right, of course. He went to Coventry City and began what has turned out to be a brilliant career. Instead of Stuart, I signed Nigel Winterburn for nothing and he did a great job for us before moving on to Arsenal.

I wanted to make sure that Stuart was happy and that we both understood the arrangement. I was joining as general manager and would not interfere with team matters unless he asked me to – which I didn't expect that he would. That was how it stood and, for me, that was the final hurdle. I had already spoken to my wife, Christine, and she was delighted that I would be moving so that I could live at home again. From my house to the City Ground is only about an hour's drive so there was no longer any need of a flat elsewhere with just occasional trips home.

Joining Forest had some extra novelty value for me, too. As general manager I was to be involved in transfers. The most that I had ever spent on a player before was the million I used to buy Neil Shipperley for Palace from Southampton the previous October. Prior to that I had always been dealing in six figures, so the step up to seven was quite a challenge!

I had also quite liked Forest. Their exploits in Europe had been outstanding and in Brian Clough they had had a legend of a manager. They were not at all pretentious, just a workmanlike club with a long and successful history, one of the cornerstones of English football. It was quite a thrill to drive into the City Ground for the first time as general manager.

My first engagement, though, was at the club's away match at Tottenham. I had been appointed on the Thursday and went to White Hart Lane on the Saturday. It was a good day. I met everyone and was well received by the supporters. The result could not have been better as Dean Saunders scored after 18 minutes and that was it. We took home three points and there was almost a jubilant mood in the dressing-room.

It was obvious to everyone that the squad was in need of strengthening and the director of football, Irving Scholar, and I looked at several players. Stuart took care of team selection and match preparation and I was on hand if he wanted to have a chat. The decisions were all his as far as the team was concerned. It was not easy for either of us, but we made the best of it.

We did not need a brilliant soccer technician to tell us that we needed to score more goals and that was our priority. When Chris Waddle's agent informed us that he was free to leave Bradford City at any time and join a bigger club, we were naturally very interested. Who wouldn't have been interested in having one of the best play-makers in the game in their squad? As it happened we were led well up the garden path. Bradford City shut the door on our fingers, making it very clear that Waddle was not free to leave at any time. Perhaps we could have negotiated, but I was pretty disgusted that an agent had actually instigated the matter knowing full well that things were not the way that he was leading us to believe. If the agent and the player don't know what is in their contract – then who does? Isn't that what agents are for? Are they not supposed to do a little more than just introduce players to clubs?

We dropped interest in Chris Waddle like he was a hot potato, although I have to say that my admiration for his skills was not in any way diminished. He went to Sunderland but was unable to prevent them from being relegated even though his performances, as ever, were first class.

Our attention turned to Scotland where Pierre van Hooijdonk was keen to leave Celtic. Suddenly the club was spending £4.5 million on a new player. It was almost eerie! It was a record for the club but Hooijdonk had shown what he could do, both for Celtic and for Holland – and if you want class you have to pay for it. That much I had learned.

This would probably be a good time to talk about the van Hooijdonk saga. The Celtic fans loved him, of course, because he had been delivering on the park but his reputation within the game was low. He had alienated a lot of people by making comments which were totally unnecessary.

We bought him with this knowledge and expected that he would stay with us for a season or two before moving on again. We did not think he could do much damage in that time, but could certainly be of value on the pitch. We had to take a chance that we could get the best out of him and that his goals would be worth any hassle. I have always thought that character was of greater importance than talent, and when I look back at van Hooijdonk's overall contribution to Forest, I stand by that view.

We also tracked young Ian Moore and spent £700,000 on signing him from Tranmere. It was not that he was going to solve all our problems instantly but we were already building for the future whether that future was to be in the Premiership or in the First Division. The chance to buy Moore was there and he has a lot of obvious talent – the sort of talent that we needed at the City Ground.

My first home game was on the following Wednesday, after the Spurs game. A 3–0 home defeat by Sheffield Wednesday was a real blow and this was followed by a 2–0 loss at Arsenal. A few days later we were at Blackburn for Hooijdonk's debut. We drew 1–1, which was not a bad result, but it was spoiled for me by Brian Roy throwing a tantrum when he was substituted. It was not the sort of conduct that I expected to see from a professional player who had been a World Cup international for his country. I let him know it, too. It was a disgrace and it underlined the fact that he put himself way ahead of any feeling for the team. When you are in a fight for either promotion or relegation, you don't need that.

After the 1–1 with Blackburn we recorded the same scoreline in each of our next three games – at home to Liverpool, and away to Sunderland and Middlesbrough. Being undefeated for four games was good, but each time we dropped two points we were signing our own travel warrant to Division One.

When Southampton beat us 3–1 at the City Ground it was virtually the knock-out punch. We were second from the bottom and fast running out of games. Stuart took the squad away to Bournemouth for a few days to play some golf, train a little and try to get some focus back for the remaining matches. Internationals meant that there was a break for the Premiership, and we hoped that it might work to our advantage.

While all this was going on, I found myself in the usual demand from the media. It appeared that some thought I was in a cloak-and-dagger role, secretly pulling all the team strings while Stuart Pearce acted as front-man. Others saw me as some sort of vulture, sitting on the crossbar watching the team manager's job become my prey. I seemed to be forever in the position of explaining to everyone that I was merely doing the job that had been announced when I first joined the club.

When Nigel Clough returned to Manchester City after an extended loan with Forest, there were those who thought that it was me who had put him on the train. Not so! When Nigel returned to Maine Road I was away in Italy on business and the decision had nothing to do with me. I was enjoying the discovery of what life was like as a general manager with no team responsibilities.

Stuart Pearce had taken on the job as team manager for the rest of the season and it would then be decided if he was going to remain in that capacity. If he decided that he wanted to revert to being a player then we would talk about the possibility of me becoming manager – but not before. I have never knowingly stitched anybody up in my life, and I was not going to start in the back end of my career.

I also took the opportunity of having a go at the constant talk of my having been brought in to 'save' Forest from relegation. I have been tagged 'Harry Houdini' for years because of the various scrapes that I have come through with my teams – but I'm no lucky rabbit's foot, or some superman who turns up just when the world is about to fall apart and puts it all back together again. If it was as easy as that to save a club I would be earning more than Alex Ferguson. I could charge an arm and a leg for guaranteeing that clubs would not be relegated!

No – I had no magic wand for Forest! If I had, I would have gift-wrapped it and sent it to them much earlier in the season, because that was when the die was cast. Their relegation form had begun almost as soon as the season had started. A real miracle was needed to save them, not some trick from 'Harry Houdini's' repertoire.

After that Southampton beating, we were facing a home fixture against Leeds, who had one of the meanest defences in the Premiership, but also had one of the worst scoring records in the entire League. Their last games had been a typical 0–0 draw at home to Blackburn and a 2–0 defeat at Wimbledon, so I don't think the Forest fans were expecting a thrill-a-minute game when they visited the City Ground. I wouldn't have been surprised if some of them had brought a good book to read. We were bottom of the table – three points adrift of safety – and had played a game more than most of our close rivals.

Our performance was a little better. Brian O'Neal, on loan from Celtic, had a good game and Pierre van Hooijdonk scored after six minutes. An hour later and we were holding our heads in our hands. Chris Bart-Williams almost scored an own-goal when he sliced the ball while trying to clear. It hit the post and Brian Deane – of all people – stabbed the ball home. But for a great performance from Nigel Martyn in the Leeds goal I think we might have scored another and grabbed all three points. Nigel was outstanding and I was wishing that I had not sold him to Leeds when I was at Palace! Once again we had a 1–1 draw – the fifth in six games.

With three games left the writing was not just on the wall – it was plastered all over it in letters ten feet high! The press began to speculate about the future of Stuart Pearce. If Forest were relegated, would he quit the club? It amazed me that, even after all this time, some of the media did not know him better. Stuart Pearce never has been, and never will be, a quitter. He might make changes to his situation but he lives life the way he plays football with honesty and integrity, and we all know that he is one of the best international defenders ever. You don't get to play like that by being a quitter. Stuart shrugged off the questions and just reminded everyone that he still had several years of his playing contract left and that he had no intention of tearing that up.

Our midweek local derby against Derby was not a bad game, although it never actually achieved the thrills and spills that you might expect. There were a few niggling moments that earned yellow cards, but there were no goals. Derby still weren't mathematically safe but near enough and so for them the result was not a matter of life-and-death as it was to us. Once again we had taken one point where we needed all three.

The England World Cup game against Georgia meant that there was another break in the fixture calendar. It was prolonging the agony really. Our next game was at home – to Wimbledon! We needed maximum points to stand any chance at all, however remote, of staying up. In theory we did have a mathematical chance of avoiding the drop – in practice we had about as much chance of survival as a parachutist who had forgotten to put his pack on his back.

After about a quarter of an hour we lost Stuart Pearce with an injury. A minute before he left the pitch, Wimbledon went ahead through Leonhardsen. On the hour Brian Roy put us back on terms and we were set for an exciting half-hour. Both Alan Fettis in our goal and Neil Sullivan in the Don's goal were in top form and you probably don't need me to tell you that the game ended with yet another 1–1 draw. My old club had finished off my new club. Forest were definitely relegated. Shoulders drooped, heads bowed, and there were even a few tears. It was a little ironic because the last time that Forest were relegated I had been manager of Sheffield United — the last club they had played before the drop. Now I was at Forest — and on the receiving end.

We had just one game left — away to Newcastle who were pushing to get runners-up spot in the Premiership which would mean that they would qualify for the new-look European Champions Cup. It is not good to be going to St James's Park at any time, but when the Geordies were likely to be going full throttle to gain more than just the points, it was far from the ideal fixture for us.

After the game, Stuart announced that he did not want to remain as manager beyond the end of the season. It was not the relegation. He had done what all of us do — he had discussed it with his wife and decided that it was not yet the right time for him to be manager of a football club. He was probably right. I am certain that if I was in his position — a class player, still in demand at international level, and with the possibility of ending my international career in the 1998 World Cup in France — I would have taken exactly the same decision. His day as manager will come. In the meantime he had gained some valuable experience and in the January had even won the Manager of the Month Award, which is not a bad thing for his CV when he does step into management full time.

I was approached by the board with a view to taking

over the job. I did not hesitate and it was decided that my appointment would take effect after the Newcastle game, leaving Stuart in charge to the actual end of the season as had been arranged in the first place. I didn't envy him one bit. Newcastle, of course, were up for it and hammered five goals past us without reply It secured for them the second place they wanted and closed the curtain on our season with a finale that summed it all up – we were not in the same league!

Sunderland and Middlesbrough joined us on the elevator to the lower floor and as I looked to see how my old clubs fared – Wimbledon finished in eighth place, just outside a UEFA Cup spot, Crystal Palace and Sheffield United both made the Wembley First Division Play-off, with Palace winning promotion to the Premiership, and Watford finished in the middle of Division Two. Looking down the Second Division I saw that Notts County finished bottom just as we had finished bottom in the Premiership. It had not been a good season for the city of Nottingham.

Steve Coppell was very kind when he commented on Crystal Palace's success that season, saying that I had made a great contribution towards the club's success. He need not have said that and it showed once again that Steve is a very decent man who deserved better treatment than he ultimately received by the new regime at Crystal Palace.

History has it that I took over as manager of Nottingham Forest and reflected on the fact that, for the first time in my career, I was in charge of a club that actually seemed to have a bit of financial clout. I made no bones about the fact that I had not been very impressed with some of the supposed star players, and that we were going to have to spend some money and have a change of attitude. The First Division is a tough competition and you don't win promotion just by turning up and showing everyone your past achievements.

19

Forest Ups and Downs

WHEN YOU GET RELEGATED, there is the danger that you may continue slipping. There have been a number of examples of clubs that have slipped out of the top division and fallen all the way to the bottom division. There was no way I could consider that happening to Forest while I was in charge and I was aware that the Board would be closely monitoring our progress.

I am not sure how the Forest fans greeted the news that I was their new team manager. They were all very friendly, but I suspect that they were hoping for some Kenny Dalglish-type of character. Most adopted a wait-and-see stance.

Jon Olav Hjelde joined us for £500,000 from Rosenborg; Alan Rogers was a £2 million signing from Tranmere; Andy Johnson was another £2 million signing from Norwich; Swiss international goalkeeper Marco Pascalo was signed for £600,000 from Caliagri and Thierry Bonalair and Geoff Thomas were free signings.

While all this was going on, there were other developments. Paul Hart joined us a Youth Coach from Leeds. I had been looking at the youth set-up at Forest and knew it needed an overhaul. Paul was the man for the job and, of course, he has since become manager of the club. I believe that the fruits of that Forest youth scheme are yet to be realised but I am sure they will be.

We went on a pre-season tour of Finland and I felt that it did much to bring the players together. We had a few laughs as usual and, with a number of new players having joined Forest, I felt that it was important for everyone to get to know each other properly. We also played Notts County in a pre-season friendly, and Leeds, who we beat 1-0, but at a cost. A tackle by Jimmy Floyd Hasselbaink left Colin Cooper with 16 stitches and put him out for the first ten games of the season. It was a disgraceful tackle and it was that which led to us signing Hjelde earlier than we had planned.

The 1997-98 season got underway with a 1-0 win at Port Vale, so that settled us straight away. A few days later, we went to Doncaster for a League Cup match, which we won 8-0 and set a new club away record. I know that might not seem a big deal, but sometimes results like that can perform miracles for confidence.

Just a few days after that, we had our first home game. It was on a Friday night so that Sky could show it. Norwich were the visitors and we won 4-1. Three wins on the trot was not a bad start but there was a down side because both of our goalkeepers, Mark Crossley and Pascalo, were added to our injury list and suddenly we needed a goalie. That's when we signed Dave Beasant on a month's loan and he proved to be a revelation, even though he was then 38 years old.

By the end of August, we had won 1-0 at Oxford, beaten Doncaster in the League Cup return leg and then beat QPR 4-0 at home with van Hooijdonk getting his first hat-trick of the season. Life was looking good as we topped the First Division with 12 points out of 12 and ten goals for with only one against. A few people started talking about us taking the championship, but that was ridiculous at that stage of the season.

I was delighted to be named Manager of the Month for August but it all went a bit strange the following month, when we went suddenly goal shy. Having hit 20 goals in six games in August, we went down to five goals in seven games in September. There was a bit of controversy when I put van Hooijdonk, who just 24 hours previously had returned from international duty, on the bench at Swindon. As the manager, though, I reserve the right to make the selection of the team. I felt it was the right move and still do. The player made a bit of a song and dance about it, but that was his way.

During that month, I also called on the Forest supporters to stop barracking Kevin Campbell. He had had a bit of a bad spell prior to me joining, but he was doing his best to get over it and he was still wearing a Forest shirt, so I thought the fans could have been a bit more supportive of him rather than making matters worse. We also lost Geoff Thomas for three months with a back injury and Steve Stone had not yet recovered from a hernia operation. So, all in all, we had been battered a bit during September. Having said that, we had still lost only one League match and still topped the First Division.

There was a bit of unrest in the dressing room over van Hooijdonk that had to be smoothed over because team spirit was very important. I think that he was a victim of his own ego and some of the players were already starting to kick back against it.

One lighter moment came when some people turned up from the FA to routinely drug test the players. However, they turned up on the players' day off so they went away again empty-handed.

The ups and downs continued until the end of the year. Dean Saunders left us to start a new life with Sheffield United; our expensive Italian, Andrea Silenzi, who was bought before my arrival and proved to be something of a disappointment, was paid off because he just did not make the grade. Dave Beasant joined us on a permanent deal; and we kept getting results that were good enough to keep us joint top of the table with Middlesbrough. A 5-2 win over one of our nearest rivals, Charlton, was a great result although they got their revenge at the start of 1998 when they knocked us out of the FA Cup with a 4-1 win.

Going out of the cup was almost a minor disturbance compared with allegations of 'misconduct' against the club. It was nothing at all to do with me or the current players, but was to do with some allegations during the Clough era. I told the players to ignore the whole thing and get on with the job in hand.

It was a blow when we lost my assistant Bobby Houghton who left to become national coach to China. It was a great opportunity for him and I didn't blame him for going, but I was sorry to see him go. The good news was that we finished January back in charge of Division One, two points clear of Middlesbrough. There was an additional pat on the back as we had the best disciplinary record in the country. I enjoyed that.

The season was bubbling along quite nicely. Glyn Hodges joined us on a free transfer from Hull. I valued his experience and knew that he would be good to maintain team spirit and I also knew that we were going to need plenty of that during the run-in.

I had been expecting a decent amount of money for buying new players and I would be telling a lie if I said I wasn't disappointed that it did not materialise. As deadline day approached in March, I managed to get Christian Edwards from Swansea for £175,000 and that was it.

One of my favourite sayings at the time was that everything at Forest was not quite as it had appeared in the brochure when I joined. What I mean by that is that I had been promised things that were not ultimately there for me. As I have mentioned, I joined the club with a sense of excitement that sprang from the promise of no end of money to spend. Of course, the money had been there at the start as we bought the likes of Van Hooijdonk for sizeable fees and on good wages. But already – only six or seven months after I had taken over from Stuart Pearce – I began to realise that all was not as I had been told.

Any manager will tell you that there is a time during a season, however successful, when injuries or suspensions or problems with form mean that you have to strengthen your squad. At Forest during this time, I wanted to do it while things were going well and not wait until the pressure situation of the promotion run-in. There is nothing worse than panic-buying. As it happened, all I wanted was a couple of loan players to keep us going, but the board wouldn't have it. They told me they couldn't afford the wages and that was that. We were still top of the table at the time so I shrugged my shoulders and got on with it. But, as will be revealed later, this period of financial stringency was a sign of things to come.

I would have been more worried if we had not been enjoying a good run, but, as it happens, we were still going well. Only two clubs would guarantee gaining promotion and I wanted to make sure we were one of them. There were three serious contenders – ourselves, Middlesbrough and Sunderland. A 4-0 win over Middlesbrough in March helped our cause no end, but when, the following Wednesday, we lost 3-0 to Sunderland it brought home the fact that this was likely to go to the wire.

Our last home match of the season was against Reading and victory would guarantee promotion without having to go into the play-offs. Most of our supporters thought it would be a routine victory, but it wasn't to be. It turned out to be one of our most nervous afternoons of the season. As can often be the case in these situations, we played poorly and with only about 15 minutes left, Reading hit the inside of a post with a shot that rolled along the goal-line behind Dave Beasant and to safety. We breathed a sigh of relief and not long after, Chris Bart-Williams showed the great technical ability he has always had to turn on a sixpence and score the goal that sent us up.

A few days later, I was doing a TV pundit job with Yorkshire TV, when news came that Sunderland had lost and we knew then that we were Champions. A 1-1 draw at West Brom on the last day of the season sealed the whole thing and we finished top of the table, with Middlesbrough second, three points behind us.

For once, I did not go crazy with celebrations. For me, it was a great moment, but I always felt that it was only half the job. We were back in the Premiership, but the real test was going to be next season when we would have to show what we could do against Manchester United, Liverpool, Arsenal and the others. I left the bulk of the celebrations to everyone else and had a brief holiday with my family, all the way plotting how we were going to keep our place in the Premiership.

When you have been in football management for a while, you become quite philosophical about your future. You know that from the day you start your job you are already a day nearer to the parting of the ways. Having said that, you push it to the back of your mind and assume that you are going to be allowed to get on with your job, do your best and hopefully be in that seat for an indefinite period.

That summer, as I prepared for our first season back in the Premiership, it never crossed my mind that I was months away from clearing my desk at the City Ground. When I left for that holiday, I did so knowing which players I felt I needed in order to give us a fighting chance in the Premiership and confident that I could secure one or two of my present group on new contracts. How naïve that turned out to be. Instead, I returned to find that the rug had been well and truly pulled from beneath my feet. Given that Campbell and Van Hooijdonk had scored 52 goals for us the previous season and were going to be the nucleus of my attack in the Premiership, I understandably was a little miffed to discover that in my absence

Campbell had been sold to Trabzonspor in Turkey.

With hindsight, this was the beginning of the end, both for me and for Forest as a credible top flight club. I had gone away believing that Campbell was on the verge of signing a new deal and while I cannot say that he was sold behind my back – I was told what was happening over the telephone – it was certainly done over my head. I didn't want Campbell sold, and the club, Irving Scholar and the rest of the board damn well knew it.

My relationship with Irving had not been that good for some time and it certainly did not improve when Campbell was sold. He loves being involved in football and being at the centre of all the decision-making processes. In my opinion, Irving is much too fond of direct contact with players and their agents. During much of my time at the club, he was also involved in a bitter dispute with the Chief Executive, Phil Soar. Both had been part of the consortium that had bought the club only a year or so earlier, but it was not long before they were at each others throats. I am still not sure what exactly the problem was – apart from a clash of personalities – but it was a distraction that both I and the club didn't need and it was one that I believe was to negatively influence life at the City Ground long after I had left. It was an argument I tried to keep out of. For much of my time at Forest, I didn't always feel that the board totally supported everything that I was trying to do.

During my early time at the City Ground, for example, there were two transfers that I and my chief scout Ian Storey-Moore thought would have been good for the club and the fact that I wasn't allowed to complete either was indicative of the short-sighted nature of the people running the show. The first was young striker Matt Jensen at Carlisle. Available for £1 million, Jansen seemed an excellent investment, but the board would not have it. He eventually moved to Crystal Palace and was subsequently sold to Blackburn for £8 million. He is now an England international. The other is less well-known, a Swedish centre forward called Marcus Allback who was going for £300,000. Again, we were knocked back. Allback is now Henrik Larsson's partner for Sweden and has been transferred to Aston Villa for £2 million. Neither of those incidents were as potentially damaging as another crisis that myself and my youth director Paul Hart narrowly managed to avoid. Hart and I were understandably keen to establish a youth academy at the club that would hopefully produce and nurture the Forest players of the future. The board were all for it until it came to the matter of stumping up the £1 million required to seal the deal on a plot of land we had found.

I was astonished. How could they do this? I eventually went to a board meeting and battered them into submission in support of the youth scheme. Hart and I got our money and Forest now has a flourishing academy that has already produced the likes of Jermaine Jenas, the young midfielder recently sold to Newcastle for £5 million. You could say that the £1 million has already been more than recovered!

During the promotion season, I developed a good relationship with the Forest reporter on the local paper, Ian Ladyman. I learned to trust him and, in return, I like to think I helped him out with as many good stories as I could. In other words, it's exactly how a relationship between a manager and the local rag should be. Ladyman was aware of the conditions that I was working in. He knew that the board were not quite delivering what they had promised and on several occasions encouraged me to speak out, telling me I would be doing so from a position of strength at the top of the Division One table. I never did and, before long, things had got a lot worse.

If losing Campbell was the equivalent of tying one arm behind my back, then the troublesome Van

Hooijdonk effectively chopped the other one off by going on strike before the season started. Through the press Van Hooijdonk claimed that he thought the club was not showing the necessary ambition. On that point, he and I were in perfect harmony – for just about the first, and only, time!! – but while I and the rest of the players were prepared to stick around and fight, he chose to sit around on his backside in Holland and moan. To me, he was a coward and a disgrace and I said so.

As far as I was concerned, he could have stayed in Holland under contract to us without pay since he had gone on strike. If he did not have the decency to come back to train with his team mates and air his views man to man, then I was quite prepared to wash my hands of him and let him wreck his own career by not kicking a competitive ball for the rest of his contract with us. I thought his conduct was disgraceful and unprofessional. Basically he thought everything revolved around him and that he should be the star player, the coach, the manager and probably the Chairman as well, given half a chance.

The problem managers have, though, is that players are worth money, and, at Forest, the cash was in short supply. We simply could not afford to have a £4.5 million player sitting on his backside doing nothing. I was all for selling him and using the money to get a couple of decent alternatives. He had been a problem at Celtic and I'd been warned about him when I wanted to buy him, but I thought he would be all right for a season or two. I didn't expect him to go off the rails quite so quickly but there is no doubt that his goals played a major part in our promotion, which is why we bought him.

Because of his reputation, most people realised that his actions were not the club's fault. The Forest players did not particularly like him anyway, so there was no problem with them as far as I was concerned. He used to slag off English football in general, so he hadn't made any friends in the dressing room. I was annoyed at the Board's reluctance to sell van Hooijdonk. They seemed to be prepared to humour him, whatever the cost to team spirit.

Personally, I had lost all respect for van Hooijdonk. He thought he was a big star, but I wanted to see him prove himself in the Premiership. When he had joined the club originally, it was during the relegation period in the Premiership and he hadn't set the world on fire then. He had delivered in Division One, but if he had really wanted to make a name for himself, he had to show that he was a top striker in the Premiership.

While all this was going on, we had to get ready for the new 1998-99 season, and I knew that we had to add to the squad somehow, especially when our club captain Colin Cooper was sold to Middlesbrough for just over £2.6 million. I think a lot of people thought that I wanted him to go, but that was not true. I liked him and didn't want to lose him. Despite this, Cooper had an influence in the dressing room that I didn't think was always healthy. When I bought central defender Jon Hjelde a year earlier, he had bags of promise and I had expected great things from him. But Cooper and his mate and defensive partner, Steve Chettle, seemed determined to undermine him. Hjelde's big problem was that he lacked confidence – both on and off the field – and Cooper and Chettle seemed to exploit this in order to keep him *out* – and in turn the two of them *in* – the team. You could argue that Hjelde should have been big enough to overcome this and perhaps that was the case. But the offer for Cooper was a good one and we certainly needed the cash. If the financial situation at the club had been better, then perhaps I wouldn't have done it. Looking back, I wish I had kept Cooper but I thought we would be alright. He was a great asset, but I also knew that we needed the cash to try and acquire some extra power up front.

I spent £1.5 million on Neil Shipperley from Crystal

Palace. Palace needed the money and I had worked with Shipps before and knew him to be a good, honest centre-forward. I brought Jean-Claude Darcheville on loan from France, but he proved to be a disappointment. I sympathised with the fact that he had been through a trauma when his girlfriend was killed in a car crash, and hoped that bringing him to England meant that he would have a fresh start. He was quite promising in the early days, but then his fitness went down. I also bought Nigel Quashie from QPR for £2 million and, with hindsight, I think it was probably too soon for him. A lot of people had been raving about him and he certainly had all the potential, but he was a bit immature and not ready for the Premiership. Looking back, I made a mistake with Nigel because I was buying for the future, not for our immediate needs.

The season started with the van Hooijdonk business unresolved, and we had to travel to Arsenal on the opening day. We were live on Sky on the Monday night against the defending champions and my team included the raw Darcheville, young Craig Armstrong and veterans Glyn Hodges and Geoff Thomas. No disrespect to any of those players – least of all Glyn and Geoff who have been great pros – but ideally they wouldn't have been in my first choice team. The Summer had seen me try – and fail – to land players like Dutch International Wim Jonk, fresh from the World Cup. Instead, I was already having to mix and match and, to my despair, I found myself starting the season with a worse team than the one that had ended the previous season. As it happened, that night, young Armstrong played a blinder, Darcheville scared the life out of Martin Keown with his pace and Thomas scored the Goal of the Month. It was a great performance – full of guts, heart and commitment. We lost 2-1, but I was proud of my players. If Van Hooijdonk was at home watching on TV – and I am sure he was – then he should have felt embarrassed and ashamed.

We had lost our opening game, but I was not too disappointed about that, especially when we beat Coventry at home the following weekend. It was only 1-0, but that didn't matter, especially when we went to Southampton a week later and won 2-1. It wasn't a bad start for us.

If the season had ended as August came to a close, we would all have been fairly happy, but it didn't and it all went pear-shaped after that. Other than beating Leyton Orient and Cambridge United in the League Cup, we didn't win another game throughout the rest of 1998. I am not going to offer any hard-luck stories, but we drew a lot of games that we should have won, allowing other sides to come back when we were leading and in control of the game.

I think there was a lack of self-belief and concentration at times and that led to mistakes. I also think that the players just didn't get the breaks, which happens when you are in that situation. On a number of occasions we were two goals to the good and then some error allowed the opposition – Aston Villa and Blackburn are examples – to pull a goal back and the Forest players' heads would go down. It was as if they had resigned themselves to it all going wrong. There is little a manager can do about that when the game is underway, especially in the second half. I am not using that as an excuse, because there were plenty of other reasons why it was not working out, but it is a factor.

The bottom line is, however, that the players were simply not good enough. I had finished the previous season telling the board that we needed to strengthen but instead we grew weaker. It wasn't fair on the fans and it certainly wasn't fair on the players who had worked so hard to get us promoted. I got some stick for some of my decisions and that's fair enough. I can cope with that. As I said, Quashie was a mistake and maybe I shouldn't have sold Cooper. But I got a particularly hard time for buying strikers Shipperley and Dougie Freedman and I didn't think that was fair. All of a sudden I was trying to replace Van Hooijdonk but had hardly any money to do so. Shipps and Dougie are both good players, but we needed proven Premiership quality. During the course of the season, I think I used more than ten strike pairings up front and that said everything about how desperate we were for goals.

During November, van Hooijdonk returned, said a few unpleasant things and got on with his job. During all that time, the club had to suspend him every two weeks, otherwise his contract would have been deemed to have been terminated and he would have been free to go somewhere else without a transfer fee.

Irving Scholar thought that van Hooijdonk would come back and save us, but I knew that wasn't going to happen. I had lost all patience with the player, and when someone suggested that the Dutchman might be offering an olive branch, I remember giving an opinion as to where I thought he should put it.

I was disappointed with the players' reaction to his return. Some ignored him, others spoke to him a bit, but there were quite a few who chatted to him as if nothing had happened. They didn't seem to have the gumption to realise that this so-called team mate had let them down badly. I know if he had been a team mate of mine, I would have ended up punching him. It showed a lack of character that they greeted his return very weakly.

I think in many ways, the players' reaction said much about the way the modern footballer thinks. Too many of them earn too much and care too little. I know one thing – had I had the likes of Vinnie Jones or Stuart Pearce in my dressing room, then Van Hooijdonk would have been a much quieter character. The week he returned, one incident summed him up. Van Hooijdonk bumped into our goalkeeper Mark Crossley in a Nottingham restaurant and he thought it was only decent to approach his team-mate to say hello. To Crossley's intense embarrassment, Van Hooijdonk blanked him. Just what hope did we have from then on?

Everyone thought he was going to become the saviour, but he was never a battling player. So I didn't expect him to roll up his sleeves and fight for Forest. To be honest, I just wanted him banned or sold. Leeds offered £4.5 million for him but Scholar said we should hold on for £6 million. There was no way that was going to be paid, so the sale was lost, and, eventually, at the end of the season he went to Arnhem for £3.5 million. Had he been sold to Leeds when he returned, we could have strengthened the side a bit more.

During his exile, I came up with an idea for the top 14 Premiership sides to donate £500,000 to help us buy a new striker for about £7 million. I know it sounds a bit crazy, but the point was to keep van Hooijdonk in exile and keep the power with the clubs rather than the players. Gordon Strachan was one of those in favour of the idea, but most of the others thought I was being foolish. It has come home to roost now, though, as we see player power running football. If action had been taken over the van Hooijdonk affair, then a lot of other player-club problems might have been avoided.

The Blackburn game before Christmas knocked the players' confidence even more. There we were, cruising to a 2-0 victory, but we let Blackburn back in for a 2-2 draw and that was another two points lost. To make matters worse, we travelled to Old Trafford to play Manchester United on Boxing Day. We were doing well for the first half-hour, but then they popped in two goals before half time and another just after the restart to seal the match. Once it had gone to 3-0,they started doing all their clever stuff and I remember hoping that our players didn't annoy them by pulling one back, because they might have started popping in a lot more goals.

We started the New Year by getting knocked out of the FA Cup when Portsmouth beat us 1-0. Talk of Bassett getting the sack was already rife, and the supporters aired their views in the way that supporters do, although most of their annoyance seemed to be directed at the Board rather than Bassett.

It was the manner of my departure that disappointed me. As I have said, I hadn't been getting on very well with Irving Scholar. The promises of money for players had not materialised and there was the rift between him and Phil Soar, the club's Chief Executive. It was very difficult getting on with things when all that was going on.

For some weeks, it had been obvious that, unless we could get into the transfer market, we would be facing relegation at the end of the season. When we lost to Portsmouth, I started to hear that Ron Atkinson was being lined up for my job. I had heard nothing from anyone at the club.

On the Monday following the Portsmouth defeat, I went to watch Arsenal play Preston with Mickey Adams (now the Leicester City manager) who had been brought in to replace Bob Houghton. After the game, my phone started ringing. It was the press, telling me that I was going to get the sack the following morning. I was upset because Irving Scholar had said nothing to me at that stage, but I knew the press had got it right as it confirmed the rumours I had been hearing and I knew that at least one of the reporters was a pal of Irving's.

Irving was at his home in Monaco. I was not going to give him the chance to sack me over the phone, so I switched off my phone and went to work the next morning as usual. Phil Soar came over and handed me the letter which terminated my contract and that was it.

It was typical of the bumbling way that Forest went

about their business that they couldn't even get this right. Soar was a well meaning man and a huge Forest fan, but he could also be very naïve. In the absence of Irving Scholar and plc chairman Nigel Wray, Soar was effectively ordered across to my office to slit my throat, so to speak. As he read out a statement to the press about my departure, he actually stated that I was leaving by mutual consent. Needless to say, I was quick to assure him and the media that I was not! Nobody likes to be sacked, but this was a particularly upsetting day for me. There I was, hung out to dry by people who couldn't even be bothered to turn up to say farewell. I thought I had done my best for Forest and this was my reward. I don't mind admitting there were a few tears as I cleared my desk, as I had genuinely hoped I would be at Forest for a long time. Irving Scholar and the members of the board were slaughtered in the press – both national and local – the following day and I can't say now that I disagree with much of what was written.

I thought that the way it was done was disgraceful. Some others would have either come over from Monaco or arranged for me to go over there so that they could tell me face to face. Irving was the Director of Football and it was his role to tell me. The silly thing was that Ron Atkinson was in Barbados and he wasn't going to rush back. Mickey Adams had to take charge of the team for the following game, which resulted in a 4-0 loss at Coventry. That wasn't Mickey's fault. I don't think anyone could have done any better under those circumstances.

Eventually, I did see Irving and told him what I thought, and, to be fair, I know that if he and the other directors could turn the clock back, they would. They have all been in touch since and have told me that they wished it had been handled better. For all the differences I have had with him, I must say that Irving is not the sort of person I could dislike. I just wish that he had been more open with me. I still believe that his direct line with van Hooijdonk was a big mistake and influenced his manner of dealing with things.

I haven't spoken to Irving since then, but I expect I shall because there is no point in being silly about the whole thing. His wife Julia is a nice lady, and, along with my wife Christine, the four of us had enjoyed each other's company.

When Ron Atkinson arrived, he was able to spend a bit and do a bit more wheeling and dealing than I had been able to. He was assisted by Peter Shreeves and I think they thought they might be able to save the club from relegation. I told Ron at the time that he couldn't.

He also thought that he would be able to handle van Hooijdonk, but they soon fell out, and on the training ground, Ron actually sent the Dutchman back to the dressing room. Van Hooijdonk retaliated by calling Ron a pub manager, which was in reference to a TV advert Ron had done.

I received a lot of phone calls and letters of support and there was one particular call which I really appreciated. It was from Alex Ferguson, who said that he thought I had been treated badly and offered me a job as a scout for Manchester United. I was grateful to him for that and for the rest of the season, I scouted players and went to watch their opposition before European games. They went on to record a memorable treble of European Cup, Premier League Championship and FA Cup winners, a feat that I believe will never be repeated in the modern game. A fantastic team, led by a fantastic manager.

It was a little ironic that United chalked up an 8-1 win at the City Ground when they played there the February after my departure. That morning, Carlton Palmer, one of Ron's new signings, was quoted in the papers as saying that Ron Atkinson should have taken over from Dave Bassett much earlier and that relegation would have been avoided because they now had a good, solid defence. I guess those eight goals were accidents. It gave me a giggle.

When I left Forest, they should have given the job to Paul Hart there and then, but they didn't and wasted more money. Even when Ron left they called in David Platt which was another decision which didn't work out as well as expected. Today, Forest are still struggling financially and will continue to do so unless Paul Hart can produce a miraculous promotion – but it is a tall order.

Still, that was Forest and my life had to move on.

20

Off to Oakwell

I CONTINUED WITH MANCHESTER UNITED until the end of the season and waited to see what vacancies would arise. John Hendrie parted company with Barnsley and Eric Winstanley became caretaker manager for the last few games. A few people suggested that Barnsley were interested in me, but I heard nothing from the club itself, so I took it all with a pinch of salt.

Meanwhile, I did have an approach from Aberdeen. I met the directors in London and they impressed me. I spoke to Alex Ferguson and he spoke well of the club and said that they needed a bit of a personality to put some life into them. I did seriously consider it, but then I made up my mind that I didn't really want to live that far north, so I thanked them for their interest and wished them all the best, but declined their offer. I guessed that something else would turn up eventually.

However, shortly after, I did receive a call from John Dennis, chairman of Barnsley, who invited me to have a chat. I knew I wasn't the first he had spoken to about the job. Others had already been interviewed including, ironically, two other former Sheffield United managers Steve Bruce and Nigel Spackman. Anyway, I went to see Mr Dennis at his house and had a talk with him and Barry Taylor, another director, and we spent a couple of hours discussing the club. We went our separate ways at the end of the discussion, and the next day, John phoned me and offered me the job. I asked for time to think about it because I felt that it needed proper consideration.

There had been a few managers in and out of the club in recent years; but expectations were high because Barnsley had sampled a season in the Premiership, even though they had just been relegated and I knew there was not much money to play with.

Danny Wilson, then manager of Sheffield Wednesday FC and an ex-Barnsley manager, told me that the Board were keen for me to take the job and, after some thought, I decided that it was worth a try. Just as I was making my mind up about Barnsley, Bernard Proctor, a Director and old friend from Sheffield United, offered me the job at Bramall Lane. However, the die was cast and I had given my word to Barnsley.

Barnsley had certainly progressed a great deal since I had first moved to South Yorkshire. Oakwell had changed considerably and was now a really good football ground with excellent facilities.

I have to admit that there was still one nagging little doubt gnawing away in the back of my mind even as I agreed to take on the challenge there. In my meeting with John Dennis and Barry Taylor I detected a lack of realism in their expectations. Ambition, of course, is something to be applauded, and everyone should set their sights as high as they possibly can regardless of the walk of life they are in.

You have also got to know and accept your limits. Nowhere is that more true than in football, where finances now dictate that the rich get richer and the poor are simply glad to survive. No disrespect to Barnsley but, let's face it, Manchester United – or Brazil! - they are not and never will be. But, in their case maybe a little success, like a little knowledge, was a dangerous thing.

They had sampled life in the top flight for the first time in their history, and they clearly loved the experience of rubbing shoulders with the elite. So, of course, they wanted to sample it again – and there's absolutely nothing wrong with that. The only problem was I rather got the impression from John and Barry that they believed Premiership football was Barnsley's by rights. That never was the case and never will be. Clubs the size of Barnsley can no longer hope to ever be Premier League heavyweights.

The Board was also a little worried about the staff I might want to bring in. Eric Winstanley was still with Barnsley, and he had been there for years as player, coach and caretaker manager. Peter Shirtliff was also there, along with Mark Smith who was well known for his time with Sheffield Wednesday. I had an open mind on the staff situation.

But the situation with Eric was an intriguing one and, perhaps, underlines how the club remains at odds with itself over its identity. It wants to mix it with the big boys, yet still tries to cling to this reputation it has for being a close-knit family club that rewards loyal servants like Winstanley with a job for life.

In my younger, more impetuous and intolerant days, I would have been apprehensive about keeping on someone with Eric's background at the club. But I told the directors I was more than happy to work with the current staff as long as they worked the way I wanted them to. And I had an agreement that, if they were not up to it, then I could replace them and bring in my own men.

There was about £1million available for the transfer market and we signed Neil Shipperly from Forest for £700,000. I knew he didn't figure in David Platt's plans and I knew he would do a good job for us at Barnsley. I also signed Geoff Thomas on a free transfer from Forest. We were also desperate for an experienced goalkeeper and I knew that that was a problem that would have to be solved and solved quickly.

In order to get to know each other, I took the players to Sweden for a pre-season tour and that proved to be useful as it gave us the chance to try new systems as well as whip up team spirit.

Before my arrival, Barnsley had been playing the sweeper system for a good while. I had no problem with that at all. After all, I had used it to pretty good effect at Crystal Palace the season they came all the way through the play-offs to win promotion to the Premiership.

However, I felt it would be better for Barnsley to play a more flexible 4-4-2 formation, and we experimented with this in our pre-season games. I know Eric Winstanley was not altogether happy because he favoured playing three at the back. But he showed his open-mindedness by not being at all negative about my favoured system.

When you first join a club, you are never totally sure of the ability, strengths and weaknesses of its players, even though you know plenty about them as opponents. Even with the help of Eric and the rest of the backroom staff, I knew it would be difficult to fit the pieces of the jigsaw together in the early games and settle on my best team.

We didn't start the season very well, losing 3-1 at Charlton and then being beaten 3-2 at home by Crystal Palace. The 4-2 Worthington Cup win over Lincoln between those matches was small consolation. It was evident that we needed another experienced goalkeeper and managed to sign Kevin Miller from Crystal Palace for £250,000. Even though we didn't sign him in time for our trip to Blackburn, we still came away with a 2-0 victory. That's football, and I felt that our season then started properly, especially since we hammered Portsmouth 6-0 in our next home match.

Suddenly, things were looking good again but, as is often the case, we were brought down to earth with a big bump when we lost 6-1 at Ipswich in Kevin's first game for us. I still thought he was our Man of the Match despite the six goals, so it shows what the rest were like! We had gained our biggest victory and our worst defeat of the season all in a matter of days.

I still thought we were heading in the right direction though, and I was particularly pleased with the way Shipperley and Miller had bedded down. They were players of undoubted Premiership pedigree, and they certainly added a real touch of extra class to my team. Neil and Kevin took the top flight in their stride, so there was never going to be a question mark about their ability to operate at First Division level.

In September, I had also added David Tuttle to our defence in a £150,000 transfer from Palace. As it happens, he did not stay that long and we later sold him to Millwall for £200,000, but he did a good job while he was with us.

It was just that we had Chris Morgan coming through and he established himself as first choice. I also heard that Steve Chettle might be available from Forest and secured him on a free transfer. His experience would be invaluable to us.

There was talk of me making a move in November as Blackburn Rovers were looking for a new manager. Brian Kidd had just left and Blackburn did approach me indirectly. I told John Dennis and he made it quite plain that he didn't want me to go. He was, in fact, at his wits' end as I learned later from Mike Morgan, the *Sun*'s football writer who, over the years has become a good friend and one of the few journalists in whom I have implicit trust. John knew that Mike and I were close, so he confided to him just how fearful he was of losing me.

Indeed, I recall Mike writing an article for his paper on the strength of his phone conversation with the Chairman, in which John was quoted as saying that there was a job for life for me at Oakwell and that when I'd had enough of management I could become Director of Football or even have a place on the Board!

What he told Mike privately was that he was amazed by my knowledge of the game and the extent of my contacts, and that he did not want all that to be lost to his club when I decided to jack it in as manager.

John was nick-named the 'Fat Controller' during my time at Oakwell because he was like the character from *Thomas the Tank Engine* when he got agitated. But some of the press boys who cover Barnsley came up with their own, typically brutal, nickname for him. They reckon that, when he gets flustered, his face reddens and takes on the look of a bilious baby. So one or two of them simply refer to him as 'Bilious'.

Anyway, back to the dilemma of whether I should stay loyal to Barnsley or take-up the tantalising challenge on offer at Ewood Park. I had only been at Oakwell a short time and I was torn because the money available and the management possibilities were so much better at Blackburn.

If I'd had a crystal ball and known what was going to happen at Blackburn, I would probably have stayed out of work that previous summer until the opportunity arose. Having said that, Blackburn said that they had been impressed by what I had already done at Barnsley, so who knows?

Blackburn did offer me the job and I regret now that I didn't take it. I just couldn't bring myself to drop Barnsley in it during what was an important season for them. I have always tried to be loyal and I couldn't change my nature at that time. It was a mistake; I should have taken the job because I was not to receive sufficient support from Barnsley later on when it mattered. It was probably just the wrong time for me. Christine told me that I was stupid and didn't talk to me for a week. She told me not to moan to her when it all went wrong at Barnsley, and she was right, of course. I should have shown loyalty to Bassett for a change.

Christine wasn't the only one to get on my case. Trevor Francis, a big mate from our days together in Sheffield, when I was manager at United and he at

Wednesday, also gave me an ear-bashing. At the time Blackburn offered me the job, we beat Trevor's Birmingham City 2-1 in a league game. And afterwards he told me: 'You must be mad to turn them down. You really ought to go to Ewood Park.'

At Barnsley, we continued to have our ups and downs, but by the end of 1999 we were in a good position in the top five of the First Division. We had moved right up there after being bottom after the opening few games of the season, and maybe that coloured my thinking a little bit, too. After beating Birmingham, we went on an excellent run through December and entered the New Year in the top three. The whole place was buzzing. Momentum and expectation was gathering in the town, and there was a genuine belief that we could go on and win promotion.

We had been drawn against my old team, Wimbledon, in the third round of the FA Cup. I was touched by a tribute on the front page of the match programme that day penned by Sam Hammam.
It read:

> *Today we salute Dave Bassett, hero of Wimbledon, manager of the millennium. What you did by taking us from the Fourth to the First Division will never be equalled. Other wonderful managers continued the miracle, but it was you who made it possible. You may well be in the rival dug-out today, but there will always be a part of us in you and you in us. This will always be your spiritual home. It is an honour to welcome you back.*
> *Sam.*

It might seem a bit indulgent including that in this book, but it was a lovely surprise when I was handed a programme and found that on its cover. It was embarrassing but still a great and unexpected gesture. Sam later took Christine and me out for a meal, so, apart from the match result, it was an enjoyable return to Wimbledon.

Wimbledon beat us 1-0, so they were happy, but our chairman, John Dennis, was none to pleased about our Cup exit. As for me, I thought it was a bit of a blessing in disguise. Sure, the cash from a Cup run would have been nice, but I felt a lengthy run in that competition might well have damaged our promotion push.

Just before Christmas, we had a bit of an injury crisis and Alex Ferguson let us have John Curtis on loan to help us through. I was delighted because he was a very good player and I hoped that we might be able to sign him permanently at the end of the season. If things had worked out a little differently, that might have been possible. But, at the end of the season, he signed for Blackburn. All of which re-emphasised that Barnsley really is a small club, because it was players of John's quality that we should have been holding on to, in order to help us move to a higher level.

We had some good results over Christmas although, after beating Blackburn 5-1 at home, we then lost 3-0 at Portsmouth. We lost a vital home game to Ipswich 2-0, but then we beat Manchester City 2-1. We seemed to take two steps forward then one back, but we stayed in the top five, finished the season in fourth place and ended up with more points than when Barnsley went up to the Premiership under Danny Wilson.Charlton and Manchester City won automatic promotion and the third place was fought out between ourselves, fifth-placed Birmingham, third-placed Ipswich and sixth-placed Bolton.

During the busy run-up to the end of the season, after the Walsall game, Christine and I were invited to a black-tie dinner to celebrate Sir Alex Ferguson's testimonial. All the 'great and good' of football were invited – and me! I even managed to get David Beckham's autograph!

We went head-to-head with Trevor Francis' Birmingham. He was convinced that his side would beat us. However, we trounced them 4-0 in the first leg at St Andrews, and that victory just about wrapped up the semi-final in our favour. Trevor was devastated and I felt quite sorry for him, but the result was what we wanted and for which we had worked and planned. We had changed our tactics for the first leg, and I think that threw Trevor's own plans into disarray.

Birmingham won the return leg at Oakwell 2-1, but that didn't stop the party. Barnsley was going to Wembley for the first time in the club's history and the whole town wanted to celebrate in style.

People have often said to me since, that the play-off final must have been an awful disappointment. To be honest, it wasn't. Sure, the defeat hurt – and hurt badly for a long time. But the day, the occasion itself was simply marvellous for all those wonderful Barnsley fans who had waited for a lifetime to see their club at Wembley.

We had selection problems going into the game that would decide our whole season. Nicky Eaden had a question mark against his fitness, so I decided to play John Curtis instead and he didn't give us one of his best performances. With hindsight, I would have been better off chancing Nicky on that particular day.

We made errors in the play-off final and paid the penalty. You can look back on any important game and reel off a list of things that didn't go right. Darren Barnard failed with a penalty kick, the defence made some mistakes, the attack didn't create the chances they should have done. On the day we were just below par, while Ipswich were on good form. But there is still no getting away from the feeling that we were just a penalty kick away from the promised land of the Premiership. I remain convinced to this day that, had Darren scored with that spot-kick, we would have gone on to win the final.

We were ahead after just six minutes, let them back in, fluffed the penalty just on half-time, and then didn't have the answers in the second-half. The 4-2 result was probably a fair reflection on the game, but defeat was still incredibly painful to take. We had our moments – like Georgi Hristov's point-blank header which brought a breathtaking reflex save from Richard Wright in the Ipswich goal – but simply didn't make them count.

At the end of the day, one team wins and goes up and one team loses and stays down which can make the season's other successes seem null and void. Lives are affected on the strength of a match result, as I have said before.

We had to face up to a new challenge the following season. Finances had to be taken more seriously because the money that was allotted to us because of relegation from the Premiership was no longer available and we had to look at ways of cutting the wage bill and balancing the books.

First of all, though, I had a family holiday and a break from the game. How often those holidays include phone calls about players and events going on back home.

Craig Hignett wanted to continue his career in the Premiership and I knew we could transfer him for a reasonable fee, some of which could benefit the facilities of the club's youth academy.

So Craig was sold to Blackburn for £2.2 million, of which I had £1million to spend on players, hoping to replace our leading goalscorer. Craig had been brilliant for us that season, influencing matches dramatically and ramming in 22 goals from midfield – a terrific return.

His understanding and link-up play with Shipperley was a joy to behold, and one of the big reasons why we went so far in that campaign. Shipps revelled in playing alongside Craig, and his form blossomed to such an extent that they shared an incredible 40 goals between them.

I sometimes still wonder whether Barnsley's board really are as ambitious as they like to have everybody believe. Despite the end of the parachute payments from the Premiership that summer, surely more could have been done to try and keep Craig at Oakwell. After all, we should have been building a team around the likes of him and Shipps if we were deadly serious about having another crack at promotion the following season.

Nicky Eaden is another one we should have held onto. But he was allowed to leave on a Bosman free for Birmingham after Barnsley had failed to agree a new deal with him during the season. We really should have kept Nicky.

On top of that, John Curtis went to Blackburn; Eric Tinkler was injured while on international duty for South Africa and he was out for the whole of the next season, although we did not know that at the time; Georgi Hristov left us for NEC Nijmegen. We lost half a team of quality players that summer, when we should have been pulling out all the stops to keep them for the task ahead.

We signed Lee Jones on a free from Tranmere. Lee had a good goalscoring record, and I felt he was ready and eager to move his career forward. Unfortunately, that proved not to be the case, and he turned out to be a major disappointment. He is now back at Wrexham – where, perhaps, he should have stayed all his life!

I brought in Alex Neil from Airdrie for £25,000 and Carl Reagan from Everton for the same amount. They were two young players with little experience but we were still building for the future of the club. I think that the fans were expecting a repeat performance at least, but, in truth, we were building for the future and it was difficult to get that message across, even to the chairman. John Dennis listened to my appraisal – perhaps privately he was thinking that Harry Houdini would still get them in the play-offs again.

Mitch Ward was also signed on a free from Everton. As an ex-Blade, I was well aware of his ability. Matteo Corbo, an ex-Uruguayan international, was signed from Real Oviado for an initial £100,000. He became quite a favourite with the fans and I felt, given time to settle in, he would have been an excellent acquisition. However, after I left, he dropped out of favour and eventually left the club.

That summer we signed a new shirt sponsorship deal with a computer company called Big Thing. As you can imagine, the jokes flowed thick and fast about having Big Thing emblazoned upon your chest. I was simply relieved that it wasn't plastered all over the front of our shorts! Anyway, they turned out to be no Big Thing at all. The company went the same way as the club they were sponsoring – belly up.

We won our first game of the new season at home to Norwich, although Reagan was sent off. It was a good start but then we went to Watford and lost 1-0 with the last kick of the game going against us. Then we beat West Brom 4-1 and that led to talk of Gary Megson, their manager, getting the sack. He didn't and they went on to make the play-offs at the end of the season followed by promotion 12 months later. It shows yet again that there really is no need or room for panic decisions in football.

Birmingham gained some revenge when they beat us 4-1 and we became inconsistent again. We beat Sheffield Wednesday in an all-important local derby which was a great result, then we had an awful game against Sheffield United at home and drew 0-0. We were not just a team of different games but of different halves. We sometimes looked like champions for 45 minutes and relegation candidates for the rest of the game.

My relationship with the Chairman began to deteriorate quite a bit because of our mid-table position, and our discussions became increasingly unconstructive. I knew there was still a few bob to spend but I couldn't get specific information. There were all the classic signs of a parting of the ways. I held on, though, and tried to continue as if everything was normal. The last thing the players needed was further distraction.

It all probably came to a head when we lost 2-0 to Stockport. In the first half we were all over them, playing quite brilliantly. The problem was failing to score. We let them off the hook by missing a load of chances. But our second-half performance was dismal, to put it mildly. They popped up with two goals to send us home licking our wounds over a 2-0 defeat.

All because of that one season in the Premiership, Barnsley don't ever see themselves losing to the Stockports or Crewes of this world. That emphasises yet again that, in footballing terms, they are living in a fantasy world.

When I came out of our dressing-room door at Edgeley Park, I was immediately and acutely aware of people avoiding me. I was walking down the corridor to meet the press boys when Barry Taylor came into view. When he saw me, he ducked out of the way and I did not like that at all. It provided further proof – if any were needed – that the knives were out for me.

I was determined to tough it out and made my mind up that the team needed stimulating with an injection of fresh blood. I sat down with the coaching staff, ran my ideas by them, and they all agreed that changes had to be made with new players coming into the team. I still had almost £1 million left in the kitty, and I was in the process of selling defender Adie Moses to Huddersfield Town for £200,000.

That £1.2 million would nicely cover the cost of my intended buys. I had targeted striker Richard Cresswell, who would cost £750,000 from Leicester, and Kilmarnock's £400,000-rated Gary Holt. But Preston jumped in to snatch Cresswell while Norwich landed Holt. I was deeply frustrated at losing the pair of them.

The day after the Stockport defeat I rang the Chairman and asked if we could have a meeting after Monday's training session. I felt we needed to clear the air, and my intention was to inform him of how I wanted to get the team back on track.

As I outlined my plans, I could see his face growing redder by the second. He then started to pour with sweat when I told him I wanted to spend some money. He was clearly surprised when I started talking about the changes to the squad that were needed, and I did not get a particularly positive response from him.

In fact, he really shocked me by telling me he thought I had come to see him to resign, and that he was due to see the rest of the Board at a pre-arranged meeting. He indicated that two directors were up for sacking me, although he insisted that he could not justify doing that – and wouldn't – because a year earlier I had stayed loyal to Barnsley when I could have gone to Blackburn.

He also stressed that he felt there was no reason to sack a manager who had taken the club to the play-off final just a few months earlier – especially as Barnsley were currently 12th in the First Division and in no danger of being relegated, despite being in a transitional stage. But it still came home to me that I was not going to get the support I needed and deserved. I knew exactly what the scene was, but I was still going to make him sweat. No way was I going to give him an easy ride out of this situation.

I couldn't get away from the fact that the Chairman's words and body language gave more than an indication that the conclusion of these events was inevitable, not least because of the Chairman's attitude after I had referred to a pocket of 'sad anoraks' among the Barnsley support in a local radio phone-in. It wasn't a sweeping generalisation or anything like a total condemnation of Oakwell supporters. It was merely a reference to the tiny minority of fans who couldn't – or wouldn't – understand what was happening at the club and what we were trying to do to make it better in difficult financial circumstances.

The local paper, the *Barnsley Chronicle*, hadn't helped my cause by giving the impression that I was attacking all the Barnsley supporters. I was already fully aware of how John manipulated the local paper. This was something he clearly enjoyed doing. And being looked upon as 'Mr Barnsley' in the town was something he craved and needed.

The business with the fans could have been nipped in the bud by John. But, instead, he disappointed me by not coming out and defending me and telling the fans that I did not tar them all with the same brush. I had a healthy respect for the vast majority of the club's followers and their knowledge and understanding of the game in general and Barnsley in particular. The Chairman knew that full well.

After that fruitless meeting with John, I went home and talked it out with Christine who said that I should do whatever my gut feeling was telling me. I decided that, in the best interests of the club, I would leave.

The next morning I rang John Dennis at 7.00 am to say I wanted a further meeting with him. This took place at his business headquarters in Barnsley, where I told him that I was disappointed with him and the rest of the Board and that it was in the best interests of all concerned that we split and go our separate ways. He didn't put up much of a fight for me to stay, so I knew that I had made the right decision. I would not stay where I was not especially wanted. The usual statement was issued to the press.

I had 18 happy months at Oakwell and had the pleasure of taking the club to Wembley for the first time – something that will always be a cherished memory. I look back with pride on the job I did there, and the circumstances in which I did it. I also reflect on the fact that my successors Nigel Spackman, and then Steve Parkin also paid the price for not delivering what John Dennis and his directors arrogantly thought they were entitled to. Steve was unable to alter the trend after coming in from Rochdale, and Barnsley now start life in the Second Division. Yet, two seasons earlier, they were in the play-off final and just a penalty kick away from the promised land. Sad, very sad.

As for my feelings towards John Dennis. Well, in a way I can't help but quite like him still. He can be charming, intelligent, self-confident, cynical of mind and caustic of tongue. And I wonder if he thinks, looking back on it all now, whether letting me go was in the best interests of the club he loves so much.

No matter. The fact was that Harry was available again, although in no rush to find just any job. This time, it just had to be the RIGHT job.

21

Into the Foxes' Lair

DURING THE EARLY PART OF 2001, I continued with my 5 Live and Sky TV work. I was also doing player assessment for a number of my friends in football.

Unfortunately, early in March, my father died suddenly. He was 83, in good health, kept his bungalow clean and tidy as a new pin, and still had his wits about him. I could ask for no more than that myself. It is always at times like this that you wish you had done more for your parents, but such is life. I will miss him.

Soon after the funeral, I was approached by both Queen's Park Rangers and Portsmouth, who were then looking for new managers. I wasn't impressed by those that interviewed me from QPR, and although I liked Milan Mandaric, the Chairman of Portsmouth, very much and was tempted to say 'yes', it was just a little too far south. Harry Redknapp, a good friend, is now Manager at Fratton Park and I wish him well.

I had been out of the game for nine months when Peter Taylor became the first Premiership managerial casualty of the 2001-2 campaign in September. As is always the case in these circumstances, every out-of-work manager finds himself being pitched into the reckoning. I was in the fortunate position where I did not have to return to work through financial necessity but I was at a stage where I was starting to get itchy feet. I'd done the shopping expeditions to Meadowhall with my wife Christine and gone for those casual afternoon strolls through the South Yorkshire countryside. I wasn't quite yet ready to don the carpet slippers and, if truth be known, Christine was probably getting fed up with me under her feet at home. My first concrete approach for the Leicester position did not come from any official at Filbert Street. Instead, I received a call from Harry Redknapp. Harry, who was then Director of Football at Portsmouth, had explained there was an interest in him at Leicester and asked if I fancied being his assistant alongside Frank Lampard. Harry was putting together a very experienced managerial and coaching team and I said that I definitely would be interested. I believe that Harry had a few chats with the Leicester board but felt a debt of loyalty to Portsmouth and his chairman Milan Mandaric, with whom he had struck up a very good relationship.

Harry rang me to explain he was withdrawing his interest but enquired whether I would fancy going for the job as number one. Shortly afterwards, I received a phone call at home from chairman John Elsom asking if I could come down to meet him and some of his fellow directors. We arranged to meet at a hotel in Oakham on a Sunday lunchtime. I travelled down and was met by John, Director Martin George, Club Secretary Andrew Neville and Communications Director Paul Mace. We had a good chat and, in contrast to some of the other managerial interviews I had attended, this was very professionally organised and I knew exactly where I stood with them from the moment I walked in the door.

It was made crystal clear to me that not only was there no money to spend but that I would be expected to raise approximately £2 million from the sale of players. The board had backed the previous manager to the hilt with the summer signings of Dennis Wise, James Scowcroft and Ian Walker and it had always been on the agenda to recoup some of those monies by selling other members of the squad. Perhaps it was not exactly what I wanted to hear but ask any manager and he will tell you that he needs to know exactly what parameters he is working within and not to have any unexpected surprises. Cardiff City were also showing an interest in me. Sam Hamman, with whom I forged a strong bond at Wimbledon, was setting about trying to recreate that atmosphere and success story in the Welsh capital. Sam can be very persuasive but the opportunity to manage again in the Premiership was a major lure. I was under no illusions that this was going to be a massive task, most probably the toughest I had faced in my managerial career. But I knew it was going to be a job I would accept if I was offered the position.

The Leicester board were particularly keen to establish who I would appoint as my number two. They wanted someone who would be able to eventually take over the managerial reins from me and were looking for a hungry young manager who had proven himself in the lower divisions. I had worked with Mickey Adams before at Nottingham Forest and he was doing a first-rate job with Brighton, where he had taken them to the Third Division championship and the Seagulls were currently top of Division Two. I suggested Mickey would be a suitable candidate and, after 90 minutes, we agreed to meet again the following day for further talks.

I was verbally offered the position and it was agreed that an official approach should be made to the Brighton chairman Dick Knight, for Leicester to speak to Mickey about the position of Foxes assistant manager. Those talks duly took place and everything seemed to be dropping into place. Nine days had now elapsed since the club's last game with Peter Taylor in charge – a 2-0 defeat at Charlton. On the Tuesday night, the club had a Worthington Cup tie with Leeds United at Filbert Street. Rather than watch this game and draw too much attention to myself, I decided to go along to the Coventry v Chelsea game at Highfield Road. Leicester were playing Chelsea on the Saturday and this was an ideal opportunity for me to take a look at them. After the game, I stopped to get a curry and was halfway through my chicken tikka masala and pilau rice when my mobile phone rang. It was John Elsom. 'Bad news, I'm afraid. We lost 6-0. I was wondering if you still wanted the job,' was his opening gambit. John is a very honest man with the club's best intentions at heart and I reassured him that I most certainly did.

During the next 24 hours, we tied up the loose ends of mine and Mickey's contracts in John's sun lounge, over some coffee and biscuits courtesy of John's wife Janet. The club arranged for a press conference on the Wednesday afternoon. It was probably fair to say that I was not the most popular man for the job among Foxes fans. There had been a few chants during the Leeds game, but that in no way affected my decision or my enthusiasm for the job. George Graham had been one of the managers linked with the position and I could quite understand fans preferring George but there has to be a degree of reality. Under the constraints and parameters of the job, there was no way a George Graham type was coming to Leicester.

From day one we made it clear that Mickey was being groomed to take over the reins which was why I signed an 18-month agreement and Mickey signed an extra 12 months. The club had enjoyed great success with managers who learned their craft in the lower divisions. Martin O'Neill and Brian Little had both cut their teeth with Conference-winning sides Wycombe and Darlington and Mickey fitted perfectly this identikit of a manager. One of the most quotable lines that came out of the press conference was a one-liner I used to describe myself as 'the old codger' and Mickey as 'the sexy young thing'. My comment made all the national papers the following day.

I also added Peter Shirtliff to my management team. I was aware of his talents whilst we were at Barnsley together, and I always appreciated how loyal and supportive he was. He and his wife Jackie have become firm friends of mine, and he remains at Leicester, doing well as reserve team coach.

Sky Television probably had more of an inkling than most that I was about to be unveiled. It wasn't anything I had said but more the actions of my daughter, Carly, who works at Sky headquarters in Isleworth. When she heard I was to be announced she booked the day off from Sky. It's a similar scenario with Kelly Dalglish, daughter of Kenny, who always booked a day off whenever there was a major announcement relating to her father.

Just after I joined Leicester, Tony Pritchett, who had recently retired as the football reporter on the *Sheffield Star and Green'un*, died after a brave fight against cancer. We had both chuckled to one another that, in our dotage when we retired, we would regularly play golf together. Tony was a fine 'old fashioned' honest football writer in the old tradition. He was loyal in the dark days at Sheffield and I will always be grateful for that support.

I've never been one to kid myself and I was under no illusions about the size of the task ahead of us. Aside from having to sell players to recoup monies, the squad was already being stretched with the injuries to Gerry Taggart and Darren Eadie. Little did I realise that this was only the tip of the iceberg: in the coming weeks and months, just about every senior professional was struck down.

My first two games in charge were at Chelsea and at home to Liverpool. Welcome to the Premiership. Not that you'd find me complaining. I was very proud and privileged to be in a band of just 20 Premiership managers and I had thought that the only way I would become one of them would be to have got a club promoted out of the Nationwide League. In truth, there was little bearing either myself or Mickey could have had on Chelsea. The players worked hard but individual errors cost us in a 2-0 defeat. It did surprise me after the game, though, that board directors told me we had played better and created chances.

The margin of defeat against Liverpool was larger. Robbie Fowler helped himself to a hat-trick in a 4-1 scoreline. Little did I realise that Fowler was to remain the highest goalscorer at Filbert Street for the rest of the season! But my lasting memory of that game will always be our own centre forward Ade Akinbiyi, who took some fearful criticism from the fans. He had four great chances that day against a very miserly Liverpool defence but missed them all. To be fair, he should take credit for getting into excellent scoring positions but at the end of the game I did worry for him.

In the coming weeks we worked hard to stem the flow of goals. Call it building from the back if you like but the side had conceded 12 goals in its last three games against Leeds, Chelsea and Liverpool. The players responded well and we put together a run of four clean sheets in five games, two victories and two draws and hauled ourselves out of the bottom three. It was no mean achievement but even at that time I couldn't help but think we had thrown away points by not converting goalless draws into victories at Blackburn and at home to Everton.

Ultimately, our lack of goals was to cost us dearly. But there could be few complaints and the scenes which greeted our victory over Sunderland in front of the Sky cameras were fantastic. I don't think there is anyone in football who can't picture Ade wheeling away in triumph with that fantastic toned torso after he scored the winning goal.

We had hauled ourselves up into 17th place and were then entertaining Southampton, the bottom club, at home. Everyone felt the club had turned the corner and we found ourselves in the very rare position of starting a game as favourites. I detected a feeling not just among supporters, but the players as well, that we only had to turn up to win it. I was very uneasy about the game although I must admit I was not bracing myself for a 4-0 stuffing. I was disappointed with the response of the players after we went a goal down and that was to manifest itself later in crucial stages of the season.

With very little money to spend, I knew that I would have to wheel and deal to bring in any new players. There was some talk about Dean Sturridge who I allowed to go out on loan to Wolves shortly after my arrival. Dean went on to score a lot of goals while at Molineux which did not entirely surprise me. What it did mean, of course, was supporters questioning why I had allowed him to go there. Managers have to make decisions on players all the time. I knew that Dean was capable of scoring a lot of goals in the First Division, but I did not feel he was what we needed at Premiership level. I felt that our chances would be better served by making a move for Brian Deane which I was able to do after protracted negotiations with Middlesbrough. Brian was a player I knew well from our time together at Sheffield United and with his eye for a goal and ability to lead the line, I felt he would do well for the club in its present position

Alan Rogers was another player whom I signed for a nominal fee from Nottingham Forest as I sought to freshen up the squad. I had spent £2million on Alan when I was at Forest, but he was now looking to get away from the City Ground and Forest were prepared to sell at a significantly reduced price given he was out of contract at the end of the season. What I had not bargained for was the string of serious injuries that was to manifest itself. Gary Rowett played in my first game at Chelsea and I was not to see him in Premiership action again until April after he needed a knee operation. Dennis Wise was to become a major casualty in January, and Matt Jones was to require cruciate ligament surgery a month later.

I'm a firm believer that there are defining moments in any campaign. The Christmas and New Year programme was certainly a defining moment as far as we were concerned. We had a series of games against clubs around us in the bottom half of the table. Our first game was against West Ham just three days before Christmas. We had scored the all-important first goal through Muzzy Izzet and were not in any real danger until our club captain Matt Elliott made an ill-advised challenge on Joe Cole. It was a penalty and to compound our problems Matty got himself sent off with his reactions afterwards. That was the turning point of the game. Paolo Di Canio scored from the spot with one of those audacious chips and we were probably relieved to hear the final whistle. Nothing should disguise the fact, though, that we had the three points in the bag and handed West Ham a lifeline they had not looked like creating for themselves.

Boxing Day provided us with one of those real six-pointers at Ipswich. Again, for the first hour of the match I felt we were the better team and the side much more likely to score. Once again, we went behind to a goal and capitulated. I was furious in the dressing room afterwards and told the lads a few home truths. I questioned their attitude, their desire and their commitment. Afterwards I was quoted as saying that I would have hit them with a baseball bat. I had not meant it literally but my comments were borne out of a frustration to try and knock some sense into the lads.

This game was quickly followed by a trip to Bolton, who had beaten Leicester 5-0 at Filbert Street on the opening day of the season. A few weeks earlier, I had agreed to take part in a *Tonight with Trevor McDonald* ITV documentary programme on the stress of being a Premiership manager. We had done some filming beforehand and myself and Sam Alladyce both agreed to be 'wired up' for the match. I don't believe the producers could believe their luck with what transpired during the game. When the programme was broadcast a few days later I also got a little fed up with the constant references to a slightly irregular heart-beat which was diagnosed several years previously. As a consequence I spent the next few weeks assuring everyone that I was not about to keel over. In actual fact, I've had tests since then which have proved reassuring. I felt that the programme tried to sensationalise the stress that managers are under.

Inside the opening 25 minutes at the Reebok Stadium, we found ourselves two goals up and Bolton were reduced to nine men after having Paul Warhurst and Dean Holdsworth both sent off. It was a very volatile atmosphere and I ended up having to take off Robbie Savage for his own protection. Now if you're a parks team two goals up against nine men you expect to go on to win the game very comfortably. If you're a Premiership team, it should be meat and drink. Well, we allowed Bolton to pull a goal back before half time. In the second half, Muzzy Izzet was very unfortunate to be yellow carded for diving when he should, in fact, have been given a penalty he was a little foolish, though, to collect a second yellow for throwing the ball away and in the closing minutes we were hanging on for dear life. It was now 10 against nine and the hunters were being hunted. We thought luck might be on our side when a free kick ricocheted off the inside of a post only for Michael Ricketts to head home a Bolton equaliser in the dying seconds. To say I was gutted would be an understatement. In all my years in football I have never ever witnessed anything like that before. I was so perplexed that I was not really sure what to say to the players. If truth be known, Bolton had wanted the game more than us. I was particularly despondent and felt that this was a defining game we failed to take advantage of. I was of the opinion that this team was particularly soft and didn't relish a battle.

It was at that stage that I really began to realise we would do well to pull ourselves out of this situation. We had slipped to the bottom of the Premiership and had thrown points away against West Ham, Ipswich and Bolton. We had taken two points when really we should have come out with seven. From there on in we were going to have to show good form against clubs like Newcastle, Arsenal, Liverpool and Manchester United which we were always going to find very difficult. That's exactly the way it turned out because our next Premiership victory was not going to be until March 30 when we beat Blackburn 2-1.

Christmas and New Year proved an equally eventful time off the pitch as well, when the club found itself on the back pages of the national newspapers as a result of the players' Christmas party. In this day and age, the players' party is always fraught with danger and it was our luck that we should get 'caught out'. The first I knew of any problem was while the staff were having our own Christmas night out (a much more sedate affair, I hasten to add). Communications Director Paul Mace took a call at the bar of The Quay pub, just a few hundred yards from Filbert Street, from the *Daily Mirror* to say they were working on a story about a disagreement between Robbie Savage and Dennis Wise and did we have any comment.

It was all a storm in a teacup, but there were a few lurid headlines the next day about the content of the disagreement. We agreed that the best way to deal with the situation was to get the players together and hold a press conference to explain the situation. Paul arranged for Robbie, Dennis and the club captain, Matty Elliott, to sit down and meet the press. I always find in these situations that it's best to meet it head on and deal with it quickly and sharply and get on with your life. Throughout my career, I have always believed firmly that you must co-operate fully with the press and set aside time for them. The media put a lot of money into football and it is only right that they have the appropriate access they require. Of course, when you get those sort of headlines, the temptation is to turn your back on them and blank them but that doesn't really get you anywhere. You have to take it on the chin and get on with life.

It was in January that we said goodbye to Ade Akinbiyi. When I first came to the club, I wanted to give him a chance and there was certainly no faulting his application or commitment. He was a superbly-honed athlete. However, as a striker, it is very difficult to retain your confidence if you are not scoring goals, especially if your team is struggling to get a result. After giving him several chances, I felt the time came to allow him to move on and rebuild his confidence at a new club. My old pal Trevor Francis, newly installed as manager at Crystal Palace showed the biggest interest and we were able to structure a deal.

There was not even to be much respite from the Premiership for us in the FA Cup. We navigated a potential banana-skin tie in the third round at home to Mansfield 2-1 and were rewarded with a Midlands derby at West Bromwich Albion. It was always going to be tight game and we were edged out 1-0. Lady luck certainly wasn't on our side when we lost due to a hotly-disputed penalty awarded to one of my former Forest lads, Andy Johnson, who appeared to take a dive in the box. Now, we could concentrate totally on the League.

Earlier, I spoke of defining moments in a season and the next was to be the home game against Derby in late February. It was a battle of the Premiership's bottom two and inevitably whoever won that game would feel they stood a chance of survival, while the loser would be in extremely serious trouble. As had been the case on more than one occasion, I felt we started okay and looked much the stronger team. A deflected Georgi Kinkladze goal, however, was to prove our undoing and we ended up losing the match 3-0. With it, I felt, went any realistic chance we had of avoiding relegation.

The Derby result was an even bigger kick in the teeth on the back of our previous home defeat against Chelsea. We played extremely well that afternoon and were twice in front and I really did feel we were on our way to all three points. However, I reckoned without a free kick special from Gianfranco Zola and the finishing prowess of Jimmy Floyd Hassalbaink who took the score to 3-2 in the dying moments.

I must say that I did not feel there was, or is, a single bad apple among the players at the football club. I have been at other clubs where there have been divisions in dressing rooms and major personality clashes, though this has not necessarily had a detrimental effect on results. Here at Leicester the players were an enthusiastic, good set of lads who wanted to do well. Sadly, however, over the course of time I think they found it hard as a group of players to get results. Perhaps some of them had slipped into a comfort zone. The club had done spectacularly well under Martin O'Neill and, in the eyes of many outsiders, had over-achieved.

After Martin's departure, Peter Taylor took over and, in the second half of that season, the club struggled to get results. For whatever reasons, the players found it hard to turn it around. They had not been used to not getting results and found it a very difficult trench to dig themselves out of. This continued into the following season and the mental toughness which was required could not manifest itself. During my time as manager I could count on one hand the number of times I had a real volley at them. They were committed, worked hard on the training ground but when it came to getting over the fine dividing line between winning and losing and success and failure it could not be jumped. Had Wimbledon been in a similar position they would have quite literally tried to fight their way out of it. In Leicester's case, the players were all decent lads but just could not get out of it.

When you're down, they say you get a good kicking. I had to admit I afforded myself a wry smile in hindsight before our home game against Charlton Athletic. I was making my usual trip down the M1 from Sheffield to Leicester to arrive in plenty of time at around midday. Unfortunately, I forgot that I was running rather low on petrol. So low, in fact, that I spluttered to a halt somewhere just after Junction 26. I felt like a bit of a fool as I rang the emergency services for a garage to bring me down some petrol. The guy on the phone recognised my voice and had a good laugh at my expense. After waiting for over half an hour, I wondered whether he was even going to bother. I made a few calls to the club and, to cut a long story short, it was worked out that Carlton TV sports presenter Dennis Coath was only a couple of junctions further south of me. He was despatched northwards but, by the time he had arrived, the garage mechanic arrived with a petrol can and some much-needed unleaded. There was no chance of keeping it quiet and, soon after I arrived, former player Alan Birchenall came into the dressing room with an empty petrol can.

Another time, I nearly choked on my cornflakes. A few months previously I had gone along to a Leeds Champions League game as a guest of a managing director friend of mine, Len McCormack. I was introduced to a few of his guests and made the usual polite conversation you do in those sort of circumstances. I thought nothing more about it until I got a call one morning from Paul Mace. 'Have you seen the *Sun*,' he asked. 'You're not going to like this but a guy in court has claimed you told him to visit a local brothel in Leeds.'

What had transpired was that this guy was appearing

in court on a serious charge as a result of an incident arising after that Leeds game. He was one of the guests I was introduced to but I can categorically assure you I know of no houses of ill-repute in Leeds, or anywhere else for that matter. This guy had the cheek to claim – in court – that I had told him where to go. It was reported in the *Sun* newspaper so I immediately got onto the paper and they agreed to publish a retraction after the case was completed. I'm not too sure the jury believed him either because he was found guilty. As you might imagine, I took a fair bit of stick over the incident.

While my focus was solely on producing a Premiership point or two from somewhere, I was vaguely aware that I was approaching my 1000 games as a manager. However, I was a little surprised to receive a telephone call from football journalist Glen Moore of the *Independent*. 'I've got news for you, Harry, you've now been a manager for 1006 matches,' he told me. Unbeknown to me – and everyone else for that matter – I had actually made my 1000th managerial appearance in a midweek trip to Anfield in January. We lost 1-0 to a late Emile Heskey goal. Coming up that weekend was my 1007th goal in charge at home to Leeds. After discussions with the League Managers Association it was agreed that I would receive a trophy to mark the feat before our home game with Manchester United. Sir Alex Ferguson kindly agreed to make the presentation before the match and I received a great ovation from Leicester supporters. It was an unusually emotional afternoon because it marked my final game in charge before handing over to Mickey Adams and, unfortunately, a 1-0 defeat meant that we were mathematically relegated. Nothing will ever dim the memories of that game, however. It was my 1010th senior game as a manager – 1009 after my managerial debut in charge of Wimbledon at Port Vale in Division Four back in 1981.

In the subsequent 21 years, I was fortunate enough

to win more games than I lost, to enjoy more promotions than relegations and generally to reflect what a fantastic and fortunate life I have been able to lead. I feel quite humble to be only the sixth manager to clock up 1,000 games after Alec Stock, Brian Clough, Dario Gradi, Jim Smith and Graham Taylor. It's a very exclusive band and one that I am delighted to be a member of .

Losing games at a professional football club can be a very draining experience. Not only is it important that you do everything possible to keep the players' spirits up but you need to ensure that you and your staff are also motivated. One of the little things we did throughout the season was to have our own staff matches on a Friday lunchtime. Former City player and now club co-ordinator Alan Birchenall and Paul Mace were two of the key figures behind organising the games and from little acorns grew quite competitive affairs with just about everyone involved. I may be 57 but I still like a kickabout and we had some good match-ups. Usually it involved a coaching staff side taking on an Academy team and they tended to be no-holds-barred affairs. The games took place in the indoor gymnasium at the training ground and the players themselves would come in and watch. One of the more aggressive participants was the club vicar who used to take great delight in chopping down a few from behind at knee height. I often used to remind him to say a few words for us every Saturday afternoon. Unfortunately, my request seemed to fall on deaf ears.

Managers are often asked how they feel about suffering relegation. It's very hard to put it into words. I don't think I will ever forget the feeling of complete desolation when Sheffield United were relegated at Chelsea. Supporters are totally gutted when their club is relegated. Although it is professional business for managers and players, the disappointment is no easier to bear. After every Saturday you lose, your whole weekend is ruined. You don't want to go out and you don't make very good company for your family and friends. I had gone to Leicester desperate to keep them in the Premiership. I felt that I could do it and professional pride inevitably takes a hit when you cannot achieve your objective.

The record at Leicester was, unfortunately, one of the worst of my career although it's probably fair to say that it was a significantly bigger job than I had imagined. It did seem as if fate was conspiring against us. Apart from the catalogue of serious injuries suffered by senior players, I had not banked on Muzzy Izzet handing in a transfer request just a few days after my arrival. I had no problems with Muzzy whatsoever. He was as good as gold and gave us his all for the club for the subsequent seven months while he was on the transfer list. But let's just say I was not too impressed with Muzzy's agent, Jonathan Barnett, when he came in asking for all sorts of things before I had even got my feet under the table. We did agree a £6 million fee with Middlesbrough for Muzzy but he exercised his right not to move at that time. A little part of me can't help but wonder whether we might have been able to change things around if Muzzy had gone. The money from Muzzy's departure would have given me more flexibility in the transfer market and the capability to bring in players not available to me on free transfers and nominal fees. Whatever the situation, however, we still had to get on with the job.

Although the fans might not have been totally convinced about me when I first arrived, I must congratulate them for the support they gave me and the club in the following months when, to be honest, they had very little to cheer about. I genuinely have a fond affection for the club and I felt the supporters were very realistic about the club's situation. They were supportive and stayed with the players when they could have easily turned against them. During conversations with them, most understood what we were trying to do and were full of support. After all the successful years of the Martin O'Neill era, the fans were very pragmatic and realistic about the situation of the club. They hoped against hope but prepared themselves for the worst when the curtain was brought down by Manchester United. It was a fantastic demonstration of support and unity when, for the closing 15 minutes, they kept chanting and pledging their allegiance at a time when a glorious six year reign in the Premiership was to come to an end.

I was disappointed for them, the players, the coaching staff and myself. No-one likes to fail, least of all me. I had made up my mind that if we were relegated I would hand over the managerial reins to Mickey Adams which was only right and proper. I still feel I have something to offer and that I could have done a good job in attempting to bring the club straight back. But there was no doubt in my mind that now was the time to step aside and give Mickey his chance. My thoughts were at a time when other changes were about to be announced within the club and it was very much a period of change. Club chairman John Elsom stepped down to be replaced by Martin George and a change of plc chairman was also announced with Greg Clarke to take over from Sir Rodney Walker. I was sorry for John that I had not been able to keep the club in the Premiership. I got on well with him and his wife Janet. He was an honest man, completely committed to the success of Leicester City and I know he felt the relegation more than most.

My changeover with Mickey seemed a natural progression. That changeover did not quite go as seamlessly as we might have hoped. Before our trip to Southampton in March, Mickey made a throwaway line at the end of a television interview about his managerial future lying at Leicester or elsewhere. It was inevitably picked up by newspapers but my respect and appreciation of Mickey's abilities were not going to be clouded by one inopportune comment. The following Monday, Mickey himself admitted to the media that he regretted the comment and that it had bruised his relationship with me. As far as I was concerned, it was all water under the bridge and within three weeks we had agreed Mickey would take over as manager with myself in a new role of Director of Football.

The final four Premiership games afforded Mickey a chance to take a closer look at his squad and begin his preparations for the following season in earnest. We drew three and won the final game of the season at home to Spurs, which is a base upon which to build for next season. Our players had suffered a lot of defeats and it was important for them to get out of that habit. Matthew Piper scored the final ever goal at Filbert Street which was quite fitting. A young local lad, he forced his way into the team and stayed there. An exciting player who can operate down either flank, he clearly has a great potential future in the game. He was the pick of the many young players we 'blooded' into the Premiership.

Circumstances dictated that half a dozen lads from the Academy were thrust into the first team picture in the closing games. As well as Matt Piper, Jon Ashton was another who took his chance well, along with Jon Stevenson who scored his first Premiership goal in a 2-2 draw with Aston Villa. Although injuries meant those youngsters got an earlier chance than otherwise might have been the case, it will have been a terrific learning experience for them. How they turn that to their advantage we will have to wait and see but those games, I'm sure will live with them for the rest of their lives.

* * *

My new role as Director of Football is a departure from my last 21 years in front-line management but it is a challenge I am relishing. The position is still a relatively new one in the English game although there are precedents at Newcastle with Gordon Milne, Southampton and Laurie McMenamy, Spurs and David Pleat, Stoke and John Rudge and Bournemouth and Mel Machin. It is a job that I believe will grow, in keeping with many of the structures in place in European football.

I do not think we should undervalue the importance of having experience in football. Bobby Robson (now a very deserved Knight of the Realm) is the oldest manager operating in the Premiership but he is also one of the most successful. I hope to bring all the experience to bear for the benefit of Leicester City that I have learned during my long career. Managing a football club is a major operation these days, far too big for one man to handle everything.

As Director of Football, I will act as a buffer between Mickey and the board and be an independent advisor to the board on football matters. The Academy, for instance, will come under my remit and I also believe I can offer value when it comes to negotiating players' contracts, selling players and any areas for which the manager does not wish to assume direct responsibility. For instance, in the month of May, at the end of the season in which Leicester were relegated, I was busy arranging the outgoing transfers of Gary Rowett to Charlton and Robbie Savage to Birmingham, as well as structuring new deals for young first-teamers Matthew Piper and Jon Ashton.

What I will not be, however, is a parrot sat on Mickey's shoulder. Mickey's job is to manage and he would not wish for any interference from me. Nor will he get any. He has said he will stand and fall by his results and that's the way it should be. I would feel exactly the same. I am always there for advice should Mickey ask for it and we shall talk regularly but I know where the line has been drawn and I will not cross that.

A lot of people have asked me how I will cope not being the main man of management. I've been in the firing line for over two decades, and I'm now excited by my new challenge as Director of Football. It may be that Leicester decide I am not the right man for the job at the end of my final year, or maybe I will get itchy feet.

I'm certainly not thinking like that. I genuinely like Leicester as a club and I want to play my part in helping them win an instant return to the Premiership. The development of the new Walkers Stadium is a monumental step forward. It's what the club has needed for many years and, now it has taken that step, the building blocks are in place for the club to recapture past glories. There is, of course, a tremendous amount of hard work to be done but everyone is up for the challenge.

As for me, I've loved the last 21 years in management and the previous 15 on the pitch as a player. I'm embarking on a new era myself and maybe, just maybe, there's a little bit of life left in the old codger.